THE MAKING OF
THE AMERICAN DREAM

Volume I

THE MAKING OF THE AMERICAN DREAM

An Unconventional History of
the United States from 1607 to 1900

Volume I: The Making of a Republic

Lewis E. Kaplan

Algora Publishing
New York

Library of Congress Cataloging-in-Publication Data —

Kaplan, Lewis E.
    The making of the American dream : an unconventional history of the United States
from 1607 to 1900 / Lewis E. Kaplan.
        p. cm.
    Includes bibliographical references.
    ISBN 978-0-87586-693-2 (trade paper: alk. paper) — ISBN 978-0-87586-694-9 (hard
cover: alk. paper) — ISBN 978-0-87586-695-6 (ebook) 1. United States—History. 2.
United States—Politics and government. I. Title.
    E178.K17 2009
    973—dc22
                            2009014415

Printed in the United States

To my wife Carolyn
and to the next generations of Kaplans,
with heartfelt appreciation to my son Sam.

Table of Contents

Introduction   1

Chapter 1. The English Settlements in North America   5

Chapter 2. The Colonies Come of Age   17

Chapter 3. The Rocky Road to Independence   31

Chapter 4. The Revolutionary War   69

Chapter 5. The Tortuous Path to a New Nation   73

Chapter 6. A Nation in Transition   81

Chapter 7. The Emergence of the Republican Dynasty   89

Chapter 8. The War of 1812   93

Chapter 9. America Sheds Its Adolescence   101

Chapter 10. The Emergence of Political Parties   113

Chapter 11. The Mexican War   149

Chapter 12. The Coming Crisis   159

Chapter 13. The Inevitable Demise of One Nation   189

Recommended Readings   215

Introduction

> Deep into that darkness peering, long
> I stood there, wondering, fearing,
> Doubting, dreaming dreams no mortal
> ever dared to dream before.
> — Edgar Allen Poe, *The Raven*, 1845

This stanza from Poe's most famous poem must describe the feelings and emotions of the first English settlers better than any string of words in prose. Those who arrived in Jamestown, Virginia, in 1607, surely experienced just those fears and doubts when they first sighted land in the early morning darkness — while retaining visions of returning to England laden with gold and silver. Thirteen years later a persecuted religious sect which came to be known as the Pilgrims also set sail for the unknown. Its rationale for undertaking this dangerous voyage in the middle of winter was the desire to escape the discrimination imposed on any dissenting sect by the Church of England. Whether their emotional reaction when they came ashore on Plymouth Rock was the same as those who landed at Jamestown is doubtful. The former dreamt of material well-being; the dreams of the latter centered on freedom to practice their own faith. These two dreams would shape the future psyche of this nation.

What these English men and women had in common was their role as the vanguard of what would eventually become the United States. Each of their visions of this new world — wealth and freedom — was made possible by their accidental landing on that part of the North American continent whose climatic conditions lent to the development of a civilization. Its vast land mass, sparsely occupied by three million primitive Amerindians, enabled these pioneers and those who followed to exploit and conquer not only the native inhabitants but the lands they occupied. In the seventeenth century, land represented freedom as well as wealth; if land was available in unlimited quantity and quality, as it was for these settlers, their descendants and those who came after them would enjoy both.

This book recounts the first 300 years of this new nation's history, from its original settlements to the end of the nineteenth century when it had emerged as the richest and most powerful nation in the world. Its influence on every other nation remains unparalleled. In one way or another, the ideas and ideals it has propounded have shaped the form of most other governments and have come to be viewed as the *sine qua non* of what a good government should aspire to become. Still, because of its incredible wealth and the economic, political and military power that stem from that wealth, it is both feared and admired at the same time.

There is a specific reason why this book is divided in two parts. One era began with the earliest settlements and ended when the distinct difference in the economies of the North and South could be resolved only via the bloodiest war in the nation's history. Another era extended from the inception of those hostilities to the end of the nineteenth century, when the growth and diversity of the American population and of America's economy prompted the need for fundamental changes in the original Constitution and eventually led to what the United States is presumed to be today — a democracy.

However, there is more to this book than the narration of the first 300 years of US history through a different lens than that which is usually associated with the subject. A century ago, American history ranked just below reading, writing and arithmetic. Today it is glossed over in the schools and is subjected to the censorship of political correctness. As a result, the overwhelming majority of Americans who consider themselves to be educated, those with college degrees (a sizeable percentage of the population, as compared to a hundred years ago), haven't the vaguest notion of this country's history. As a matter of fact, for those people who did not major in the subject in college, the principal references to the nation's early history are the current spate of biographies of such famous Americans as Benjamin Franklin, John Adams and Alexander Hamilton, coupled with the docudramas on public television and of course, the continuous supply of books dealing with various aspects of Lincoln's life and death.

This book is not the work of a professional historian but that of an amateur history buff determined to educate himself on this subject and in the process pass along to the lay reader in two volumes the information accumulated in his studies. But there is another facet to this work as well. While the author is indebted to professional historians for the facts used in the writing, it does not follow necessarily that the author's interpretation of these events or people will coincide with theirs. As a result, the conclusions offered in this book may differ drastically from those usually associated with the events.

Chapter 1. The English Settlements in North America

Of the original thirteen colonies, only four received their original charters from the King of England for the ostensible purpose of seeking freedom to worship as they pleased: Massachusetts, first for the Pilgrims and later for the Puritans, New Hampshire for an offshoot of the Puritans, Maryland for the Catholics and Pennsylvania for the Quakers. Connecticut and Rhode Island were settled by dissenters from the Puritans and received their charters later. Virginia's initial charter was issued to a private company hoping to duplicate the treasure trove of gold and silver that the Spanish had discovered. The charter for the Carolinas, given to English planters from the sugar island of Barbados, was for the express purpose of producing sugar cane; when the climate was found impractical for that product, they switched to the production of other commodities. New York was wrested from the Dutch West Indies Company in 1664; like all Dutch possessions in the New World, it was founded as a commercial venture originally intended to enrich the stockholders in Holland. Georgia, the last of the colonies to be settled, was the brainchild of General James Oglethorpe and some Anglican ministers; their avowed goal was to rehabilitate the thousands of derelicts who swarmed the streets of London by transporting them to a salubrious environment in pristine lands where they would not be subjected to the vices associated with a large city.

Delaware and New Jersey, like New York, were originally settled and claimed by the Dutch. Their subsequent history, however, differed dramatically; while New Jersey was adjacent to the major Dutch settlements on Manhattan and Staten Island, Delaware was 90 miles away, and its Western area later would be claimed to be part of the grant issued to Lord Baltimore as Maryland. The Netherlands was restricted in the number of colonists it could send to its far-flung possessions and was hampered in its efforts to compete in the New World because of its small population, most of which was already gainfully employed. In addition, unlike England, it lacked the religious conflict that provided impetus for many to relocate to America. While the Dutch laid claim to Brooklyn and Long Island, most of the population were Englishmen who had crossed over from Connecticut.

Delaware, on the other hand, in the first third of the seventeenth century, had no English colonists to draw upon. Instead, it owed its population growth to Peter Minuit, the Director-General of the colony of New Amsterdam (and the man famous for having purchased the island of Manhattan for beads and trinkets worth $24). When he was recalled to Amsterdam by the proprietors of the Dutch West India Company and cashiered (ostensibly for speculation), he contacted the King of Sweden through a friend and convinced the King of the potential wealth the New World afforded.

Colonies of Swedes and Finns were established in Wilmington, Delaware and southern New Jersey. Although Minuit was lost at sea on his return voyage to Europe, the Swedish presence in both colonies continued to grow. The Anglo–Dutch sea wars of the mid-seventeenth century would put an end to the Dutch colonies on the North American mainland. James II, Duke of York and Lord Admiral of the English navy, sent a fleet of English warships into New York's harbor, forcing it to surrender. England acquired the Dutch colony of Delaware as well as the peninsula just west and south of Manhattan (which the Dutch considered to be an appendage of New Amsterdam). James named the Dutch appendage New Jersey, after the Isle of Jersey, but granted the lands comprising it to two friends, Sir George Carteret and Lord Berkeley, who divided it into East and West Jersey. In order to attract colonists, religious freedom was guaranteed to all, provided they paid a quitrent to the new proprietors. Sir George Carteret was named the governor of the colony; once the Quakers settled in bordering Pennsylvania, a wealthy Quaker purchased Lord Berkeley's interest.

In 1702, Queen Anne merged the two colonies and appointed Edward Hyde, Lord Cornbury, as the first governor of the royal colony. Unfortunately, the governor viewed his new post strictly as an opportunity to increase his fortune and he was relieved of his post. From then until 1738 the colony was placed under the governorship of New York. It was Judge Edward Morris who led the fight for New Jersey's independence from New York, and in 1738 the state achieved its independence with Morris appointed royal governor.

Delaware faced a different problem. While the Swedes had no other possessions in or near the North American mainland, as the number of their colonists increased in Delaware, they viewed the original Dutch settlers living there as intruders rather than as the *de facto* owners. Peter Stuyvesant, the Director-General of New Amsterdam, whose duties included overseeing the other Dutch possessions on the mainland, corrected any misapprehensions the Swedes may have had by dispatching an armed force to the colony. Once the English seized New Amsterdam, Delaware became an English colony even if it was not populated by former residents of England. This situation changed in 1681 when Charles II delivered to William Penn the last tract of unoccupied land north of the Potomac River as a refuge for his co-religionists, the Quakers. The land grant was in repayment for a debt he owed Penn's father, Admiral William Penn. Like many Quakers, he was able to separate the tenets of his faith from those of a practical businessman. Given the enormous amount of land to be gainfully exploited, Penn dispatched agents to Germany to invite Protestant sects to come over. He offered a liberal religious policy, allowing colonists to worship as they pleased, and thus attracted dissident Protestants to his colony. The only thing his new colony lacked was a major outlet to the sea; when he called on Charles's brother James, asking him to lease him the three counties that constituted the territory of Delaware, James willingly complied.

The next problem Penn faced was the difference in languages between the two populations — the English he had settled in Philadelphia and the nearby counties, and the Dutch and Swedes living in Delaware. This dilemma was finally resolved in the early eighteenth century with each colony possessing its own assembly and the appointed governor of Pennsylvania presiding over both assemblies. While this appeared to resolve whatever friction existed between the residents of the two colonies, it did not eliminate the border dispute between Pennsylvania and Maryland. The heirs of Lord Baltimore and William Penn fought this out in the chancery court in London without arriving at an agreement. Finally, in 1767, the heirs agreed to engage the services of two English surveyors, Charles Mason and Jeremiah Dixon, who determined the western borders of Pennsylvania and in turn, Delaware. This was the origin of the famous Mason–Dixon Line which would later divide the nation between those states where slavery was permitted and those where it was prohibited. Despite this division, because southern Delaware's economy was devoted to the cultivation of tobacco, Delaware would remain a slave state until the passage of the thirteenth amendment to the Constitution.

The one subject all thirteen colonies had in common with each other was their relationship with the Amerindians, the various tribes already settled on the lands they intended to occupy. How could a civilization with its own customs and mores coexist with a different one, especially one which had yet to advance to its stage of development? Take something as simple as domesticated animals, which caused the initial friction between the first settlers in Virginia and the local population. The Indians found more than enough game in the surrounding woods to satisfy their carnivorous needs. But the new settlers allowed pigs to run free and this devastated their crops of corn. It didn't take too long for the local tribes to understand that these newcomers viewed them not as fellow human beings but as savages standing in the way of civilization. It was only when they grasped that fact that a life-and-death struggle ensued, a struggle that would culminate 300 years later with the genocide of approximately three million Amerindians and with the survivors relegated to reservations. This course of events was akin to the Holocaust, even if the treatment of the Amerindians has never been depicted as such.

The Pilgrims made an effort to "civilize" the Indians and have them adopt the customs and religion of the English settlers. Where Indian women were accustomed to work in the fields and plant and cultivate the corn, Indian men now took over this role. Where the Indians in this region were accustomed to share their women, monogamy was introduced. They were obliged to change their mode of dress and conform to that of their "benefactors." They were introduced to the Protestant faith and were expected to live the life of a good Christian.

Unfortunately, the neighboring tribes viewed this experiment with alarm. One of the Indian chiefs, Metacom, saw it as a ruse whose purpose was to appropriate their lands. This set in motion what came to be known as King Phillip's War. Outlying communities of settlers were brutally massacred. The English colonists were unaccustomed to Indian warfare. Eventually the leaders recognized they would have to make alliances with other Indian tribes if they were to defeat Metacom.

Somehow they stumbled upon a cultural defect that made most of the Amerindians vulnerable to destruction — their societies had never evolved past the stage where the role of the men was restricted to that of the hunter-warrior with all the other roles left to the women. The warring of one tribe against another was not motivated by coveting the lands they occupied. In pristine North America, there was more than enough game and fish to feed double the native population. Women and children were the coveted prizes, since monogamy was not part of their projective system. In their culture, everything was shared. Once the colonists understood the motive for warfare, they tried to set one tribe against the other, with the goal of occupying the lands of the defeated. To attain this goal they offered the one thing the Amerindians sought, firearms. At the same time, there were valuable products the Indians could supply, such as fur pelts and animal skins that could be sold in Europe or used domestically. The colonists also discovered how vulnerable the Amerindian men were to alcohol, and utilized this weakness when signing treaties for land or to get the Amerindian leaders drunk and then kill them. Diseases, especially smallpox, also took a heavy toll. As far as the settlers were concerned, the end justified the means, and the end was the land the Amerindians occupied

Whether it was the rocky soil of New England or the rich soil of Pennsylvania or the swamps of South Carolina, used for growing rice, these large tracts of land had no liens upon them. Whereas in England most of the land had been seques-tered, either by the nobility, the gentry, the church or the king, in the colonies there was land for anyone willing to work it and make it productive. The cultiva-tion of tobacco, and the creation of a large and profitable market for it, eventu-ally made the Jamestown colony viable. It was this fact more than any other that doomed the Amerindians and at the same time insured the steady growth of the colonies.

Likewise, guaranteeing indentured servants 50 acres of their own land fol-lowing seven years of servitude insured a plentiful supply of labor. There is no better example of the importance of labor to the success of a colony than the program instituted by Lord Calvert when he arrived in Maryland. Although the lands for the colony were supposed to serve as a religious haven for Catholics, he immediately offered 100 acres of land to any Protestant crossing over from adja-cent Virginia — as compared to the 50 acres the colony of Virginia granted. As a fillip, he threw in an additional 50 acres for each male child over the age of 16. Both colonies needed manpower to enrich the colony as well as to cope with the Indian tribes who gradually came to realize that they were in a struggle for their very existence. While there was a steady flow of immigrants into the New Eng-land colonies, Virginia, and Maryland prior to the nine-year-long English Civil War between Parliament and Charles I, the defeat and beheading of the King altered that pattern. Supporters of the King fled to Virginia, while those seek-ing religious freedom no longer sought asylum under the dictatorship of Oliver Cromwell and his son.

By the time Charles II was returned to the English throne in 1660, there were about 50,000 English settlers in the various colonies, along with some Negroes, most of whom were free, and a certain percentage of indentured servants who could earn their freedom and 50 acres of land. The presence of Negroes in the Virginia colony was the result of a Dutch slave ship destined for one of the Span-ish islands in the Caribbean being driven off course and seeking food and water. Since the ship needed stores and Jamestown was desperate for any kind of labor, a deal was consummated and the Negroes were employed as indentured servants. The year was 1620 and the only historical record of slavery at that time was when a Negro was indentured to another Negro who refused to release him after he had completed his seven years of indenture. Moreover, the Negroes in the colony enjoyed the same rights and privileges as their white counterparts.

A number of reasons and conjectures have been offered to explain the use of slave labor in Virginia and Maryland starting in the 1670s. The one which seems to be the most credible was the growth of larger plantations in line with the continuing growth of the tobacco export business. More significant was the de-cision by the sugar planters on the English island of Barbados to change their labor force from indentured English servants to enslaved Africans. A number of reasons led to that decision. First was the high incidence of mortality among indentured servants. While it was relatively cheap to employ the detritus from the slums of London, given the state of their health when they arrived, they were particularly prone to such tropical diseases as malaria and yellow fever. The second was the close relationship of the English planters with the Dutch, who, at that time in history, dominated the African slave trade. The close relationships began when the Dutch lost out to the Portuguese in the struggle for control of Brazil, the largest producer of sugar cane. When the Dutch were ousted from Brazil, they removed the machinery necessary to process sugar cane into the finished product. The English had just entered the sugar business after seizing the island of Barbados from the Spanish. The Dutch struck a deal with the English planters, exchanging the machinery for an agreement that the finished product would be shipped exclusively in Dutch ships. The Dutch also found it a natural extension of their shipping circuit to bring in Africans as slaves. While they were far more expensive than white workers, initially, they could withstand the tropical diseases that were decimating the current labor force. To prove this premise the Dutch pointed to the fact that, in Brazil, the Portuguese employed only slave labor. Whether the Virginians were privy to this arrangement on the sugar island or the Virginia planters now possessed the funds to buy slaves is a moot point. Once the die had been cast, slavery became an integral part of the economies of Virginia and Maryland. At the same time, the flow of indentured servants continued since the colonists lacked the specie necessary to purchase slaves.

While some historians view Nathaniel Bacon's successful rebellion of 1676 against the ruling oligarchy and Governor William Berkeley as having played a major role in the introduction of slavery into Virginia, their theory does not jibe with the facts. For 50 years poor whites, whether independent farmers or indentured servants, had been living side by side with their Negro counterparts. Since neither group had a voice in the affairs of the colony, it was natural for both groups to rally around Bacon who was attempting to overthrow the existing order. The premise behind the theory is that reducing the Negroes to perpetual servitude created a status divide between the two races. This was borne out when only whites were allowed the right to vote for representatives to the House of Burgesses.

In addition to the conscious elimination of three million Amerindians, the institution of slavery remains a major blight on the history of this country. It must be added, however, that when African-Americans look with pride on their African heritage they should not gloss over the fact that Africans themselves were the ones who rounded up their own fellow Africans and delivered them to the white slave traders to be sent into slavery.

It was no accident that a representative form of government should first make its appearance in Virginia with the creation of the House of Burgesses. Once John

Rolfe introduced a strain of sweet tobacco from one of the Caribbean islands in 1612, and its cultivation in quantity produced the first return on their investment, the proprietors realized that they were in a race against time. Like most charters issued to private individuals by the Crown, theirs carried a term of 20 years. After that, the lands would revert to the Crown. The first change they initiated was to privatize some of the lands, which provided a greater incentive to cultivate as much tobacco as possible. The unforeseen result was to create the landed gentry, which soon demanded a greater voice in the affairs of the colony. By 1619, it was obvious that they would have to share some of the decision making process with their benefactors. Their appointed governor now appointed a council of six of the leading citizens, along with representatives from the 11 boroughs that had developed from the original settlement on the James River. To further placate these breadwinners, the following year they sent over a boatload of women who were to become the brides of the colonists. It was only in 1627, when tobacco exports had become profitable, that the Crown exercised it prerogative and took control of the colony under a Royal charter. Even though the colony now was under the control of a royal appointed governor and his own council, the House of Burgess retained its original status.

A similar development towards representative government did not hold true for the New England colonies. On the contrary, the governments which emerged could best be described as the dictatorships of the ministers who determined and enforced the laws of the colony. It was this dictatorial method of governance that sent some of the colonists into the adjoining lands, soon to become the colonies of Connecticut and Rhode Island. The Salem witch trials were only the prime example of the excesses of a state–church government. So strong was the influence of these Puritan ministers that they co-opted the original government of New Hampshire which had its own charter and placed it under their rule.

The man who would destroy the power of these ministers and indirectly lead to the famous New England town meetings and the concept of representative government was James II, the brother of King Charles II and heir to the throne of England. Following the beheading of his father, Charles I, James along with his older brother, Charles, fled to France, where James served in the French Army under Vicomte de Turenne in the war against Spain. Later James would serve with the Spanish Army and was offered the lucrative post of Admiral in the Spanish Navy prior to his brother being restored to the throne. As already noted, it was under James' command that the English Navy had seized New York, which forced the Dutch to surrender their other possessions, New Jersey and Delaware. Left to his own devices by his brother, James decided to reorganize the English possessions on the mainland. He sought to extend the ongoing sea war with Holland to the American colonies. He had Parliament pass the Navigation Act, which restricted all commercial shipment to English or American ships. He then set out to reorganize the New England colonies so they came under the control of a single appointed authority. His first step in that direction was to revoke the original charters of all the colonies and incorporate them along with New York into one entity headed by the former governor of New York, Sir Edmund Andros. Andros established his headquarters in Boston, while his assistant, Frances Nicholson, remained in New York.

James' vision of the American colonies was similar to that of the French: a single authority controlling every element of society. Recognizing that the major opposition to his reforms would come from the ministerial class and their use of the pulpit on Sunday, he attacked them where they were most vulnerable, the pocketbook. He made the Anglican Church the official religion of all the colonies so the tithes formerly paid to the Puritan ministers now went to Anglican ministers. The next enemies whose influence he sought to curb were the lawyers and the judges. This he accomplished by centering all court activities in Boston, making litigation difficult and expensive. At the same time, he reorganized the courts and the militia, placing them under the control of the governor. His most lethal weapon against the existing order was to revoke the previous land grants given to the colonists, thereby revising their land holdings, and as a further burden he added a new tax to their properties. Nor did he focus his efforts solely on the northern English colonies. To increase the revenues coming to the Crown he raised the duties on sugar and tobacco. As for those foolish enough to object to the newly created dominion, they were summarily jailed. James did not stop there. He viewed the fragmentation of the colonies as inimical to an orderly government. The separate colonies of Pilgrims and Puritans in Massachusetts were merged with Boston, now the sole capital, and he merged the two capitals in Connecticut, that of New Haven and Hartford, into Hartford. Finally New Hampshire, which had been under the jurisdiction of the Puritans in Massachusetts, was granted its independence.

For two decades, or until the Glorious Revolution of 1688, when James was forced to abandon the throne he had inherited on the death of his brother, Charles II, the northern colonies lived under the rules and regulations promulgated by James. It was during these 20 years that the precepts and concepts that had dominated their lives since their foundation gradually disappeared. A different New England would emerge. In place of religious rules, the secular aspects of life now took over. With their newly acquired freedoms, the northern colonies were to flourish and prosper. The ministers still preached from the pulpits but salvation and the next world now had to compete with the present one.

While James was restructuring England's American possessions, a group of investors from the Barbados Island were petitioning Charles II for a huge tract of land on the mainland on which they aimed to produce sugar cane, which would swell the coffers of the Crown. The King, always on the lookout for additional revenue and aware of the success of English planters on Barbados, and to a lesser degree on Jamaica, approved a charter for the new colony, which they named after his queen, calling it the Carolinas. While these investors were astute politicians, they were ignorant when it came to geography or climate conditions. Upon landing in Charleston, South Carolina, they discovered to their dismay that the tracts of land they had acquired were not tropical in climate and could not produce sugar cane. Since they were beholden to their investors in London and had brought their slaves and indentured servants with them, they would have to make the best of an unfortunate mistake.

Known as the Goose Creek men, because they settled four miles from Charlestown near a spot known as Goose Creek, they soon came to dominate the politics and economics of the colony. Since they had a first-class port in Charleston and were closer to Barbados and Jamaica than the New England colonies were, they became the major provider of food and other necessities for the islands. They also discovered, probably from their African slaves, that the swamps around Charleston were ideal for the cultivation of rice; from the local Indian tribes they learned that the region abounded in a plant that could produce the rare dye, indigo blue. Finally, having lived and worked on Barbados they knew that Indian women and young children were highly prized possessions and could be traded for the male African slaves necessary to labor in the rice swamps.

To acquire these captives the Goose Creek men devised a strategy of playing off one Indian tribe against the other in order to provoke warfare. First they would insinuate themselves with the tribal leaders by taking Indian women for their wives. Once they had acquired their confidence, they would cement their relationship by selling their leaders guns and ammunition as well as blankets and alcohol in exchange for deerskins. Armed with superior weaponry, it didn't take much urging for the armed tribe to launch an attack against a neighboring tribe. The custom in tribal warfare was to slay the men and keep the women and children as trophies, and the Goose Creek men were allotted their share of the captives. In addition, they also acquired the land occupied by the defeated tribe and would sell it to incoming colonists. Finally, since Indian women were proficient at drying deer skins so they could be fashioned into leathers for sale in Europe, they were able to exploit their wives for that purpose. Within a relatively short period of time, because of the wealth they had amassed, the Goose Creek men became the dominant force in the colony.

The settlers in the northern regions of the Carolinas, whose products for export were limited to lumber from the pine trees, tar and to a limited extent, tobacco, were left at a distinct disadvantage compared with the Goose Creek men who were exporting large quantities of rice and indigo. Moreover, with the colony's assembly located in Charleston, South Carolina they had no input when it came to taxes or other decisions that affected their livelihood. To rectify their status they petitioned the London proprietors to have their own Assembly so the taxes imposed would service their needs. While their petition was granted and they achieved a degree of independence, the proprietors decided that only one governor would oversee both colonies, and naturally he resided in Charleston. In 1729, when the proprietors sold out to the Crown, the two colonies were separated, with a royal appointed governor for each.

As already noted, the next to last colony to be settled, Pennsylvania, was among the largest and was endowed with the most fertile soil as well as an abundance of minerals. In addition to being a good Quaker as well as a libertine, Penn was an extraordinary shrewd businessman. Instead of offering land grants to his settlers from England and Germany, he leased them the land for which they paid a quitrent. As a result the lessees were responsible for any tax assessments on the land and any improvements they made on their property. On the other hand, he created the first modern city in the colonies, Philadelphia, laying it out in grids so its future growth would be rationale and not haphazard. Penn also endowed it with the first public library in the colonies and was eminently fair in his dealings with the various Indian tribes. The last colony to be settled was Georgia, the brainchild of George Oglethorpe along with some influential Anglican ministers. He sought to create a healthy environment for the destitute people who crowded the streets of London and were a drain on the resources of the church. Granted a 20-year charter by King George, after whom the colony was named, Oglethorpe intended to create an atmosphere for these unfortunates that would enable them to live meaningful lives. To make sure that they wouldn't backtrack, alcohol, slaves and lawyers were banned from entering the colony.

Like so many do-gooders, Oglethorpe became aware that his efforts were in vain. Colonists from South Carolina in search of unoccupied lands soon crossed into Georgia, and when Oglethorpe's charter expired, the Crown took over. All the vices he had sought to eliminate now flourished — as did the colony.

While these English colonies enjoyed a large degree of independence, in many ways they still were inextricably bound to events taking place in the mother country. The Glorious Revolution of 1688, which saw King James flee the country for the second time, removed the yoke of authority he had imposed on the northern colonies since the governors he had appointed fled from their posts leaving a vacuum to be filled. It also elevated Parliament to a new role it had never enjoyed before — master of the nation's purse strings. To attain both of these goals, Parliament had to agree to a dual rulership of Mary, James' daughter from his first marriage, and her husband, William of Orange, the head of the Dutch Republic. The significance of this *mariage de convenance* was that William could call upon English troops in his never-ending war with Louis XIV of France. Upon their deaths, the Crown ascended to Mary's younger sister who became Queen Anne, and English troops under the leadership of the Duke of Marlborough defeated the French forces in a series of battles.

When the only heir Anne produced died at the age of eleven, the only direct descendant in line for the throne was Charles, the young son James had produced with his second wife. Since he had been raised as a Catholic, his ascendancy to the throne was out of the question.

There were a number of economic reasons for the merger of England and Wales with Scotland and Northern Ireland, but overriding these was the fact that the Stuarts were of Scottish descent and still popular with the Scottish people. It was the potential threat of Charles using this popularity to seize the throne by landing in Scotland and invading England that overcame the major obstacle to the merger of these two countries — religion. The Scots were Presbyterians and refused to accept the Church of England as the official religion. Once England was prepared to accept that Scotland would continue to maintain its own Kirk, or Presbyterian Council, the other points of contention could be worked out, namely representation in Parliament and the House of Lords. After much haggling, Scotland was allotted 42 seats in Parliament and fourteen in the House of Lords. In 1707, the merger of the two nations was ratified. For Scotland, the union that created Great Britain was a huge economic boon. It opened up Scotland not only to trade with England and Wales but also with England's far flung possessions. Scottish merchants now could compete with those of London. Scottish manufactures now could be sold in England and in its colonies. With the potential for these new markets, Scottish manufacturers expanded their factory productions to meet this potential demand. Free trade benefitted the economies of both nations.

The American colonies profited the most from this union. Tens of thousands of Scots and Scots-Irish migrated to the colonies to seek their fortunes. Among them were doctors and merchants as well as artisans and mechanics and those merely in quest of a new beginning to their lives. It was this wave of immigrants and those who followed that expanded the economies of the various colonies. At the turn of the century, the population in the American colonies was guessed to be about 250,000, which included whites as well as Negroes, most of whom were slaves; by 1776, prior to the revolution, the population had swelled to approximately 2,500,000, again including Negroes as well as whites. When the first census was taken in 1790, the actual figures were 3,300,000 whites and 763,000 Negroes or a little more than four million people. A large percentage of this increase could be attributed to the high birth rate among women who produced ten or more children during their child-bearing years. On the other hand, the mortality rate also was high, although lower than that of Europe. The combination of a continuous flow of immigrants and the high birth rate accounted for the rapid growth of these colonies and their evolution into a nation.

CHAPTER 2. THE COLONIES COME OF AGE

By the end of the first third of the eighteenth century, the English colonies in North America had undergone dramatic changes. The most significant was communication. Where before there had been Indian paths linking communities, now there were roads that could accommodate a stagecoach. Boston, New York, Philadelphia and Charleston had newspapers, as did the capitals of the other colonies. With the advent of larger ships and more experienced captains, crossing the Atlantic no longer posed the danger it once had; where before it had taken months, now it could be done in two to three weeks. A very primitive mail system, initiated in 1692 under the reign of William and Mary, soon would be expanded. Given Britain's law of primogeniture, where properties were left exclusively to the oldest son, many of the younger siblings residing in Britain now sought to make a fortune in America. Moreover, living in Colonial America no longer carried the stigma it once had. Wealthy colonials now sent their sons to study in England either to become lawyers or to receive a classical education. With the death of Robert "King" Carter in 1732, Colonial America could boast of its first millionaire. Born in 1663, this Virginian, in the course of his lifetime, had amassed a fortune that included the ownership of 300,000 acres of land, 1,000 slaves and £10,000 in British sterling. In addition, he owned ships and warehouses, yet when he died he was still residing in the wooden structure from which he conducted his business affairs. It was left to some of his sons to build the stately mansions for which Virginia would become famous.

By British standards, however, while £10,000 sterling was a considerable fortune, in no way did it make Carter one of today's millionaires; Carter's fortune, much like those of less wealthy plantation owners in Virginia, Maryland and South Carolina, was tied up in land and slaves. Specie was rare in the Southern colonies and in the Mid-Atlantic and New England states as well. When Massachusetts attempted to issue its own paper currency, in order to facilitate commerce between the regions of its colony, its request immediately was rejected by the Governor. Americans were land rich and cash poor. Most of the wealthy plantation owners in Virginia and Maryland were over their heads in debt to English and Scottish merchants in London and Edinburgh and remained in that condition up until the American Revolution when commerce between the mother country and the colonies came to a halt. It was only the merchants in Boston, New York, Philadelphia and Charleston, as well as some of the ship captains engaged in foreign trade, who had access to specie. Most of the commerce within the various colonies was conducted on the basis of barter.

While Virginia by far was the wealthiest as well as the largest colony in Colonial America, merchants in Philadelphia, Boston and New York also were building up personal fortunes and constructing homes that reflected their growing wealth. The American colonies were emerging from their primitive state to that of a society including class distinctions determined by wealth. It was still democratic in the sense that upward mobility was open to all, but personal wealth had replaced the rigid class structure of the mother country. Even the clergy, which had once occupied a dominant role in the New England colonies, no longer carried the cachet they once had. In Virginia and Maryland wealthy tobacco planters now imitated the lifestyles of the English gentry with fox hunts, horse races, cock fights and gambling, while dutifully attending church services and assuming positions in their churches. In Charleston, the Goose Creek men built stately mansions to reflect their growing wealth. British magazines and newspapers, as well as personal libraries of books, were commonplace among the wealthy and the not-so-wealthy in the colonies. Lawyers, some educated at the bar in London or Edinburgh, others home grown, began to proliferate and become important members of the rising bourgeoisie. Colonial America was in the process of developing its own civilization. While British influence still predominated, especially among the rising upper classes, the overwhelming majority of Americans had begun to develop their own projective system.

Into this relatively isolated world, separated by 3,000 miles of ocean, European factionalism and concomitant wars were now to intrude upon these isolated British colonies. As was the case with the war of Spanish Succession, it was the death of a ruler that would shatter the peace in Europe. Instead of Spain, this time it was the death of the Emperor of the Hapsburg Empire, and the mad scramble began for his replacement. Actually, the war was precipitated in 1740, when Frederick II of Prussia, soon to become known as Frederick the Great, invaded Silesia, a Hapsburg property; he defeated the Austrians in battle and seized what was formerly an appendage to Austria. Since none of the other great powers in Europe had taken notice of Prussia until this moment in time, the assumption was made by France and its Catholic ally Bavaria that the Austrian Army was terribly weak and that there would be no problem placing the King of Bavaria on the Hapsburg throne. But while Austria had underestimated the weakness of the Prussian Army, so too had France and Bavaria underestimated the strength of the Austrian Army. George II now sat on the British throne; he still remained the Elector of Hanover. Thus, in the usual shuffling of military alliances that followed, for the second time Britain found itself engaged in a land war on the Continent, this time dragged into the conflict by its Hanoverian king. Since Hanover was one of the Protestant states that were part of the Hapsburg Empire, George II deemed it important that whoever sat on the Hapsburg throne should not be controlled by Catholic France. In essence, this war was a continuation of the religious war that had dominated the seventeenth century. What was significant about this conflict was that for the first time the American colonists would take part in a war not of their own making. In American history, it is known as King George's War, which is an accurate description since if he hadn't been Elector of Hanover as well as King of Britain, the British never would have become involved. The war in North America was a continuation of Britain's continuing war with France on the Continent. With the British Army, led by George II occupied in a war on the Continent, Charles Edward Stuart, the son of James II, and the pretender to the British throne, assembled a French fleet to invade England and recover his throne. The fleet was destroyed in a storm but Bonnie Prince Charles, as he is known in Scottish lore, was determined to persevere without French help. In May 1745, he and a group of his supporters landed in Scotland and were greeted by the population. He won one battle after another including the capture of Edinburgh, and his Army now was prepared to invade England. News of his growing Army and their victories reached the Continent, and George and his Army returned to England to defend his throne. In the ensuing battles on English soil Charles was defeated and fled back to France. Although the Prince had acted independently and without French support, as far as King George was concerned France had to be taught a lesson. Thus, a war over the successor to the Hapsburg Empire would be transferred to the Americas.

Not only would it would produce the only major English victory in the War of Austrian Succession but it would be accomplished by American colonials from Massachusetts and other parts of New England in conjunction with the British navy. The man responsible for organizing this victory was William Shirley, governor of Massachusetts since 1741. Shirley, a lawyer, had come to the Bay Colony in 1733 as an Admiralty Judge and a year later was appointed the King's Judge Advocate. Shirley, unlike so many other governors who were sent over from Great Britain, had lived and worked in the colony for eight years before assuming the governorship, and as a result, had a personal relationship with members of the colonial establishment. Upon becoming governor, one of his first priorities was to build up the fortifications in the state to prevent the frequent incursions by the French and the Indians in the northern part of the state. At that time, what is now the state of Maine was an integral part of the Commonwealth of Massachusetts. In 1745, a decision was made in London to reduce and capture Fort Louisburg. It was located on Cape Breton, just off the coast of Nova Scotia which had been ceded to Great Britain along with Newfoundland following the conclusion of the war of Spanish Succession. Since the loss of those two major possessions, the French had built up Fort Louisburg, considering it as the sole guardian to the entrance of the St. Lawrence River, the waterway that led to the city of Quebec, the capital of France in Canada. Not only was the fort considered impregnable because of its huge guns but the French maintained a garrison of 2,000 soldiers to defend it.

Under the naval command of Sir William Pepperell, Shirley and his American colonial soldiers began the siege of the fort. The colonials may not have made great soldiers in the European sense of strict discipline, which sought men who automatically obeyed the commands of their officers; but, what they brought to the concept of soldiering instead was a degree of flexibility and individuality and the ability to take advantage of circumstances as they opened up. The French soldiers and their officers were unaccustomed to the free-wheeling approach of the Americans conducting the siege. As their British counterparts were to learn during the retreat from Concord and Lexington, the Americans did not fight according to the rules of the Marquis of Queensbury. The siege of the fort would last for 48 days until the French finally capitulated and surrendered. Governor Shirley, as commander of the colonial forces, would receive the credit for the victory. But it was the colonials with their unorthodox approach to siege warfare who had carried the day. That was 1745. Three years later at the treaty of Aix-La-Chapelle, Fort Louisburg along with Nova Scotia was returned to France as part of the final settlement. The American colonials, who as the attacking party had suffered the major casualties in terms of dead and wounded, were to learn the first lesson about their mother country. They were merely pawns in the conflict between England and France. It would take another 30 years before they comprehended that as far as Great Britain was concerned, their only importance in the big picture of the British Empire was to be exploited for the benefit of the mother country.

Robert Dinwiddie, the Lieutenant Governor of Virginia, held a unique position. While the royal appointed governor remained in England, Dinwiddie was acting as his surrogate. Determined to make the most of this opportunity to enrich himself, he had allied himself with the wealthy planters in the colony who had responded by giving him a partnership in the Ohio Company, which had been formed to exploit the lands in the Ohio Valley. The basis for their claim to these lands, currently occupied by the French, was the original charter issued by James I, which extended the boundaries of Virginia all the way to the Pacific Ocean. It was only upon learning that the French had established a military outpost on this land claimed by the Ohio Company that Dinwiddie, with a vested interest in securing these lands, decided to use his authority as governor to oust the French.

Enter onto the American scene, George Washington. Washington was one of those men born to a great destiny where fortune would shine on him throughout his life. Upon the death of his father, at the age of eleven he became the ward of his half brother Lawrence. Prior to this time, Washington had been given little more than a minimal education by his father. Lawrence, who had married into the prestigious Fairfax family of Virginia and who had served in the British navy, where he was one of the few Americans to receive a commission as an officer, was in colonial parlance considered to be a man of the world. Thus this gangly youth of eleven, barely formed, was exposed to what passed in Virginia society as the world of sophistication. There were books, copies of English publications such as the *Spectator* and *Tattler*, balls, dancing, cards, billiards, cock fights, horse racing and all the social amenities that enabled the leading families of Virginia to emulate the landed gentry in England. Then in 1752, fortune smiled upon him for the second time when his half brother, Lawrence, died. He had named George executor of his estate and his heir in the event his only daughter, Sarah, died without any issue. When Sarah died two months after the death of her father, George Washington, at the age of 20, became heir to one of the leading estates in Virginia, Mount Vernon, with 2,500 acres and about 18 slaves. By age 16, Washington had grown to his full height of six feet two inches and was ready for a career. Through family contacts, he became an assistant surveyor. Two years later, again thanks to the intercession of Lord Fairfax, who owned five million acres of land in the colony, he was made official surveyor of Culpepper County and soon added Frederick and Augusta counties as well. Even more important was his venture into the unoccupied Western lands that Virginia laid claim to. Thus, although he was merely 23, in 1754 he had already been named adjutant for the southern district of Virginia with a salary of £100 a year, and shortly after, additional areas were added to his duties. So it was not unreasonable for Governor Dinwiddie to send this new member of the Virginia establishment, with a background in surveying, on a mission to notify the French that they were trespassing on Virginia lands and should immediately vacate them.

Washington left with a guide, a translator and four other men to make this hazardous journey while winter still blanketed the landscape. When he arrived at Fort Le Boeuf, where the French garrison was stationed, he delivered the governor's message to the commander of the fort and awaited a reply. There is some confusion about the actual reply of the French. The actual fact was that England and France were not at war, and the implied threat from Governor Dinwiddie did not reflect British foreign policy but rather the assumption by the members of the Ohio Company, of whom the Governor was only one, that this was their land to develop and that the French were intruding on private property. According to one version, given the nature of the hierarchical system of the French system of governance in North America, the Commander wrote the Governor that all decisions were made in Quebec and that he would have to forward his request to General Duquesne for an official reply. This made sense since the French believed that all decisions should be entrusted to a single authority. But that was not the reply that Governor Dinwiddie expected to send to London. A messenger back and forth to Quebec in the middle of winter would take months, if not longer, and even then, it did not mean necessarily that headquarters in Quebec would take his threat seriously. Instead, the Governor sent a message to London reporting that one of the French officers was overheard to say that the French intended to remain in Ohio and that the British would have to expel them by force if they wanted the territory. When Washington arrived back in Williamsburg in January 1754, since he had a Dutch translator, he was innocent of what message the Governor intended to send to London. There is little doubt that the Governor was intent upon inflaming the British authorities, and he did his best to publicize the threat made by the French officer. But Dinwiddie was not waiting for London to act. He commissioned an Indian trader in Pennsylvania, by the name of Trent, to hire some men and construct a fort on the disputed territory of what is now Pittsburgh. Acting on his own, he would have a showdown with the French. What appears obvious is that he had strong contacts through the officially appointed governor within both the government and the Parliament in order to take such precipitate actions.

Uncertain as to what was taking place with Trent and his workers, Dinwiddie decided to commission George Washington as a Lieutenant Colonel in a Virginia regiment the governor had organized and send him with 160 men to reinforce the fort. By the time that Washington and his men reached Cumberland, Maryland, he learned from the Indians that Trent and his workers had been expelled from the fort by the French and that the French had taken it over and renamed it Fort Duquesne. Determined to find out exactly what had transpired, and somewhat guided by a sense of self-importance because of his first military commission, he pushed on to within 40 miles of the fort. There he and his troops, along with their Indian allies, began construction of a new fort, which he named Fort Necessity. In his defense, it must be said that while Washington may have been a professional surveyor of land, as a military strategist he was a novice. The site he chose for his fort was a water-logged creek bed surrounded by dry highlands.

As to what happened next, the story remains murky. According to the French, a company of about 30 men approached the fort with a flag of truce and were fired upon, with Washington's men killing the commanding officer, Joseph Coulon de Villers, the Sieur de Jumonville, along with seven other soldiers. According to Washington, they were a hostile force that his men had driven off. Dinwiddie, upon learning of the engagement, was overjoyed, raised Washington to the rank of a colonel, and dispatched reinforcements from the militia of Virginia and North Carolina to reinforce the fort. Washington did not know that the officer who had been killed was none other than the half brother of the commander of Fort Duquesne, Louis Coulon de Villers. Washington would soon learn this fact to his utter dismay.

Believing himself safe, what with the arrival of reinforcements, Washington put the finishing touches to Fort Necessity. Naive and inexperienced, he did not realize the vulnerability of the site that he had selected. When the French finally attacked the fort with more than double the manpower available to the young Colonel, within 24 hours he was forced to surrender. Washington, after signing a pledge that there would be no more military activity in the region for one year and signing a paper in which he took full responsibility for the murder of Louis Coulon de Villers' brother Joseph, was allowed to depart, with his troops, after leaving two of his officers as hostages to bear witness to the agreement. Only when he and his remaining troops marched out of the fort and returned to Williamsburg did he learn that his translator had misinterpreted the document he had signed which allowed for him and his men to return. He not only had taken responsibility for the death of Joseph Coulon de Villers but admitted to being the actual assassin. While Governor Dinwiddie was ecstatic, viewing the abject surrender as the means to engage Great Britain in the conflict, Washington was depressed and handed in his commission.

Dinwiddie, on the other hand, forwarded the relevant papers to Sir Horace Walpole, then British Prime Minister, who in turn passed them on to the King, George II. Dinwiddie would have his war, and the Ohio Company and its investors would have possession of their valuable investments. The King's possessions had been attacked without provocation and forced to surrender. At this time, there was no official state of war between France and England. That would wait until 1756, with the start of the Seven Years War, a European conflict that had nothing to do with French or English possessions in the Americas. Despite the fact that the two nations were not at war, the King dispatched Major General Edward Braddock as Commander-in-Chief of all British and Colonial forces in America with the limited purpose of driving all French armed forces out of territory that the English considered to be part of their possessions. This included the Ohio Valley and areas in upper New York State, where the French had established a fort on Lake Champlain and one on Niagara. To Governor William Shirley was given the role of conquering Fort Niagara, after the successful campaign in which he and the American colonials had forced the surrender of the fortress of

Louisburg on Cape Breton; to Sir William Johnson was given the role of subduing the fort on Crown Point situated on Lake Champlain.

On the surface, it seems absurd that George II would commit Britain to the expense of engaging in a war 3,000 miles away without the full knowledge of the circumstances that had led to Washington's surrender. The King's decision, however, was not based on that incident but on being forced by Parliament to agree to the terms of the Treaty of Aix-la-Chapelle, relinquishing Fort Louisburg. Now he sought some recompense for having to relinquish Cape Breton. Even more important to understand is that, prior to 1756, the British had no intention of attacking the French possessions in Canada or in the upper reaches of Michigan where the French had established garrisons around Detroit and further west. The purpose of the campaign was limited to removing the French from lands they had illegally occupied; foremost among these was Pittsburgh, the gateway to the Ohio Valley. In the meantime, Washington, who had tendered in his commission, initially refused to participate in the forthcoming campaign. When General Edward Braddock landed with his three regiments of British troops, Washington's unwillingness to serve was predicated on pride. Although he held the rank of colonel, now that he did not hold his commission from the King, any officer in the British Army automatically outranked him. Braddock, realizing that he was totally unfamiliar with the terrain he was about to invade, stroked the young man's sensibilities and invited him to join the British forces as his aide de camp with a promise that once the campaign was over Braddock would guarantee Washington a commission in the British Army. To duplicate what his half brother Lawrence had achieved — a commission as an officer in his Majesty's armed forces — had been the life's dream of this young man. It was this decision, made grudgingly at the last moment, which would launch Washington on his military career and lead him to the pinnacle of success in his life.

Thus, Washington and his regiment of militia were to accompany the General on his march to Three Forks. As far as Braddock was concerned, they represented nothing more than a supplementary force whose role in the forthcoming siege and battle was incidental. It was 110 miles from the starting point to reach the Monongahela River where Fort Duquesne had been built by the French. The march would have to take place through the wilderness. To get the big guns across streams and rivers as well as marsh lands and rocks was quite an engineering feat. Since progress was so slow, Braddock decided to send ahead some light battalions that would establish camp before he arrived with the bulk of his troops and the big guns.

When the lead units arrived at the Monongahela River and set up camp in preparation for Braddock and the bulk of the Army to arrive, it was assumed that the French and their Indian allies would give token resistance as a matter of form and then surrender once the big artillery pieces began devastating their fort. It was a classic case of British arrogance taking precedence over common-sense. In their hubris, following the successful navigation of the forest and all of its obstacles, the lead elements of Braddock's Army encamped in an open field, surrounded by forests, in a wilderness they had never experienced before and failed to take any precautions against an unexpected attack. The officers leading the advanced party were so cocksure of their success that they failed to send out advanced parties of Indian scouts who were accompanying them, to scout out the surrounding terrain. Thus, they were taken by total surprise when they were suddenly attacked by Indians and white men dressed as Indians. At first, the Indians panicked when the light artillery seemed to blast them from their hiding posts behind the trees but under French leadership, they soon reformed and began picking off, first the officers, then the men in the light battalions that were Braddock's advance guard. Unused to this kind of warfare where they could not see or reach their enemy, they began a retreat that soon turned into a rout. To complicate matters, at that very time the main forces of Braddock's Army arrived on the scene they were caught up in the path of the retreating troops, thereby adding to the confusion and allowing the French and Indian forces to get in the rear of the main army. Braddock's forces now were surrounded on four sides. A disaster in the making became a total disaster. Massed together, the British and colonial forces became a shooting gallery for the French and their Indian allies. Compounding the disaster was the reaction of the Virginia militia, which Washington commanded, since they were the first to panic and set in motion the ensuing confusion on the battlefield. Braddock had six horses shot out from under him in a vain effort to rally his forces before he was killed. The death of the commanding general only added to the overall confusion. In the midst of this slaughter, no one knew who was in command, or whether to stand and fight or organize an orderly retreat. With Braddock along with a third of his officers killed, and the remainder of the regiments and the colonials fleeing in disarray, it appeared that a major disaster was inevitable. As for the wounded, they were left to die on the battlefield, soon victims to be scalped by the Indians.

It was in the midst of this massacre that Washington first showed his genius for extricating defeated troops from a total disaster, a skill that he would successfully employ when he led the Continental Army in the American Revolution. Assuming leadership, he would gradually extricate what remained of the British and colonial forces and successfully bring the remaining members of the decimated armies to Pennsylvania. The British had their introduction to warfare on the frontier. It was definitely different than fighting on the Continent where masses of troops on one side faced masses of troops on the other. Nor was the loss of officers and soldiers the only setback for his Majesty's armed forces. All of their supplies, including the huge siege guns, now were in the hands of the French. But it was only the beginning of their education in warfare on the American continent.

Much has been written about the colonials, that is to say, the English Americans who fought with the regulars from the British Army. Almost all of the accounts, at least those written by the British, were negative in the extreme. The British blamed the colonials for the panic that ensued, claiming that it was the fear of these raw troops that had infected their own. While the performance of the colonials was anything but exemplary, the basic factor leading to the panic of the British soldiers was the loss of one third of their officers and their commanding general, Braddock. The British soldier was instructed to obey blindly the commands of his officer. Without specific orders, he was helpless. There was good reason for the lack of performance by the colonials. First and foremost they were unaccustomed to the discipline imposed on the British regulars. Second, these were not the yeoman or farmers who were fighting for their lands and to protect their families but rather the unemployed who joined to make a fast buck. On the other hand, the confusion among the British officers and men, who were supposed to be the professional soldiers, only added to the insecurity of the colonials. For Washington it was his moment of vindication. As the only officer intimately familiar with the terrain and the Indian tribes, he led the disorganized remains of the British and colonials towards Pennsylvania rather than retracing the steps from which the invasion had been launched. Had Braddock not been killed Washington would have earned what he sought above all, a commission in the British officer corps. The war that was not an official war had begun on the wrong foot. But there was worse to come before it would be set on its right track. With Braddock dead, Governor Shirley of Massachusetts, the conqueror of Louisburg during King George's War, was made commander-in-chief of all the British and colonial forces in British North America. In addition to directing the operations against Fort Niagara on Lake Ontario, he was to supervise the combined British-colonial campaign to conquer Lake Champlain and seize Fort Ticonderoga. With Great Britain officially at war with France in 1756, having joined Prussia and Hanover in an alliance against the combined forces of France and Austria, any restrictions on where the British forces might operate were lifted. The French and Indian War, which had begun two years earlier over disputed territory that was completely unsettled, and whose avowed purpose was to insure Governor Dinwiddie and the wealthy Virginians that they would have access in the future for their land speculations, had now become a part of the Seven Years War, the first worldwide conflict in human history.

The man responsible for the later success of the British in North America was William Pitt, the elder. The younger son of a fabulously wealthy man who had made his fortune in India in the diamond trade, Pitt had limited choices for a career. He was not the oldest son, so the military was out of the question. This left him with two alternatives: either the Church or Parliament. Educated at Eton and Oxford, he joined Parliament in 1735 and immediately distinguished himself by his oratory. He was afflicted with a serious case of the gout at an early age, along with a slight touch of insanity, both of which he inherited from his father. Nevertheless, regardless of these shortcomings he was appointed by the Prime Minister to head the government's ministry overseeing the conduct of the war, despite the disapproval of King George II. The genius of Pitt is that he perceived the war not as a conflict to be waged on the European Continent but as an opportunity to cement British domination in both India and North America where it was in competition with France. Britain would support its allies on the Continent, the Prussia of Frederick the Great and the Hanoverian electorate of the King with monies, in order to pay for mercenaries, but the thrust of Britain's military efforts would be with its colonies. In a strange way, Pitt was a visionary. Despite the earlier success of the Duke of Marlborough at the beginning of the century in thwarting the efforts of Louis XIV to dominate Western Europe and impose the Catholic faith on Protestant nations, Pitt saw no advantage in deploying British forces on the Continent. Britain's strength was its Navy, the most powerful in the world, and its wealth stemmed from its far-flung colonies in North America and Asia. Britain's military effort focused on expanding its colonial possessions. Little wonder that George II was opposed to Pitt's military strategies. The King was more concerned with the fate of his own country, Hanover, than he was with these colonies of which he knew and cared nothing.

Governor Shirley, now in command of all the British and colonial armed forces in North America, was not a military man but a lawyer and an administrator. He had acquired his military reputation by leading the colonial troops from Massachusetts in the successful siege and surrender of the French fortress of Louisburg during King George's War. As a result of this feat, he had acquired the most dangerous thing for an amateur, an undeserved reputation as a military man. He would pay dearly for this — he was later charged with treason following a series of military disasters that took place under his command. At his trial in England, he was found innocent of the charge of treason. Instead, the court discovered that he was incompetent for the job he had been assigned. To put it bluntly, the British ministry, following the untimely death of General Braddock, could think of no other candidate for the job.

Shirley's role in the British plans was to capture Fort Niagara from the French, which was a threat to the British fort at Oswego, which controlled Lake Ontario. To accomplish his mission, he once again assembled an army of colonials from Massachusetts and New York, and with them, began a siege of the French fort. In his plan, he would use the British fort at Oswego as a jumping off point for his conquest of Niagara. There was only one problem. The French, through their Indian allies, had learned of his troop movements. In addition, the French now had as their commander a brilliant tactician who was a veteran of the wars in Europe, General Montcalm. Montcalm did not wait for Shirley to act. He struck first, laying siege to the British fort at Oswego and capturing it, thereby giving the French control of the all-important Lake Ontario. But Montcalm was unsatisfied with one triumph. From there he pushed his troops southward and seized Fort Henry, taking as captives all 2,500 British troops. Instead of being routed from the border between the British possessions and Canada, French troops now controlled the all-important lake and had captured British regulars, their forts and all of their material. Coming on the heels of the massacre that had befallen Braddock's troops in Pennsylvania, the outlook for the British position in North America looked to be bleak.

But it was not to be the end of the British misfortunes in America. One more disaster still awaited them. William Johnson was a man cut from a different bolt of cloth than Governor Shirley. Unlike Shirley, who was an appointed official when he came to the colonies, Johnson had emigrated in 1737 and established himself as a landowner in the Mohawk Valley. He soon accomplished two things. He established a strong and warm relationship with the Five Nation Tribes known as the Iroquois, who controlled northern New York State. To cement his relations with the tribes, following the death of his first wife, he married two Indian women from the tribe, his last wife being the sister of Joseph Brant, the famous Indian leader. At the same time, he acquired huge tracts of land in the area, making him one of the largest landholders in the country. Using his Indian allies, he would produce the only victory in the war, defeating the French at Lake George in the early fall of 1755. But the major campaign against the French took place on Lake Champlain. By now the British were not about to entrust their Army to a civilian. They would send over from England General James Abercrombie, with a large detachment of British forces, to seize that waterway and capture Fort Ticonderoga, the key to any invasion of Canada from the South. This battle the British were determined to win. A force of 15,000 men was assembled — a combination of British and colonial forces reinforced by the Indians supplied by the Iroquois Five Nations, and a massive attack was planned against the fort. Defending it was General Montcalm with little more than 3,000 troops and whatever Indian allies were still ready to support the French. With a force almost a fifth the size of Abercrombie, Montcalm routed the combined British–American–Iroquois forces, and if he had followed up on his victory, most of New York would have been open to French conquest. The British and Americans casualties numbered 2,000 while Montcalm suffered only 372 casualties.

Pitt viewed these initial disasters as temporary setbacks. His overall strategy was to keep France occupied in Europe by subsidizing mercenaries for Frederick's armies, while Britain's military operations would be limited to North America and India. In that way, he would be playing with a full deck of cards while the French would be obliged to concentrate their efforts within the European theater. The one great advantage that Britain had was that its Navy was the complete master of the seas. As a result, it could move its armed forces around the world with impunity while at the same time being assured that no naval force could attempt a landing on the British Isles. It had the additional advantage of being able to draw upon its British colonies in North America for foodstuffs, and when necessary, ship repairs. As soldiers, the colonists often appeared to be more of a liability than an asset. With Governor Shirley sent back to England to stand trial for treason and General Abercrombie disgraced by his defeat at the hands of General Montcalm, the British dispatched Lord Loudon as overall commander with headquarters in Boston. Pitt's plan was a three-pronged offense. The first would be an invasion of Canada by the sea through the St. Lawrence River and if possible the capture of Quebec. The second was to conquer Lake Champlain and Fort Ticonderoga, which would lead to a southern invasion by land, with the ultimate goal of attacking and seizing Montreal and from there moving on to take Quebec by land. The third attack would send a new expedition against Fort Duquesne, which would open up the Ohio valley.

In order to send a fleet up the St. Lawrence River to attack Quebec, the French fortress at Louisburg would have to be reduced. Otherwise, its huge guns would blow the British ships out of the water. The job was given to General Geoffrey Amherst. Using small boats to land his men on shore, he soon had the fort conquered. Now the British fleet could safely sail up the St. Lawrence River and gain a landing place on the shores opposite Quebec. General Wolfe, who had served under General Amherst, and had been instrumental in the capture of Louisburg, was the man Pitt selected for the capture of Quebec, while Amherst was dispatched to conquer Fort Ticonderoga on Lake Champlain and then move on to capture Montreal. Wolfe's first attempt to seize the eastern shore of the fortress at Beauport resulted in a disaster. Then, like any great general, he got his lucky break. A French deserter showed him a secret path that would lead to the Plains of Abraham, thereby avoiding the heavy guns of the fort, which had played such havoc with his troops at Beauport.

The surprise attack was successful since Wolfe fielded 8,500 troops to the 1,500 available to Montcalm. Prior to the attack, Montcalm had begged the French governor general for reinforcements but had been turned down. Montcalm had become too famous in France with his startling victories in New York State. Both Wolfe and Montcalm died on the Plains of Abraham. Meanwhile, Amherst, transferred to the American mainland, reorganized the shattered forces of General Abercrombie, and no longer facing an adversary like Montcalm, eventually captured Fort Ticonderoga.

William Johnson then led a force of colonials along with his Indian allies and seized Fort Niagara. The two armed forces then joined together, under the command of Major General Amherst, crossed the Canadian border and captured Montreal. The war in Canada was over. In Pennsylvania, a new British Army under the command of General Ford, along with the newly promoted brigadier general of all the armed forces in Virginia, George Washington, would follow a different route to Fort Duquesne, against the objections of George Washington. Upon approaching the fort, he discovered that the French had destroyed it and fled into the interior. With the last major outpost of the French in colonial territory gone and with Canada having capitulated, the French presence in North America was gone. Under the guidance of the Pitt ministry, Great Britain now ruled over two of the largest land masses in the world, North America and India. Pitt, however, was unable to enjoy the fruits of his policies. In 1761, his ministry would be dissolved by the incoming monarch George III, and the peace treaty would be signed two years later. France, in addition to losing Canada, had lost all of its possessions in the Caribbean. Under the peace treaty, however, it would turn over Madras in India in exchange for the return of its two sugar islands, Guadeloupe and Martinique.

For France, the war had been a disaster as far as the loss of its colonies in North America and India were concerned. Furthermore, none of the European policies it had pursued had come to fruition. The real problem that had dominated French policy was a result of King Louis XV's marriage to Marie Leszczynska, the daughter of the deposed king of Poland. His efforts to have the French candidate elected as Polish king led him into secret diplomacy, unknown to his ministers, and to an alliance with France's proverbial enemy Austria. The Austrians' only interest was the return of Silesia, which Frederick the Great of Prussia had seized arbitrarily; Austria had attempted to recover Silesia but had been defeated by the Prussian Army. As a result, Louis XV had committed France to a war that served no French interests other than deciding who would sit on the Polish throne. The only interest of Russia as an ally of the French and Austrians was to acquire a piece of Poland. Goaded by his mistress, the famous or infamous Mme. de Pompadour, the French king devoted all the energies of his country to saving Poland from dissolution. In the process, not only did France lose its overseas colonies but Poland was divided between Prussia, Russia and Austria, leaving France with an enormous debt. Pitt's policy of restricting Britain's war effort to North America and India had paid off but not as he had foreseen. Unbeknownst to him or anyone else in Britain, he had dramatically altered the economies of the American colonies and set in motion their quest for independence.

CHAPTER 3. THE ROCKY ROAD TO INDEPENDENCE

Mercantilism, the economic theory subscribed to by the leading European powers until the advent of the Industrial Revolution and the emergence of capitalism, held that the wealth of a nation was predicated on the amount of specie — gold and silver — in its treasury. To maintain and increase this balance its exports should exceed its imports. This was Britain's policy when it came to its American colonies. All America's major exports such as tobacco, rice and indigo would be shipped to Britain, which then would re-export them to acquire specie. The colonies were credited with the value of their exports and could use those credits to buy English merchandise. As a result, trade within the colonies was restricted largely to barter. In Virginia and Maryland, for instance, all government officials were paid in hogsheads of tobacco. In the northern colonies where most of the population were independent farmers, whatever tools and implements they required were bought through barter. Only merchants and ship captains who traded with the possessions of Spain, Holland and France had access to foreign specie. The infamous triangle trade of New England merchants, who bought slaves in Africa and sold them to the French sugar islands of Martinique and Guadeloupe, acquiring in return specie and molasses to convert into rum, enabled them to make a profit because France forbade the conversion of molasses into rum in order to protect its brandy and cognac industries. Thus, molasses, a by-product in the conversion of sugar cane to sugar, could be purchased for practically nothing. Once converted into rum, the national drink in the colonies, it would be bartered for tobacco or other products. Efforts by the Massachusetts legislature to issue its own paper currency were quashed by the British appointed governors. The role of the colonies was to service the needs of the mother country.

Pitt's policy of an all-out war against the French in North America would alter the economies of the Northern and Mid-Atlantic states. The presence of more than 10,000 officers and regulars spread among most of the colonies over a period of seven years would bring a wellspring of British currency. Those Americans who enlisted in the militia to serve with the British in their conquest of Canada and on the mainland, while generally more a liability than an asset, still had to be paid a bounty in specie before they would tender their services. It was American farmers from the New England and Mid-Atlantic states who profited the most. They provided food for the British Army and the British Navy as well. And, American captains and their crews were enlisted to ferry the supplies to the ships. In New York City, which the British used as its military headquarters, the price of land and real estate soared to astronomical heights. Boston, as well as other coastal cities in New England where British warships anchored for repairs, benefited from the British war effort. Tavern keepers also enjoyed this cornucopia of specie that descended on the colonies. Farmers took on mortgages to acquire additional lands and take advantage of the ever growing demand for food to supply the British armed forces. Once the Peace Treaty of Paris was signed in 1763, the bottom fell out of this ship of bounty, and for the first time in their history the American colonies experienced an economic depression. The supply of specie dried up, and those who had speculated on it lasting forever found themselves in debtor's prisons being unable to meet the payments on their mortgages.

As is the case with any artificial boom and bust cycle, not everyone was ruined. The more prudent found themselves in an enviable position if they had saved their newly acquired wealth. Real estate and farms could be acquired on the cheap. It was during the wartime period that merchants in Boston, New York, Philadelphia became prosperous. While before London and Edinburgh merchants had relied largely on customers from the Southern states, where the merchandise imported was sold on credit from present and future sales of tobacco, now they were able to expand their market to include a clientele from the Mid-Atlantic and New England colonies, flush with specie. Even products produced in the colonies enjoyed some of this unexpected largesse from the war. At the same time that merchandise was crossing the Atlantic Ocean so too were immigrants from the British Isles. Now that the threat from the French had been eliminated, the British colonies in North America looked more attractive than ever before, with potentially millions of acres of land open for settlement. No group of men was more enthusiastic about the future prospects for exploiting these lands behind the Appalachian Mountains than the wealthy Virginia planters who had invested in the Ohio Company for the sole purpose of the acquisition of these lands to increase their wealth. Nor was the Ohio Company the only consortium coveting their acquisition. A group of wealthy Pennsylvanians had organized a similar company with the same avowed purpose. Each group based its claim on charters issued to their respective proprietors by different Kings at different times. Since the charter issued to Virginia was issued 70 years earlier than that issued to William Penn, the stockholders in the Ohio Company were certain that their charter would prevail. Meanwhile, the man responsible for precipitating the French and Indian War, which made this vast territory open for exploitation, Lieutenant Governor Robert Dinwiddie, had been recalled to England in 1758. Before any litigation over ownership could begin, an Indian chief by the name of Pontiac put a damper on the expectations of both groups of investors. In 1763, shortly after the treaty of peace ending the Seven Years War was signed in Paris, George Mason, secretary-treasurer of the Ohio Company, sent his uncle John Mercer to New York City, headquarters of the British armed forces on the North American continent. His mission was to meet with the commander of the British forces, Lieutenant General Geoffrey Amherst, to present the company's documents indicating which lands it had acquired so it could begin reconstruction of a small dilapidated fort and sell off the surrounding lots. To his shock and bewilderment, Mercer was informed by General Amherst that as a result of "Pontiac's War" all construction and developments beyond the Appalachian Mountains had been terminated by his orders and that these millions of acres were for the exclusive use of the Amerindian tribes who inhabited them. Not only were the investors in the Ohio Company appalled by this policy, instituted by the British authorities, but tens of thousands of American colonials who had assumed once the peace treaty had been signed these lands would be open for development and exploitation now felt deceived.

Pontiac's War is the name ascribed to a massive uprising by more than a dozen Amerindian tribes, which began in the areas around the Great Lakes near Detroit and spread rapidly through what is now Illinois and Indiana to Ohio and into Pennsylvania. The underlying cause for this rebellion is generally attributed to the attitude of the British military once they replaced the French in their forts with their own garrisons. The approach of the French to the Amerindian tribes in the areas between the Appalachian Mountains and the Mississippi River, and extending northward to the areas of the Great Lakes, had been pragmatic from the very beginning. Since they had made no effort to colonize these regions as was the case in Canada but merely exploit them for the furs and skins to be sold in France, their policy had been to pamper the Amerindians with gifts, accept their customs and treat them as equals. Cohabiting with Indian women was common and in certain instances even marriage. The British military authorities viewed its role as that of an occupying force. Unaccustomed to dealing with half naked savages, and with no ulterior economic purpose, the British authorities saw no reason to coddle the Amerindians in any way. In a sense, the British attitude was a reflection of the difference between Gallic and Anglo-Saxon societies. Where the French applied their charm to guile the Indians, the British were matter of fact in their approach. But the greatest fear of the Amerindian tribes, and this fear the British did understand, was that tens of thousands of Americans now would cross over the chain of mountains and usurp their lands, much as they had done in the eastern part of the country.

But for the betrayal of his plans by one of his Indian allies, Pontiac and his tribes would have captured Detroit and made the British position in that part of the Midwest untenable. As it was, his warriors destroyed many of the English forts and killed the colonists in the outlying areas. The war, which lasted a year, finally ended when Pontiac lifted the siege of Detroit and the English established peace by bestowing gifts to be distributed among the warring tribes. Ostensibly, it was this war that convinced the British authorities in London that in order to maintain the peace among the Indians it would be necessary to station troops in the region. Their purpose was twofold — to prevent any further Indian uprisings and to contain the colonists from expropriating Indian land past the natural dividing line of the Appalachian Mountains. This decision by the British government to contain its colonial possessions within their present boundaries was one of the root causes that led its colonies to seek their independence. The British government had good reasons for adopting this policy of containment. The British were unconcerned with protecting both the Indians from the colonists and the colonists from the Indians. What they feared, and rightfully so, was that if these millions of acres were opened up to colonial expansion, given the continuous influx of immigrants and the high birth rate among Americans, eventually, these colonies would become too powerful to be controlled.

It was in the aftermath of this war that the first colonial complaints surfaced about the presence of British troops on the mainland. By the terms of the peace treaty, the English had acquired Florida and returned Cuba to the Spanish, and in turn, the French had turned over to their Spanish allies New Orleans in recompense. Thus, the British Empire in North America now extended from Canada in the north to the Florida Keys in the south, and from the Atlantic Ocean to the Mississippi. To control this enormous expanse of land following the end of the conflict, the British decided to leave 15 regiments of soldiers. These regiments were strung out over the newly acquired lands from St. Augustine in Florida to Halifax and Quebec in the north. A large percentage of these forces, however, were stationed in and around the Ohio valley supposedly to maintain peace with the Indian tribes, but in effect blocking the colonists from Virginia and Pennsylvania from moving into the new territories and seizing the lands of the Indians.

The state of mind of the colonists prior to the decision by the British Parliament to have the colonists pay taxes for the maintenance of these regiments was in general positive. To the New England colonists and those in upstate New York, and to a far lesser degree to those states of the Mid-Atlantic region and Virginia, the defeat of the French meant that they no longer would be subject to the depredations of the French and their Indian allies. Furthermore, the colonists now would have a monopoly on the fur trade with the Indians. At this moment in time, their loyalty to the Crown was at its apogee. And with good reason; it was thanks to George II that hostilities had been initiated, following the disaster to Braddock's Army, and the subsequent conflict had paid off handsomely in more ways than Americans ever imagined. While some of the greedy now suffered, the majority of the colonists felt they never had it so good.

The leaders of the British Parliament viewed things quite differently. They were now in control of a huge continent with a hostile French population in Canada, and to a lesser degree with the same situation in Spanish Florida. In between these two occupied areas were the English-speaking colonists that the mother country had planted and which had grown to maturity. It was time for them to chip in and bear some of the costs of the British regiments that they placed there to insure peace between the colonists and the native Indians. To the colonists, on the other hand, the presence of these regiments had only one purpose — to prevent them from acquiring these lands which were a natural extension of what they considered to be their country. To ask the colonists to pay taxes to support an Army on their land was in contradiction with Britain's own policy. The Americans pointed to the fact that the British Parliament, following the Glorious Revolution, had passed legislation prohibiting the stationing of British troops on their own mainland, other than in times of war and only with the permission of Parliament. Now, they, as English citizens, were expected to maintain the cost of a foreign Army on their soil. Neither Parliament nor the colonists understood the position of either side. To the colonists this was their country, and while they were perfectly willing to be part of a British empire, this willingness was predicated on the mother country recognizing them as British subjects entitled to the same prerogatives afforded those residing in Britain. To Parliament, however, they were colonists of British descent and subject to the laws that Parliament imposed on them. British taxpayers had paid for the removal of the French threat, and it was only fair now that the threat was gone that the colonists should share in the cost of maintaining the peace that had provided their security. To put it bluntly, as far as Parliament was concerned, by leaving the mother country they had abdicated their British citizenship, and as part of the British Empire, they were subject to Parliamentary laws. Therein lay the fundamental conflict that would lead to America's independence.

The presence of the British troops on the newly liberated territories, and to a lesser degree, within the colonies themselves, irked the colonials from the start. The Coercive Acts that followed served to exacerbate their fundamental complaint. The Sugar Act, passed in 1764, a year after the treaty of peace had been signed, was the initial effort of Parliament to control the trade of the colonists. It was designed to protect the English sugar interests on the islands of Barbados and Jamaica from the competition with the French islands of Martinique and Guadeloupe and to sweeten the deal for those who had been trading with the French islands. The price of molasses, from which rum was made, was reduced so as to be competitive with that of the French. On the other hand, the price of sugar was increased, and all trade with the French was forbidden. Since its effect on the colonists was limited and since illegal trade with the French continued, there were few (if any) remonstrances from His Majesty's subjects. But while the Sugar Act pleased and protected those members in Parliament with a financial interest in the islands, it did nothing in the way of raising revenue to pay for the British regiments stationed in America. During the French and Indian War, the British had used the requisition system to defray some of the expenses of the war, and the colonials had never raised any objection; when Lord Grenville came to power in Parliament in 1765, he thought this method to be impractical. What was most important was how to raise money to pay for the British regiments now stationed in the wilderness. What the Parliament needed was not supplies, such as had been delivered with the requisitions, but hard currency. To accomplish this, he established a tax on all legal documents, newspapers, dice and playing cards, as well as the shipment of merchandise from the ports, along with an annual tax on those who sold spirits. In theory these taxes would raise about £200,000 and help defray the cost for the maintenance of the garrisons. Since such taxes existed in Great Britain for years he assumed they would be acceptable in the colonies. Grenville made one basic error in his assumption. In the mother country, specie was common, and it was in general use throughout the British Isles. In the colonies, despite the influx of specie into New England and the Mid-Atlantic states during the French and Indian War, Virginia did not partake in this largesse once the French had abandoned Fort Duquesne, and the Carolinas and Georgia never knew a war was going on. Most transactions still were conducted on the basis of barter. These taxes, once implemented, would deplete the already meager amount of specie in the colonies when the colonial economies finally were adjusting to the concept of conducting commerce through specie.

If a government is going to levy a tax on any element of society, the last groups it should choose are lawyers and newspaper publishers; they were the two most vocal and influential groups in the colonies. Yet the initial reaction among the majority of the colonists was one of reluctant acceptance. Only in the legislative bodies of the colonies where lawyers predominated were efforts made to petition the King for relief. On the other hand, the leading members of the establishment in each colony vied to obtain the lucrative post of distributing the stamps since the distributor would be paid an annual of fee £300 sterling for his efforts. In the House of Burgess in Virginia such a petition was in the course of being drafted and was in the process of being finalized when a 29-year-old newly-elected lawyer stood up to speak and caught the attention of the one third of the representatives still sitting in session.

His first words announced the forthcoming revolution. "Caesar had his Brutus," he began, "and Charles I, his Cromwell, and George III..." The Speaker of the House interrupted him with the words "treason, treason," to which Patrick Henry calmly replied, "If that be treason, make the most of it." That last sentence attributed to Henry is actually apocryphal. According to a French visitor sitting in the gallery, Henry then apologized to the Speaker and the other members of the Assembly, a more likely scenario. Patrick Henry, the son of a moderately successful Virginia planter from the less developed western region of the colony, was a total failure as both a farmer and the owner of a store — both ventures subsidized by his father. But after he opted to study of law, whatever he had lacked in his earlier professions was more than compensated by his oratorical ability. (It was only because of this natural ability that he had been admitted to the Bar.) While his knowledge of the law was minimal, he possessed the ability to sway jurors despite the evidence. Extremely popular among the people in his region of Virginia because of his willingness to take on any case, no matter how small or how remunerative, he had just been elected to serve in the House of Burgess when he delivered his first speech to that body. Henry viewed Grenville's proposed tax on all legal documents as a personal burden since most of his clients, small farmers, lacked the specie to pay him. In bringing the suit for his client he would have to pay the proposed tax on legal documents; and on collecting his fee from his client, since he generally had to sue in order to collect it, he would be obliged to pay another fee, both of them in specie. Thus, his objection to the legislation was personal rather than in terms of principle. Nevertheless, he was determined to defeat the proposed tax on legal documents.

The petition that the members of the House of Burgess were prepared to send to the King was in its final stages when Henry rose to offer his amendments to the resolution. His first five amendments were relatively anodyne but his sixth and seventh were so revolutionary in their content that they were ordered stricken from the records of the House.

In his sixth amendment, he enunciated the soon-to-be-famous doctrine of "no taxation without representation." Henry's logic was unassailable. Ever since the institution of the House of Burgess had been created, about 150 years previously, whatever taxation had been levied on the people of the colony had been agreed by the representatives they elected to this body. From these tax receipts they had paid the salaries of the British-appointed Governor and other officials sent over by the King. Now Parliament had usurped the rights of Virginia's elected representatives by imposing their own taxes on the citizens of Virginia. Since Virginia had no representatives in Parliament, these taxes violated Virginia's laws and were therefore contrary to the wishes of the citizens of Virginia.

His seventh resolution was the most inflammatory: that since these taxes were illegal, it was incumbent upon the citizens of this colony to disregard them. With that resolution Henry challenged the authority of Parliament by calling for civil disobedience. In effect, however, he was also challenging the authority of the King, since the King's authority was derived from Parliament. This was the meaning and significance of the Glorious Revolution of 1687 that had led to the removal of James II from his kingdom and the substitution of his daughter, Mary.

These resolutions of Henry would have died and been buried had not the editor of the only newspaper in Virginia been present during the proceedings. Within a few days, all seven of Henry's resolutions were printed in the paper, which was widely disseminated throughout the colony. Even more important for the dissemination of Henry's resolutions was the postal system, originally established by the British and reformed by Benjamin Franklin, who held the appointed post of assistant postmaster general for the colonies since 1753. Within a week, copies of the Williamsburg paper were sent to the other newspapers in the colonies. Henry's words of no taxation without representation would be the spark that ignited a revolution.

Thomas Jefferson's now famous quotation — "given the choice between a government without newspapers or newspapers without a government, I should not hesitate a moment in choosing the latter" — would have been meaningless without the efficient postal system developed by Franklin for the colonies. While the newspapers were the conduit that spread those now famous words "no taxation without representation," without Franklin's natural genius that he applied to reforming the system and to making it profitable, it is doubtful if Henry's words would have reached the mass audience they did. It was not members of the establishment who would have had to pay the fees, who set in motion the repeal of the Stamp Act, but rather the working class and the unemployed still suffering from the economic depression that had ensued at the end of the war. Unable to comprehend the cause for their plight, they viewed the Stamp Act as an impediment to economic recovery and Henry's phrase as a clarion call for action. In Boston, the house of Lieutenant Governor Thomas Hutchinson was trashed, and in the process valuable documents relating to the early history of that colony were destroyed. But it was in New York that an organization referring to themselves as the Sons of Liberty set in motion a movement that led to the repeal of the Stamp Act. Only one thing is clear about the subsequent events: the crowd of 200 to 300 young men who had assembled on the pier at the foot of Manhattan was not a spontaneous gathering of individuals. It was a planned rally designed to prevent the stamps that had to be affixed to the documents from being landed. Furthermore, the rally succeeded. With no means to control the rowdy crowd, the stamps were disembarked on Governor's Island in the Bay. The frustrated crowd took out their anger by burning the carriage of the Lieutenant Governor. Were it not for the newspapers, which would have been subject to the tax, this would have remained an isolated incident. However, when newspapers throughout the colonies published an exaggerated story of the event, spontaneous clubs of Sons of Liberty emerged in all the capitals of the colonies. Members of the establishment who had not been chosen for the lucrative role of stamp distributor notified the Sons of Liberty of the names of the men who had. These men, threatened with their lives and those of their family, either burned the stamps or refused to distribute them. Without the stamps, courts were closed and merchandise couldn't be shipped out of ports, but the newspapers continued to publish even though they were in violation of the edict. When news of what was taking place in the colonies reached Parliament some of the members called for armed action against these ingrate colonists. The merchants in Boston led the way out of the impasse by calling for a boycott on all imported goods. From Boston the boycott spread to New York. When some of the Quaker merchants in Philadelphia refused to participate in the boycott, their minds were changed by the appearance of Sons of Liberty in front of their homes. If Parliament wouldn't rescind the Stamp Act then the merchants of London might respond. And respond they did. Outside of the British Isles their major clients were the colonies in North America. The pressure on Parliament from the merchants and manufacturers of the merchandise sent to the colonies worked their magic. Grenville, whom George III had never liked, was dismissed from office and replaced by someone the King had even less confidence in, the Earl of Rockingham. To Rockingham was left the job of having Parliament repeal the Stamp Act. It was not easy. Within Parliament, about one third of its members were in favor of enforcing the Act through the use of military force. It was only with the death of the leader of this movement, the Duke of Cleveland, that Rockingham was able to convince Parliament to rescind the Act. At the same time, Parliament's ruffled ego had to be satisfied. The result was the passage of the Declaratory Act: *The British Parliament had, hath, and of right ought to have all power and authority to legislate for the colonies in all cases whatsoever.* With the passage of this Act the members of Parliament felt they had drawn a line in the sand. Rockingham's attitude toward the colonists was based on pragmatism rather than on empty threats. By reducing the duty charged for the importation of molasses from three pence to one pence, the amount of smuggling was reduced, and over the next ten years, until the outbreak of the rebellion, about £300,000 in duties entered the British Treasury.

Having twisted the tail of the British lion and made him cry "uncle" proved to be a wakeup call for the American colonists if not quite yet for the British. They did not comprehend that the American merchants were prisoners of their clientele. If the public refused to purchase British merchandise the American merchants who imported these goods were as helpless as their British counterparts.

They would soon learn when a second boycott forced Parliament to remove the Townshend Acts. Lost in the enthusiasm over the repeal of the Stamp Act were the other legislative acts passed by Parliament in an effort to restrain the economic activities of its American colonists. Foremost among them, outside of the aforementioned Sugar Act, was a prohibition against the production of iron ore and clothing. British merchants, who had pressured Parliament to rescind the Stamp Act, were determined to enforce the monopoly on those products which were their bread and butter.

Many reasons have been ascribed to the events that led to the American revolution but the fundamental cause for the dissolution of relations between the colonies and Great Britain was the Americans' belief that either they were entitled to the same privileges as if they were living in England, or, if not, they had an identity of their own and were no longer subject to the laws of Great Britain. There is no better example of this attitude than the reaction to the Quartering Act, another piece of legislation passed by Parliament under the Ministry of George Grenville. Since British troops now were stationed west of the Appalachian Mountains, in order to reach their assigned destinations they would first have to pass through New York City where British military headquarters was located. During the war the colonists offered no objection to opening their homes to the officers since they were paid specie for these accommodations. But in 1765, when Parliament passed the law, the war was over, and while the troops assigned to the colonies were posted in the wilderness and not in the towns and cities, during their period of passage they would have to be provided with shelter and such amenities as beer, salt and vinegar. While the Quartering Act did not call for the colonists to open their homes to the soldiers, they could make use of inns, empty buildings and barns. The idea of the Redcoats on the streets prior to their departure for duty was anathema to New Yorkers. In essence, having to subsidize these soldiers was another form of taxation since the funds for their maintenance would come out of the taxes raised by the Assembly of New York. To a few, this was but another example of taxation without representation. To the majority, however, unaffected by the presence of the soldiers, it meant nothing. All of this would change in 1767 when New York ran afoul of the British ministry in London. New York by the last third of the eighteenth century had become the major port on the Atlantic seaboard. As a result most of the troops being sent to the interior or being repatriated passed through its port. Since the Assembly had only a limited amount of funds for military purposes it agreed to house the transients for a year, but not to provide them with the beer and other incidentals required by the Act. Outraged by this insubordination, the ministry in Britain dissolved the Assembly until it conformed to the Quartering Act. Because New York was singled out, the reaction in the rest of the colonies was muted, and when New York came up with additional funds, the action against the Assembly was lifted. Despite this supposed capitulation by the Assembly, New York still did not adhere to the full terms of the Act. The failure of the other colonies to support New York led some members of Parliament and George III to the false assumption they could divide and conquer their adversaries.

After one year, and the revocation of the Stamp Act, George III had enough of the Earl of Rockingham. Since the Whigs still controlled a majority in the Parliament, his choice of a Whig to replace the outgoing Prime Minister was limited. In desperation, he turned to his nemesis, the elder William Pitt, to form a government. The King, despite his youth and his obstinacy, was not stupid. He was well aware of Pitt's oratorical gift and his ability to sway the Parliament; at the same time the King asked Pitt to form a government, he elevated him to the House of Lords, naming him Earl of Chatham. Since Pitt was now a member of the House of Lords, no longer could he use his debating skills in Parliament. In addition to suffering from a severe case of the gout, which became more debilitating as he aged, Pitt today would be classified as a manic-depressive. Since psychotherapy had yet to emerge, his fits of extreme bursts of energy followed by periods of complete lassitude were described as madness. George III also exhibited the same symptoms, although when he was lucid he merely became obstinate. Until Pitt was chosen to form a government, it was the Lord of the Treasury who had been considered the Prime Minister since control of the nation's finances was of prime interest to the members of Parliament. Instead, Pitt chose the position of Lord Privy Seal while the third Duke of Grafton became Lord of the Treasury. Although born to Lord Fitzroy and Elizabeth Cosby, Grafton inherited his title of Duke upon the death of his grandfather, a descendant of the bastard son produced in the illicit affair between Charles II, the next to last of the Stuart Kings, and his mistress, Barbara Villiers. Since neither Pitt nor Grafton could address Parliament that role fell to Charles Townshend, Chancellor of the Exchequer.

Any monopoly by its very nature soon becomes lazy and inefficient. Such was the case with the East India Company, which held a monopoly on all exports from both India and the Far East. Although London was famous for its coffee houses, what the British public consumed in enormous quantities was tea, and all the tea coming into Britain came through the East India Company. Thanks to his father having made his fortune in India, Pitt was well aware of the corruption and inefficiency that plagued the company. When Pitt became Prime Minister in 1766, the first item on his agenda was to put an end to the monopoly held by the East India Company. Nor was he oblivious to the practices of the company, which included having key members of Parliament as stockholders, and when necessary bribing others. Prime Minister Pitt was ready to take them on. It was a close struggle, but in the end the company escaped dissolution by pledging an annual contribution of a half a million pounds to the Treasury. Frustrated by his inability to convince Parliament of the Company's forthcoming disaster, he was overtaken by one of his massive states of depression and combined with a serious attack of gout, he retired to his home in Bath where he remained in total seclusion. While he held the title of Prime Minister until 1768, the day-to-day affairs of the government were now in the hands of the 31-year-old Duke of Grafton.

The Duke's basic interests, besides womanizing, were his race horses and going to the hounds. In May 1767, under pressure from the landed Gentry who paid the bulk of the government's revenues, the tax on their land's evaluation was reduced from 3.5 shillings to the Pound to three shillings, leaving the government with a shortfall in the revenues required for its operations. With Pitt absent and Grafton not yet responsible for the direction of Pitt's administration, the problem of where to find additional revenues came under the control of the Chancellor of the Exchequer, Charles Townshend. The Chancellor's answer was to revisit the taxation of Britain's American colonies. To get around the colonies objection to internal taxation, Townshend's answer was an external tax. By placing a duty on lead, paper, glass, paints and tea, the government merely was raising the cost of these items to the consumer. Those Americans who could afford to pay the increased cost of these items would purchase them; those who could not would do without. At the same time it would reaffirm Parliament's right to tax its colonists. Townshend, noted for his charm and his glibness while in the midst of a debate, had no problem with Parliament immediately approving the legislation. In addition to these external taxes the Townshend Act also focused its attention on the collection of custom revenue. Up until the passage of this Act all disputes over the duties due the government were adjudicated in local courts where local juries generally were on the side of the accused. As a result, custom duties from American ship owners yielded only £2,000 in revenue at a cost of £9,000 in salaries and expenses. Under the Townshend Act, Admiralty Courts were established in Boston, Halifax, Philadelphia and Charlestown. Since there were no juries, the British officials who heard the cases now could rule on the evidence. As a result, the revenues collected rose from £2,000 to £30,000 while the cost of administration only increased to £13,000. Finally, an American Board of Customs was established in Boston to oversee the collection of custom duties.

Townsend died suddenly in August 1767, so he never lived to see the results of his efforts. As was the case with most members of Parliament he had no head for business. By increasing the cost of paper, lead, glass, paints and tea through his external tax, he was reducing the potential market for these items in the colonies. He had projected that these external taxes would result in an additional £40,000 in revenues for the Treasury. Instead, the funds collected from these external taxes were miniscule. It was the imposition of the Admiralty Courts that aroused the ire of the merchant class and led to the second boycott of British merchandise.

The merchants in Boston, New York and Philadelphia not only imported British merchandise but also engaged in smuggling into the colonies contraband merchandise without paying the requisite duties. Since there was an external tax on lead, glass, paper and paints, as well as tea, they would import these products either from the British sugar islands or from the Dutch and French possessions in the Caribbean. The largest and most successful merchant in Boston was the soon-to-be-famous John Hancock. When one of his ships was impounded by the British authorities because they believed he was bringing in contraband merchandise, and he knew that his trial would take place in an Admiralty Court where he was certain to be found guilty, he organized the other Boston merchants to impose a boycott on all British merchandise. Once again, the merchants of New York, Philadelphia and Charleston joined in, and British merchants and manufacturers exerted pressure on Parliament to rescind the Act. The problem facing the Whig majority in Parliament was economic, which made it political. To maintain their majority in the Parliament they had to appease the landed gentry, which they did by lowering their taxes while at the same time supporting the expense of maintaining garrisons of 10,000 troops beyond the Appalachian Mountains. Since its American colonies refused to bear any part of the cost , and in the case of Boston had become arrogant and cocky, they withdrew the troops from the territories, and instead of stationing them solely in Halifax and St. Augustine, Florida, they stationed a few of them in the capitals of the colonies. On the suggestion of General Thomas Gage, who commanded the British troops in the territories, the only trouble spot was Boston so he suggested two companies of British troops be quartered there. These actions came too late to save the Whigs. Parliament had lost confidence in their ability to deal with the economic situation or that of the American colonies. In 1770, George III asked Lord Frederick North, a Tory, to form a new government

If Britain was looking for trouble, it had chosen the perfect location. These were not Red Coats in transit as had been the case with New York, which was explicable, but troops permanently stationed in the City for no apparent reason other than perhaps, to intimidate the population. The antagonism between the soldiers stationed in Boston and the civilian population began to escalate. Schoolboys harassed and taunted the soldiers. Each side accused the other of precipitating trouble. It finally reached its culmination with the Boston Massacre in March 1770 when a free black and four Caucasians were shot by British troops. It all began with the usual epithets lodged against a group of soldiers. Within a short period of time what began as heckling by a few, turned into a large and hostile crowd. The officer in charge tried to restrain his men but as the crowd began to close in, the soldiers cocked their guns. Somebody then threw an object at the soldiers and five men lay dead in a pool of blood. Before other shots could be fired, the officer took control and the soldiers were gradually withdrawn. Strangely enough, it was John Adams who defended the four British enlisted men who had been charged along with their officer; through his arguments, the men were acquitted. But the general public was aroused; to appease the citizenry, the troops were withdrawn from the City to the outskirts. When the news of the incident reached London, members of Parliament were outraged that an officer had been put on trial; some even called for military action. Prime Minister North soon calmed them down. In an effort to appease the colonists he announced that all the Townshend duties, with the exception of that on tea, were to be withdrawn. Once again, the British were reacting rather than having a consistent policy with regard to its colonies. Nor did North or the members of Parliament realize that because the colonies possessed a free press, the news of the Boston Massacre was widely disseminated throughout the other colonies. Instead of the incident being isolated, local, it was blown out of proportion.

If Patrick Henry was considered to be a firebrand in the Virginia House of Burgess, and later at the First Continental Congress, possessing a facility for rhetoric unequaled by any of the other revolutionary politicians, Samuel Adams played an analogous role in Massachusetts, in a different way. Unlike his sedate and proper, lawyer-like cousin, John Adams, Sam never was able to succeed in any profession other than that of a gadfly; to others like Governor Hutchinson, he was nothing more than a rabble rouser. Sam Adams, on the other hand, viewed himself as a defender of the rights of Americans to enjoy the same privileges as those granted to Englishmen in the home country. By establishing the Committees of Correspondence with politicians in the other colonies, he played a major role in exposing the problems facing one colony to residents of the others. For the first time since the aborted Albany Congress of 1754, the various establishments within these colonies conducted a written discussion of common problems. Leading figures from Virginia and the Carolinas, by virtue of the Post Office system, were able to communicate with their peers in Boston, New York and Philadelphia. Unbeknownst to the British authorities in London, the first steps had been taken which eventually led to the First Continental Congress.

As the elder William Pitt had predicted in 1766, upon taking office as Prime Minister, unless the monopoly held by the East India Company over all trade with the Far East was dissolved, the Company was headed for bankruptcy. In 1773, the Board of Directors of the East India Company announced that it could not meet the voluntary contribution of £500,000, which the Company had guaranteed to the British Treasury in order to save its monopoly on merchandise shipped from the Far East. The Company was bankrupt. Its warehouses in London were overstocked with tea and spices. In order to sustain the fortunes of the Company, it had paid out dividends to its stockholders, many of whom were members of Parliament. Unless it could raise funds immediately, it would have to be dissolved. Should the Company be forced into bankruptcy, the repercussions in British financial circles would be devastating. Those members of Parliament who were stockholders in the Company appealed to Lord North to salvage the Company's business affairs before it was too late. Besides corruption, the major problem it faced was the exorbitant fee it paid to the government in order to maintain its monopoly. As a result, its tea and other products from the Far East were unable to compete with those of the Dutch East India Company. Because the price of tea even in Britain was expensive, smuggling was common. In the American colonies, even though Dutch tea was inferior in quality, it was the only tea used by the colonists. While the North ministry was unwilling to remove the fee for tea sold in the British Isles, it was prepared to waive the fee if it was distributed in the American colonies. While the author of this scheme remains unknown, once it was presented to Lord North he embraced it wholeheartedly. Here was an opportunity to kill two birds with one stone. By eliminating the usual fee paid to the government and decreasing the usual duty charged Americans from six pence to three pence, the superior teas of the East India Company would become less expensive than the Dutch tea currently used by the colonists. At the same time, retaining the low duty fee of three pence would establish in principle the right and authority of Parliament to levy taxes on the colonists. Lord North's reputation as a financial expert before he became Prime Minister was well deserved. For the first three years of his ministry the financial condition of Britain had never been in better hands. He was Lord of the Treasury as well as Prime Minister, and government revenues far exceeded expenditures. Someone gifted with financial acumen is not necessarily a good psychologist. In proposing to undercut the price of Dutch tea he was alienating the few thousand people who made their living from smuggling Dutch tea into the colonies. Had he not insisted on retaining the reduced British tax on tea, the protests of those engaged in smuggling would have fallen on deaf ears. Especially in colonial America where specie was so scarce, a bargain on such a comestible as tea would have been welcomed by colonial women, almost all of them avid tea drinkers. However, in 1773, ten years after the end of the French and Indian War, Britain's colonists no longer looked on the mother country as its savior. The Sons of Liberty, the radical groups in each of the colonies that had been instrumental in preventing the distribution of stamps, remained active and were on the alert against any further attempt by Parliament to impose taxation on the colonies. In just one decade, a large percentage of the colonists went from looking upon Britain as the country that had liberated the Americans from the threat of the French and their Indian allies, to viewing it as a nation intent upon exploiting them. Lord North and the directors of the East India Company failed to take into account this change in attitude.

Certain that the scheme that had been concocted was foolproof, the Company alerted the colonists by publicly announcing that distributorships for its products already were in place in each of the colonies. When the ships bearing the products of the East India Company arrived in the ports of each of the colonies, members of the Sons of Liberty were at the docks to greet them. Realizing that it would be impossible to unload their cargos in the face of such large and openly hostile crowds, the captains of many of these ships found their best option was to return to London. When the ships laden with tea arrived in the harbor at Boston, they received the same reception at the docks. With no possibility of unloading the cargo, the captains planned to return to London.

In Boston, however, under the orders of Governor Thomas Hutchinson, the harbor exit had been blocked by British war ships. The only native-born American to be appointed by the King as the governor of one of his colonies, Hutchinson was a direct descendant of Anne Hutchinson, who had espoused freedom of religious worship and had been banished from the Puritan colony of Massachusetts to join Roger Williams in Rhode Island. A successful merchant, he had been elected to the Massachusetts Assembly and rose to become Speaker of the Assembly before being named Lieutenant Governor of the colony. As previously noted, his animosity towards the Sons of Liberty and those who supported their programs had been heightened when they ransacked his home and in the process destroyed his valuable collection of papers on the early history of the colony. As the representative of the King, Hutchinson was determined that the cargo should be unloaded properly and stored in the warehouse. It was his obstinacy in the face of reality that would lead to the Boston Tea Party and the ensuing events that evolved into the American Revolution. Whether Samuel Adams was actually responsible for organizing the group of men who dressed up as Indians, climbed aboard the ships laden with tea sitting in the Boston Harbor, and emptied the chests loaded with tea into the harbor, is immaterial. If it was not Adams, it could have been James Otis or perhaps someone still unidentified. The fact was that no one identified either the leader or any of the participants. Since no culprits could be charged with the crime, there was no way to seek reparations for the loss of merchandise.

When Lord North and the members of Parliament received notification of the loss of tea, their outrage at this wanton destruction of property was sincere. In eighteenth century Britain property was more sacrosanct than even life. Little urchins caught stealing a penny-loaf of bread were routinely hanged as punishment. Governor Hutchinson was certain that his hated enemy, Samuel Adams, was behind the outrage but there was no way of establishing Adam's guilt in a court of law. Nor could any of the so-called fake Indians be discovered. While making the colony responsible for the loss of property, Governor Hutchinson, in conjunction with General Gage, made the radical decision to close Boston Harbor until reparations had been made for the loss of the tea. With its harbor closed to all merchant marine attempting to enter or leave, Boston was reduced to economic penury. Thousands were thrown out of work; most business came to a standstill, and martial law, if not actually pronounced, was assumed to be in effect. If the colonists thought the closing of the port of Boston was the last reaction to the anger of Parliament they were sadly mistaken. Three weeks later Parliament was to pass the Massachusetts Government Act. Under the terms of this bill, the Massachusetts Assembly no longer could appoint the governor's councilors; that was now in the hands of the Crown; and the same applied to judges and juries, now to be appointees of the governor. The original Massachusetts charter had been torn to shreds, and not only Boston but the entire state came under the control of the governor. The colony had been shorn of all its rights. Nor did it stop there. In addition, British soldiers who committed crimes no longer could be held accountable in a colonial court if it was the opinion of the governor that they were unable to enjoy a fair trial. Instead, they would be tried in England. The Quartering Act legalized the billeting of troops in people's homes. Although both Edmund Burke and the Earl of Chatham opposed these restrictions on Massachusetts, viewing them as leading toward further problems with the American colonists, King George III and the members of Parliament were not to be deterred in their efforts to quell any rebellious tendencies in the colonies. Parliament in its blind fury and its impotence to tax its American colonies was committing one blunder after another. It wrongfully assumed that the roots of the rebellion were in Boston, and that if they could be extirpated there, the problems with the other colonies would disappear. Instead, they had unleashed a nest of hornets. Food and provisions for the beleaguered citizens of Boston poured in from all the other colonies. In place of quelling an incipient rebellion, the members of Parliament were fostering one that would soon spread to all the other colonies.

The biggest blunder committed by Parliament was the passage of the Quebec Act. Long before Parliament had arrived at the conclusion that it no longer could afford the cost of stationing 10,000 officers and soldiers west of the Appalachian Mountains (in a territory that extended as far west as the Mississippi River, and from the Great Lakes in the north to the Gulf of Mexico in the south), thousands of settlers from Georgia in the south to upstate New York and New Hampshire in the north had established themselves in these forbidden lands. Once the British garrisons had been withdrawn, the number of people crossing over into the sparsely populated territories increased enormously. Since there were millions of acres still unsettled, contact with the French already living there was limited. The passage of the Quebec Act was a desperate effort by Parliament to halt this emigration. Since those French already on these lands practiced the Catholic religion, the decision was made by the British governor in Canada, whose authority extended to these lands, that henceforth the only religious faith allowed in these territories was that of the Catholic Church. Parliament in its wisdom had found a way to alienate every Protestant minister in the colonies as well as their parishioners. This was the proverbial straw that broke the camel's back. Its intent was not lost on the colonial establishment in every colony. Parliament was determined to exclude its American colonists from migrating into these territories. Meanwhile, they were aroused by the blistering sermons delivered every Sunday by their ministers; the passage of the Quebec Act was deemed to be the equivalent of bringing the Papacy to North America.

In fact, there was opposition to this Act both within and outside of Parliament, and it might have been withdrawn had George III stayed out of the picture. Until then, most Americans had viewed the King as their protector. This was the same George III who had opposed forced housing of British troops in colonial homes in order to avoid the Army becoming odious to the civilian population. From now on until the final peace agreement would be signed in 1783, he would be the single, staunchest opponent of coming to any terms with the colonists. But if the attitude of the King was adamant and petulant, that of the government and the majority that supported it in Parliament was one of frustration. The colonies were not Ireland, where British landlords had their fiefs and treated the peasants as though they were dirt. These were English Protestants, not swinish Irish Catholics, where in the event of the slightest sign of revolt the Army marched in and immediately squelched it. What was to be done to end this quasi revolt? To some, the true hard liners, the answer was to seize the leaders, Sam Adams and John Hancock, bring them back to England and hang them as traitors. Even those in Parliament who sided with the colonists in their complaint, such as Pitt, Fox and Burke, were unprepared to give the colonists their freedom from the empire. Nor did the colonists seek it now. What they failed to understand was the attitude of George III. It was he more than Lord North or Parliament that viewed the actions taken by the colonists as a personal insult because it demeaned the authority of the King.

The First Continental Congress of 1774 differed from the conclave called nine years earlier by nine of the colonial governments to protest the Stamp Act. This time there was a clarion call by eleven other colonial Assemblies to protest the action taken by the British government against a single colony, Massachusetts. Whereas the protest against the Stamp Act was nothing more than a unified protest against an act passed by Parliament that the colonists felt infringed on their basic rights as Englishmen, the closing of Boston Harbor, followed by the Massachusetts Government Act and the Quebec Act, were nothing less than a declaration of war against one of their sister colonies, with the implicit threat that members of Parliament might arbitrarily impose draconian legislation on the other colonies as well.

The British government expected Massachusetts to come groveling on its knees, to beg forgiveness, and to reimburse the East India Company for the merchandise that had been destroyed. Moreover, the troops were stationed there, and there was the threat of bringing in more troops, if necessary, to enforce Parliamentary laws. But with the actions against Boston and Massachusetts, it was apparent that this time Parliament had no intention of backing off. This reality dawned upon the majority of the delegates. There was an effort by some of the moderates and Loyalists, led by Joseph Galloway of Pennsylvania, to create some sort of joint representation between Parliament and the colonies, but the attempt came to naught. When a delegate as conservative as George Washington told the Congress that he was prepared, if necessary, to raise 1,000 men at his own cost to defend the liberties of the colonial governments, it was obvious that compromise was not in the offing. The presence of Washington and of Peyton Randolph, elected president of the Congress, made this Congress different from its predecessor. Virginia, the largest, wealthiest and most populous of all the colonies, had been absent from the Stamp Act meeting. This time Virginia was represented by Peyton Randolph, a member of one of the most powerful families in the Commonwealth, by the Lees, and by other key families including Washington's.

The only member from Virginia not drawn from the leading families was the firebrand Patrick Henry, who in his first address to the delegates established a fundamental principle of the gathering when he said: "Distinctions between [colonies] are no more. I am not a Virginian, but an American!" Whether the majority of the delegates recognized the implication of Henry's words is doubtful, but once again the Virginian had pointed out the obvious. They no longer were English expatriates who were part of the British Empire; they had their own identity. They were Americans.

With Galloway's proposal finally out of the way, the discussion centered on whether the Trade Laws regulating the commerce of the colonies were another form of taxation that should be eliminated. After much debate, the topic was finally set aside as being too controversial, and the Congress stuck to its original complaint that Parliament had no right to tax the colonies. Regarding the situation in Massachusetts, until all the laws affecting that province were withdrawn, a non-importation law would be respected by all the colonies, and a year later the same law would apply to exports as well. It was the feeling of the delegates that the only way to bring the British government to its senses was once again to hit the merchant class in the pocketbook. That would have been a solid theory if the merchant class in Great Britain controlled Parliament, but that was not the case. While they had some influence and while the non-importation acts would cause unemployment in British factories, the unpleasant fact was that the landed gentry and the nobility still controlled Parliament.

For the moment, everything was at a standstill. The King and Parliament were certain that time was on their side and that sooner rather than later the economic pressure placed on Massachusetts would force the dissident leaders from power. They would surely be replaced by moderates who would deal with Parliament and reimburse the East India Company for the loss of their merchandise. Perhaps, if they had not passed the Quebec Act, this might have occurred. But the idea of being tithed to support the Roman Catholic Church was heretical not only to the Puritan ministers in Massachusetts but to every Protestant minister, no matter his denomination.

The dilemma facing the North government was that, short of war, there was no way to coerce the colonists of what later became the Bay State. Instead, the government decided that the royal-appointed Governor, Thomas Hutchinson, the only American to have represented the Crown, was the roadblock to accommodation. If they replaced him with General Thomas Gage, commander of the British armed forces in America, who had married an American from New Jersey who had given birth to 13 of his children, perhaps appointing him would appease the people of the Bay State. In the words of Shakespeare, "wishers were ever fools." Thus, Governor Hutchinson and his family were moved to London where he later served as an advisor to Lord North and the King.

As for the delegates to the first Continental Congress, all they could hope for was that the imposition of a third boycott on British imports would bring the same results as its predecessors. The possibility of war was the last thing on their minds. The initial reaction of the Bostonians to the news that Hutchinson was leaving and General Gage was replacing him was one of jubilation, with the optimists believing that the source of contention between the colony and the mother country was the vindictiveness of Governor Hutchinson. In response to the news, the citizens of Boston organized a parade to greet Gage. In their minds, because he was married to an American woman and his children were American, he would be sympathetic to their views. But, the first step the new governor took was to reinforce the number of troops in Boston. General Gage was a professional military man, and his assignment was to break the back of the rebellion and restore British authority over the colony. Soon, both London and the colonists would wake up to reality, understanding that their respective assumptions were in error — London, in its expectation that a military man as governor somehow would cow the colonists; the colonists in thinking he was sympathetic to their cause.

The first problem facing Gage, who was still in command of British forces in America, was where to quarter all of these additional troops. The obvious purpose of their presence was to sow fear in the populace. A major portion could be lodged on Castle Island, adjacent to Boston; others could be housed in inns and empty barns, but the problem of barracks added to the confusion between the military and the townspeople. Another unforeseen factor in quartering the troops was that many of them had brought along their wives and children. Here was an Army of close to 4,000 men sitting side by side with a civilian population of 16,000. In this hostile atmosphere, a crisis was expected to occur sooner or later. Yet, despite one or two incidents, nothing comparable to the Boston Massacre of

1700 took place. While Boston appeared ready to explode, the actual outbreak of fighting would ultimately take place outside of the metropolitan area. Gage, as both the commanding officer of the British troops and the governor of Massachusetts, was well aware of the delicacy of the current situation. In order to get a reading on the mood of the local population, he employed "American agents," who for small sums of money would provide the necessary information relating to the activities of the colonial establishment. It was through these informers that Gage learned that the colonials were storing guns, cannons and ammunition in Concord. While Gage was spying on the plans of the Americans, they in turn were keeping close watch over the activities of the British military. Receiving information that Gage intended to arrest Samuel Adams and John Hancock on charges of treason and ship them to England to stand trial, and at the same time to seize the munitions stored at Concord, Paul Revere and William Dawes were assigned to alert Adams and Hancock and those patriots at Concord who had amassed the military supplies. The only missing piece of information was whether the British regiments would be leaving Boston by land or would be embarking from ships on the Charles River. If one lantern was visible in the belfry of Old North Church, the approach would be by land; if two, by sea. Revere and Dawes arrived in Lexington early enough to alert Adams and Hancock, and then continued their ride toward Concord, where the militia stored its arms. But before they could reach Concord, they were stopped by a British patrol. In a stroke of luck, before they were seized they had met up with a doctor, Samuel Prescott, who was having a tryst with a woman and was on his way home. The doctor was able to escape detention and rode on to Concord, successfully warning the militia there. Meanwhile Revere was released, *sans* horse, and was able to travel on foot to Hancock's and Adams' location and to help them escape. The news that the British were coming was not relayed by Revere, as Henry Wadsworth Longfellow immortalized in his famous poem, but by the good doctor who was having an affair.

Before dawn of that day — April 19, 1775 — area militiamen gathered on Lexington Common. At first, they simply watched as the British regulars entered the town. Neither side was planning to engage the other unless attacked first. When ordered by a British officer to lay down their arms and disperse, most of them held their ground and none laid down their arms. Nobody knows who fired the first shot, but it terminated the uneasy accord. The British charged forward with bayonets, leaving eight colonists dead; the others managed to escape. The British wrongly assumed that they had established their supremacy as an armed force and that the rebels would understand that they had no chance against his majesty's Army. On they marched to Concord where their mission was to destroy whatever armaments had been hidden there. Armed with information from Loyalist spies, they were successful in locating and smashing three heavy guns and other munitions, and dumping about 100 barrels of provisions — flour and salted food — and 550 pounds of musket balls into the millpond. (Later, the thrifty and enterprising colonists were able to recover most of these supplies.)

Meanwhile, Colonel James Barrett was commanding the militiamen who were slowly gathering in the Concord environs. When the British were marching from Lexington to Concord, his troops numbered about 250, compared to the advancing British regulars of 700, so he made the decision to reposition his men to a hill north of town, crossing the North Bridge. There, he observed the movement of the British troops, and waited for his militia to swell. And swell it did, to five full companies of Minutemen and five militias from surrounding towns, totaling at least 400 colonists, prepared to fight if necessary. When Colonel Barrett saw smoke rising from the direction of Concord's meeting house (accidentally set on fire by the British when burning some militia gun cartridges) and noted just a few British companies (totaling 95 regulars at most) in line of sight, he ordered his men to advance toward North Bridge and Concord. Realizing he was outnumbered, the British officer in command ordered his troops to retreat from the bridge.

And then it happened. The shot heard around the world. One of the British soldiers on the bridge fired his gun, probably in panic, and the American officer near the bridge gave the order for the Patriots to fire at will. It was a narrow bridge and when the two British companies searching for hidden armaments heard the fire, they returned only to see their comrades in arms dead, wounded or trying to extricate themselves from the bridge. There was pandemonium as the two missing companies joined the others to cross the bridge. A retreat was called, and the British troops began their march to return to Lexington. Following the fight at the bridge the story becomes confused, as confused as the British officers and their men were during the long retreat to Lexington. The Patriots seemed to be everywhere, shooting at the ranks and the officers in particular, from behind trees, walls and houses. Firing their guns and then running to hide behind an object to find a new position. The soldiers were at their wit's end. They were unaccustomed to this kind of warfare. When a house was used as a form of camouflage, they entered it, shot any men found there, turned the women and children out and burned the house to the ground. This uncivilized practice on the part of the regulars was a direct result of the officers having lost control of the situation on the battlefield. Since 20 percent of the officer class had been either killed or wounded, it was obvious that panic had become the new commander-in-chief. But for the arrival of Colonel Hugh Percy with reinforcements, including cannons, which tended to scatter the Patriots, it is questionable just how many of the original force of almost 2,000 men would have been able to make their escape back to the safety of Boston. It was only because Colonel Thomas Pickering with his Minutemen from Salem refused to cut off the British escape route to Charleston that the bulk of the forces were able to escape.

A number of lessons were learned by both sides as a result of the British flight from Concord. First, the British military learned that the colonials, when pushed far enough, were more than ready to fight and die, and that their method of combat did not conform to the usual standards of warfare. Second, the colonials were unimpressed by the fact that they were fighting a professional army. The message for the colonials was equally clear: the vaunted power of the British armed forces, with their highly disciplined troops, was based on their fighting on their own terms. Once the rules of the games of warfare were changed, they had been reduced to a disorganized body of men looking to save their lives. The scores from this original scrimmage told the story: among the killed, 49 Americans, 73 British; among the wounded 39 Americans versus 174 British. Twenty percent of the British troops were dead, wounded or taken prisoner. Among the soldiers still unaccounted for were five Americans and 26 British. Most of the colonials who fought and died were farmers, the majority with families who were dependent upon them, and yet they were prepared to make the supreme sacrifice of their lives. What motivated them? Was it the catchwords of freedom and liberty? Was it peer pressure? They were not professional soldiers such as their adversaries; their vocation was farming, their avocation raising a family. Their life was hard and monotonous. Yet, when they determined the situation warranted it, they were there to defend not only their own parcel of land but also that of fellow farmers who were perfect strangers. What was it that brought leaders and soldiers from Connecticut and New Hampshire to the colonial headquarters at Cambridge, Massachusetts to join the army, now under the command of Artemas Ward? To members of Parliament and General Thomas Gage it was inexplicable. There was no chain of command; no professional officer class; the men elected their own officers; yet despite these handicaps, they had managed to put to flight 2,000 of the best-trained officers and soldiers in the world. Now this band of undisciplined farmers had General Gage and his British forces penned up in Boston.

If General Gage and his officers were puzzled by the attitude of these farmers, so too were most of their fellow Americans. Despite the rhetoric of Patrick Henry, very few Americans had given any thought to the possibility of a war with Britain. Most Americans expected some kind of compromise would be reached, and once cooler heads prevailed, life would continue as it had before. The farmers gathered at the bridge in Concord had no idea that eight Americans at Lexington had been killed for no reason other than to intimidate other Americans. Yet once guns were fired on the bridge at Concord, the reaction of the Americans was instantaneous. The enemy, which they had only heard or read about, now was standing at their front door. If not now, when? Did British troops have to enter their homes as had already happened in Boston? The symbiotic relationship between a farmer and the land he cultivates is quite different than any other. The British might be professional soldiers, but the colonial viewed them as intruders on his life and that of his family. Like any armed intruders, there was only one way to deal with them — kill or be killed. It was so simple that it was difficult for the British to understand. The fact that they were armed soldiers made no impression on these farmers except that they knew enough to aim first at the officers.

The command of "don't shoot until you see the whites of their eyes" is all most Americans know about the battle of Bunker Hill. The first thing to remember is that the battle was not fought on Bunker Hill but on Breed's Hill, a hill directly in front of it. The second is that there was an argument among the three commanding officers as to which hill the Patriots were to choose to make their stand. When the decision was finally resolved, the men began building a fortification on Breed's Hill. Wishing to avoid detection by the British, the men began digging at nine in the evening of June 16, 1775, and worked throughout the night to build a parapet that would give them protection while still allowing them to shoot at the British coming up the hill. The command structure for the defense was so confused that only a small percentage of those available actually did the work. Artemas Ward was supposedly the general in charge of the operation but in reality his control of the disparate forces was pro forma rather than real. The men had been constantly at work for eight hours and yet no one had thought to send up food or water. Despite the noise and confusion, it was only with the coming of the dawn that the British realized what the Americans were doing. Prior to the setting up of the breastworks on Breed's Hill, three British generals had been sent from London to help Gage in his effort to quell the incipient rebellion in Massachusetts. They were by order of seniority, Maj. General William Howe, Lt. General Henry Clinton and Maj. General John Burgoyne. All three of them were combat veterans who had distinguished themselves in war. Howe, in the French and Indian War, led a minimal force of men up a redoubt of Quebec and held off the French troops until the main force of General Wolfe arrived. Another brother was an Admiral in the British Navy, and a third brother had died fighting with the colonials at Fort Ticonderoga during the French and Indian conflict. Clinton, whose father had been governor of New York, had been raised in America and had been in command of the New York militia. Burgoyne had been a successful commander during the Seven Years War and was known as a general who went out of his way to take care of his troops. All three were members of Parliament, and were considered friendly to America. All of the generals, with the exception of Burgoyne, had close relations with Americans, and Howe in particular, had been elected to Parliament from a district in England that supported the aims of the colonists and to whose electorate he had promised never to take action against their fellow brethren.

On the American side, most of the leading officers had seen battle in the French and Indian War and a few of them had even been offered commissions in the British Army. The battle plan of the British was simple: to drive the Americans from their positions in Cambridge, thereby dispersing the militia who had gathered there and hopefully break the back of the armed resistance. It was thus with great surprise that they learned that morning that the Americans had fortified Breed's Hill, and if they acquired large pieces of artillery, would be in a position to shell the British in Boston. In picking out an American hero for the day, among the many responsible for the psychological defeat of the British, the honor would have to go to Captain John Sparks, who arrived late on the scene with his men from New Hampshire. His troops prevented the British from turning the left flank of the defenders; in the process of defending his position, he destroyed the Light Horse Brigade and the Marines who attempted to force the position. It was shades of Tennyson's famous poem, *The Charge of the Light Brigade*, during the Crimean War. Only this time there were no cannons to the left or right of them or in front of them. Instead of cannons, there were the militia men from New Hampshire with their muskets, picking off first the officers and then the men. Yes, they charged, and when beaten back, they charged again, but it was getting difficult since the bodies of the dead and wounded men were in front of them. There were many others who contributed to the decimation of the British armed forces, the most important of whom were Colonel William Prescott in command of the Massachusetts militia, Major General Israel Putnam, who led the forces from Connecticut, and Colonel Richard Gridley, an engineer whose exploit during the French and Indian War (getting two cannons up the sheer cliffs at Quebec) resulted in the usual largess Britain bestows on its war heroes — a colonelcy in the British Army with half pay on retirement, and Magdalen Island in the Gulf of the St. Lawrence River, and 3,000 acres of land in New Hampshire. At 65, Gridley was the oldest of the three and was given command of building the fortifications on the hill. The plan he laid out for the defense of the hill was 180 feet long, 60 feet wide and six feet high. Prescott had about 1,200 men to perform that task before daylight, when the British would become aware of its presence.

Unable to turn the flank of the Americans, the only method to dislodge them from their fortification that would force them to evacuate Cambridge was a frontal attack against the hill. Commanding General William Howe gave the order to advance, and perched on his horse, was leading his men into battle. With the customary fanfare of the band playing and the junior officers on their mounts urging the troops on the lines, the Red Coats marched up the hill to overwhelm the defenders behind the dirt parapets. Besides the sounds from the band and the voices of the officers urging their troops on, there was a deadly silence until they were 20 yards from the parapets. Then all of hell broke loose; the first column of soldiers fell from the withering fire and the second column fared no better.

Panic followed when the troops discovered that their officers were either dead or wounded. A retreat was called, the lines reformed, and a second wave marched up the hill only to be greeted by the same deadly barrage with the same effect on the troops as the initial charge. For General Howe, after sustaining such casualties if he didn't capture the hill it meant a court martial, disgrace and the end of his military career. So he launched a third charge, and this time with the defenders out of ammunition, the British troops carried the day with their bayonets. However, the number of British casualties was staggering — more than 1,000, accounting for between 40 and 50 percent of the troops that were in battle; casualties among the officer corps were even worse, 19 killed and 70 wounded. In no other battle had Britain suffered such a high rate of casualties. In contrast, fewer than 450 Americans were killed or wounded. Thus, although the colonists technically lost Breed Hill, the outcome proved positive for the Americans in that they demonstrated to themselves and the rest of the world that they could hold their own against the British army. It was only when the American survivors told their story that the successful defense of the Americans could be understood. Instead of one line firing and reloading while a second line fired, both lines fired at the same time, which killed or wounded the soldiers and officers in the first and second lines at the same time. Instead of adhering to the rules ascribed to defensive warfare, they had used common sense. Until formal hostilities began, following the signing of the Declaration of Independence and the British invasion of New York, the New Englanders resorted to improvisation in their struggle against the British and forced them to evacuate Boston and Massachusetts.

The Second Continental Congress, meeting once again in Philadelphia in the late spring of 1775, had yet to mesh into a compact body with one political program. While there were few if any Loyalists present, the Congress was divided into groups of moderates and radicals. The battle at Breed's Hill had yet to take place and discussion of Britain's war effort against the colonists was limited to the actions around Lexington and Concord. Since all the fighting up until that time had taken place in Massachusetts, it was obvious that the Massachusetts delegation was most concerned with gaining the support of the other colonies. One thing was obvious to all the delegates. What had taken place at Lexington and Concord was a signal that the British intended to disarm the colonists by seizing armaments that had been stored, leaving the colonists defenseless. Once placed in this situation, the colonies would be doomed to total subjection. The question facing the delegates was how to respond to this situation. If Massachusetts was brought to heel by military force, could the same methods be applied to the other colonies? This, in turn, brought the delegates face to face with what kind of military force was open to the colonists. Obviously, the New England states were prepared to fight, if necessary, by themselves. But if that was the case, what was the purpose of the Continental Congress? If the colonies were united in opposing the mandatory decrees of Parliament, then ipso facto there would have to be a Continental Army under the direction of the Congress. Following this thought, if there was a Continental Army, the cost of maintaining it would have to be the burden of all the colonies. The Second Continental Congress was conspicuous by the presence of two newcomers and the absence of Peyton Randolph, who had recently died. Of the two who now entered the political scene, one was the most famous American of the eighteenth century, Benjamin Franklin, with an international reputation as the inventor of the lightening rod, a member of the Royal Society, the creator of *Poor Richard's Almanac*, the assistant postmaster general for the colonies, the inventor of the Franklin stove, and an agent who before he returned home represented three of the thirteen colonies in London. Franklin was a man of the world in every sense of the phrase. The other was Thomas Jefferson, a relative unknown who joined the Virginia delegation only upon the death of Peyton Randolph. Once elected to Congress, the young Virginian would leave his mark upon history.

It is difficult to explain the functioning of the Second Continental Congress because the members themselves were unsure of what their role should be. When John Adams brought up the concept of Massachusetts writing its own constitution and urged that the other states should follow suit, the suggestion was immediately rejected on the ground that such an action would mean a definitive break with Great Britain, a step the other delegates were not prepared to take at this moment in time. About the only thing that the delegates agreed upon was the need for a national Army to defend the colonies against British troops and the appointment of a commanding officer to be in charge of all military operations within the colonies. It was John Adams and his cousin Samuel Adams who recognized that although the bulk of the forces in the field would be drawn from the Massachusetts militia and its neighboring colonies — Connecticut, New Hampshire and Rhode Island, the most important problem facing the Congress was to achieve a national consensus and that meant having the Southern states play an important role in this first effort to create a national organization, an American Army. The decision to select George Washington of Virginia as the commanding general of the Continental Army was the obvious choice. First of all, Virginia was the largest and wealthiest colony; equally important, Washington already possessed a reputation as the American officer who had managed to salvage the remnants of Braddock's army. It often has been said that in military affairs the most important ingredient for success is luck. This was Napoleon's favorite lodestar. Luck comes in many shapes and forms on the battle field. Often it is the stupidity of the enemy as well as the brilliance of the victor. But this was not to be the case with Washington. In the selection of Washington the delegates had not chosen a great general — generals are only equated with greatness following victories, and Washington had none to his credit. Nor did he or the British generals he encountered in battle prove to be great and imaginative strategists. What Washington brought to his new role in life was leadership in the face of adversity. He had exhibited that unique and rare quality when General Braddock was killed and the British and colonial troops were in total panic. Had Washington failed to step in and take control of the situation and to lead what remained of these forces to the safety of Pennsylvania, there would have been a wholesale slaughter. The war for independence was not waged along the lines of conventional European wars. It was a war of attrition, and Washington's role was to keep a Continental Army in the field. The fact that he succeeded against the enormous odds he faced — a series of weak and vacillating Congresses; a general fatigue and indifference by the majority of the population; frequent desertions by the troops; and a number of cabals — is the measure of a great leader. While the war never could have been won without the support of the French, without Washington there would have been nothing for the French to support.

The choice to select Washington as commander-in-chief of a non-existent army was a far more radical step than the Declaration of Independence, which followed a year later. Aside from his reputation as the young Colonel who had extricated the remnants of Braddock's Army, he was unknown to almost all the delegates. No one was certain how the New England forces stationed outside Boston would react to this total stranger from Virginia. Even more difficult to ascertain was whether the other commanding officers would defer to their new leader. It was one thing for men from the other New England colonies to rally round Massachusetts, but would the militia from New York and Pennsylvania join in the struggle against a common enemy? In accepting this honor, Washington had agreed to serve without any remuneration other than his expenses. Before he had accepted and left for Cambridge to assume his new role, the idea of placing the responsibility for the conduct of the war in the hands of one man created doubts in the minds of some of the delegates. Some went so far as to believe that the appointment of a single commander of the Army might lead to the creation of another Oliver Cromwell and the dictatorship he imposed on England. In order to prevent such a possibility, Washington agreed that all major military decisions would be made with the approval of Congress. Since from the very onset of the hostilities the British generals would determine the course of the war and where it would be waged, the resolution adopted by Congress was meaningless. The greatest concern of John Adams, the man who had been largely responsible for elevating Washington to the command, was that all the glory and honor for the success of the revolution would redound on the military and that those civilians who had been in the forefront of setting the stage for rebellion would be forgotten. John Adams was a true patriot who suffered from an overdose of vanity. What is truly remarkable about the delegates who participated in the Second Continental Congress was the certitude of some of those present that the rebellion would succeed, not in the sense of acquiring independence from the British Empire but rather in having the rights of the colonies clearly defined and accepted by Parliament and the King. Foremost among those rights was no taxation. At the same time, there were a few prepared to break the imbecile cord that bound them to the British Empire and the King. It would take another year, marked by victories and disastrous defeats, before they were prepared to take the definitive step of divorcing themselves from the King as well as Parliament.

Throughout the New England colonies the news of the battle of Breed's Hill was widely disseminated. Some men lured by the prospect of adventure and potential fame dropped whatever they were doing and headed for Cambridge where the Massachusetts militia was headquartered. Among those who left a wife and children as well as a business behind him was Benedict Arnold, who owned a pharmacy in New Haven. It was not the first time that Arnold had abandoned the humdrum life of a citizen to seek glory. During the French and Indian War he had been among the volunteers who had fought under British General Amherst in the conquest of Fort Ticonderoga in upstate New York. On his way there, he ran into an acquaintance, Colonel Carson, and a group of men, also determined to join the Patriots. Now Benedict Arnold was no ordinary man. So he says to Carson in passing that there exists a marvelous opportunity for the Americans to seize Fort Ticonderoga which the British have left lightly garrisoned. Carson and two of his companions, totally familiar with the area, agreed with him, and after he departed, decided to engage their limited forces in that project. Arnold, unaware of these plans, headed to Cambridge where he hoped to sell his concept to the military authorities. He met with the Committee of Public Safety, and given his enthusiasm, sold them on the concept. They provided him with some papers authorizing his proposal, appointed him a Colonel, a temporary rank, and agreed to provide him with up to 400 men to achieve his goal. Meanwhile, Carson and his men ran into Ethan Allen and his Green Mountain Boys who agreed to join in the operation provided that Allen would be in command. Arnold, oblivious to the fact that Carson and Allen were determined to accomplish the same goal, met up with them prior to their assault on the fort. Arnold, with his troops still on the way, showed Allen his papers, which indicated that he was to be in command of the operation. Allen, a giant of a man, with all the men gathered there under his command refused to concede to Arnold. An altercation broke out, and peace was finally concluded by having the two of them accept a joint command. Using boats, they crossed the lake, surprised the sentry, and without a shot being fired, took possession of the fort along with the commandant and the 40-odd soldiers, most of them crippled from the French and Indian War. Without any authorization Arnold and Allen decided these captives were prisoners of war. They then marched on to seize Crown Point, also lightly defended. Up to this moment, it appeared that Allen would be in sole command of the expedition. Then the situation changed overnight. A schooner arrived with Arnold's men, and since he was the only commander capable of sailing the boat, he took off for St. Johns, completely surprising the garrison and seizing a 70-ton warship with its crew, so that the Americans now were in total control of Lake Champlain. Frustrated by Arnold's success, Allen and his men took off for Canada in the expectation of continuing the spate of victories. Unsuccessful, he returned to Ticonderoga to discover that Arnold, with further reinforcements, was totally in charge. The news of the seizure of Fort Ticonderoga and all of its guns and ammunition was communicated to the Second Continental Congress.

Totally unaware of the events that had taken place before the information was brought to the attention of the Continental Congress, that body had to come to grips with an unforeseen development. For the first time the Americans had captured soldiers and an officer of his Majesty's Army, in addition to seizing British property. Since they had yet to declare their independence from the Crown, the initial reaction of the majority was to return the forts and the guns to the British along with the prisoners of war. After much debate, the members of Congress decided that they would keep the guns and ammunition but return the forts to the British. The colonies might be united, but they were not quite ready to break their ties to the Crown. However, if most of the members of the Congress were reticent about offending Great Britain, the individual assemblies of the colonies were not. They recognized the importance of the forts in the event of any future conflict. New York, New Hampshire, Connecticut and above all Massachusetts were aware that control of the waterways was necessary for the safety of the New England colonies. At the last minute Congress changed its mind and accepted control of the forts but released the officers and the wounded soldiers. Having accomplished his mission, Colonel Arnold returned to Cambridge expecting to receive his well-deserved plaudits and the confirmation of his rank from temporary Colonel to permanent status. Instead, he was informed that he would serve under the command of General Nathaniel Greene, who had been assigned the role of dismantling the cannons and heavy guns on the fort, and packing the ammunition and supplies stored at the fort, and bringing them to Cambridge for use of the Army now under the command of George Washington. For the first, although not the last, time, Arnold was faced with the unpleasant fact that politics took precedence as far as Congress was concerned. Arnold had assumed that since it was his idea to seize the guns, all the honors associated with bringing them to the use of the Continental Army should be his as well. In a fit of petulance, he resigned his temporary commission. While Arnold was sulking, a group of men organized by General Nathaniel Greene dismantled the huge guns and cannons at Fort Ticonderoga in the middle of winter, placed them on improvised sleds and brought them to Cambridge where, once reassembled, they would force the British to evacuate Boston.

Arnold's audacity made him unique among all the military commanders who served under Washington. Washington alone understood the necessity for this trait and made good use of it at both Trenton and Princeton. Realizing that unless he redeemed himself he was destined to play no role in the conflict, Arnold sent a letter to the Second Continental Congress proposing an invasion of Canada. In his letter he outlined a plan for the invasion. He referred to the relative weakness of the British forces in Montreal and stated that he had knowledge that the British will be unable to gain the usual support they depend upon from the Indian tribes. As a rationale for the invasion, he believed that the potential loss of Canada would be a perfect bargaining chip with the British government to address the grievances of the colonies, and that this course of action would bring the conflict to an end and restore the old relationship between the colonies and the mother country by eliminating once and for all the concept of taxation without representation. In the letter, he stressed the need for speed of action before the British had a chance to reinforce their garrisons in Canada. What is most striking about his letter is not the audacity of his proposal but that it was taken seriously. No one bothered to ask who he was and how he had acquired this information. Since he was largely responsible for the seizure of Fort Ticonderoga and solely responsible for that of St. John and the seizure of British warships, every one of his claims was accepted on its face value. But the Second Continental Congress, like its predecessor, was more of a debating society than an organization prone to take action. After a month or so, Arnold's proposal was brought to the attention of Major General Philip Schuyler, who was in command of the forces in New York State. Schuyler's appointment as one of the few major generals in the Continental Army was a direct result of his wealth and his political position within New York. A soldier he was not, but fortunately his second in command, Richard Montgomery, was.

The story of Montgomery's successful attempt to conquer Montreal is filled with mishaps, blunders, desertions on the part of some of the troops, hunger, lack of supplies, and Schuyler believing misleading information. In other words, if anything could go wrong, everything did. Yet despite all of these setbacks, in the end Montreal surrendered to the Americans, setting up the second stage of the planned pincer attack for the conquest of Quebec, the stronghold of the British in Canada. Without its conquest, the position of Montgomery and his forces in Montreal would have been untenable. Reenter Benedict Arnold. He approached General Washington with a daring plan. He would lead a force of men through the woods of Maine, entering the St. Lawrence River from the other side of Quebec, and together with Montgomery, launch a two-sided attack on the fortress of Quebec. Since Quebec was the capital of British Canada, once it was seized all of Canada would follow suit. The story of Arnold's march, covering 230 miles, is perhaps one of the most amazing and brilliant feats in military history. While

Washington welcomed Arnold's daring proposal and agreed to supply him with the necessary men and supplies, before it could be launched it required the approval of Congress. While the pros and cons were being debated, early autumn turned into early winter. By the time Arnold and his men set out, the ground was covered with deep drifts of snow, temperatures were well below freezing and his armed force had to contend with all the other obstacles imposed by winter. With waterfalls to be circumvented and often with a lack of food and supplies, the trip to the St. Lawrence River was made in six weeks by sheer dint of courage. When the weary soldiers arrived on the banks of the St. Lawrence River facing Quebec, most of the men who hadn't perished or deserted were barefoot; their clothing was in a shambles; they were short on powder, and they were hardly in a condition to launch an attack on such a fortress. After a brief delay, somehow they got word to Montgomery who brought the men food, warm clothes and additional powder for their guns. Arnold's Army was truly the first American Army on the field of battle. Not only were there troops from each of the New England colonies but there were companies of men from Virginia and Pennsylvania, including one of the most famous soldiers of the revolution, Captain Daniel Morgan, who headed up the Virginia contingent. Arnold's aide de camp during the march was the famous or infamous, Aaron Burr.

The odds of the Americans attaining their objective were overwhelmingly against them, yet having come this far they were not about to retreat. The only possibility for success was a surprise attack, and in a blinding snowstorm at night they set out to conquer the most powerful fortress in North America. In the beginning, their surprise attack was successful; but then fortune turned against the Americans: Montgomery and two of his officers, who were supposed to lead the diversionary effort, were killed by cannon shot. Arnold, despite being wounded in the leg, fought on, but his French Canadian allies ran for cover. While Arnold and some of the men (including Captain Morgan) escaped capture, the blow that might have brought the war to an end fell far short of that goal. The casualties were about 60 men dead or wounded, most of them from the rifle companies who had borne the brunt of the attack, and another 400 had been taken prisoner. "General Luck" had failed the Americans. Montgomery's delay in making contact with Arnold's forces; Montgomery's accidental death along with some of his key officers; the fact that Arnold was wounded — all worked against the success of the daring plan. There would be the usual recriminations in the Congress, and blame for the defeat was foisted onto some of the individual delegates, but the real problem was that of Congress. Because of its terrible fear that a military man might usurp civilian power, it had left all military decisions in its own hands. And there were too many chefs cooking the soup. As a result, until a consensus could be reached, procrastination was the order of the day. Instead of a campaign being launched in the early fall when it had the greatest chance for success, it was delayed until early winter.

Any assessment of the British war effort in the colonies prior to the summer of 1776 when they seized New York must take into consideration the repercussions from the battle of Breed's Hill. The wholesale slaughter of so many officers and troops shocked the Secretary of War for the colonies as well as General Howe who was Commander-in-Chief of the British forces in America. While before, the military had contempt for these farmers, now they realized they faced a determined enemy. Furthermore, the British Army in Boston was in no position to take any action until it received reinforcements. So Howe sat in Boston and allowed the Americans to seize Dorchester Heights, and once the big guns from Fort Ticonderoga were in place, Howe had to fold up his tents and abandon the city. In London, heeding the advice of his Southern governors that the soft underbelly of the colonies was found in the South where most of the population were Loyalists, he sent General Clinton to seize Charleston, South Carolina by invading the city from the sea. Unfortunately, the Loyalists never made their appearance, and Clinton sailed away. He also instructed the Southern governors to organize the Loyalists in their colonies; when they attempted to carry out his orders, they were forced to flee for their lives. The North ministry was under the illusion it could quell the insurgency on the cheap. It took almost a year before it recognized that it would have to wage an all-out war if Britain was going to retain its colonies.

Nor were a majority of the delegates to the Congress convinced they should declare their independence. The more astute and less emotional viewed Britain as a military superpower and considered the chance of the colonists to succeed as remote. Others believed that obeisance to a monarch or single authority was the natural order for any government. What really kept the Congress debating the merits and demerits of independence was the absence of any military action by Great Britain. As long as Congress did not have to cope with the reality of war, it could put off any decision. In the spring of 1776, a pamphlet appeared in bookstores entitled *Common Sense*. The unknown author, Thomas Paine, seemed to have emerged from nowhere. But the thoughts expressed in the pamphlet resonated with everyone who read it. By word of mouth it became an instantaneous best seller. The simplicity of Paine's thesis made it an immediate success. Paine's pamphlet posed a question that never had been asked before. Where was it written that men could only be ruled by kings? Unlike Britain and Europe, the American colonies had grown and prospered by dint of their own efforts and those of their elected representatives. The only role kings played was to exploit their subjects for their own benefit. He then posed a second and more devastating question. Where had all the appeals to the king to redress the illegal legislation Parliament imposed on the colonies led? Did the British monarch evince any interest or make any effort for the colonists? Did the king ever show or indicate any interest in their plight? After all the remonstrance sent to George III indicating the need for his intervention, how many responses were received? No one could explain or justify the king's silence. In his summation, Paine called on the colonists to take the horse by the bit and ride him to freedom. It mattered little that the numbers of copies of *Common Sense* sold, printed or read have been grossly exaggerated. Paine managed to disarm those delegates who wanted to believe that George III would come to their rescue.

Having overcome the hurdle of the King as their salvation, it was time to consider a vote on independence. The two major holdouts were New York and Pennsylvania, two of the largest and most central states, but Maryland and New Jersey were indecisive as well. Without the approval of these states, the concept of a nation was impossible. Their geographic position was such that it would separate the New England states from those of the South; in addition, the Congress had made Philadelphia the new nation's temporary capital, and Washington and the Continental Army had moved down to New York to protect it from an invasion by the British armed forces. The maneuvering that took place between those who sought an independent government for the colonies and those who were not prepared to break with the Crown went on throughout the month of June. Little by little, with the arguments used by Paine, the forces promoting formation of an independent nation began to chip away at the concept that the colonies should stay under the "protection" of the Crown. First, the Congress passed a resolution that simply acknowledged the need for some kind of a national government. This acknowledgement was innocuous enough to pass muster. But five days later, when a preamble was added to the resolution, it delivered a knockout blow by stating bluntly that by virtue of making war on the colonies any authority of the Crown over the colonies should be suppressed and replaced under the authority of the people of the colonies. While the passage of the preamble was approved by a majority of the colonies, the delegates from New York and Pennsylvania objected violently since the preamble declared the colonies to be independent of the Crown. The pressure on the Pennsylvania Assembly to conform to the wishes of the majority continued to grow to the point where they finally relented from their obduracy and appointed a committee to bring new instructions to their delegates.

But the final blow came from the Virginia Convention that urged Congress to "declare that these United Colonies are, and of right ought to be, free and independent states ... and that all connection between them and the State of Britain is, and ought to be, totally dissolved." The tocsin had finally sounded. Virginia had called a spade a spade and those who were opposed to breaking the ties to Britain had their backs up against the wall. Congress now appointed a five-man committee to create a declaration of sorts that would conform to the general ideas of the Virginia resolution. The committee was composed of five members: Robert Livingston of New York, who was opposed to independence and would vote against it; Roger Sherman of Connecticut, a self-educated dyed-in-the-wool patriot, a man of many talents, but not necessarily gifted with a felicitous pen; John Adams, Benjamin Franklin and Thomas Jefferson. That Jefferson, the youngest member of the committee, was given the role of preparing the document rather than Franklin or Adams, both superb political writers, can be attributed to chance; neither of them realized the import that the document would have in defining the American Revolution. The writer, who Jefferson would lean upon in creating the Declaration, in addition to John Locke, and Montesquieu to a lesser degree, was George Mason, who had composed the Virginia Bill of Rights, which would become the basis for the first ten amendments to the Constitution. Mason's document began:

> That all men are by nature equally free and independent, and have certain inherent rights, of which, when they enter into a state of society, they cannot by any compact deprive or divest their posterity; namely, the enjoyment of life and liberty, with the means of acquiring and possessing property, and pursuing and obtaining happiness and safety.

Mason's thesis was derived entirely from the Second Treatise on Government written by John Locke. But Locke had listed the inherent rights of man as "life, liberty and property." There was no mention of happiness. Jefferson had found that phrase in Mason's work, but it followed that of property.

Why was property, which is a fundamental right in both Locke and Mason, excluded from the Declaration of Independence, while at the same time being preeminent in the Constitution of the United States? If the basic complaint of the colonies was "no taxation without representation" and taxation was an invasion of property, why should it be excluded from a document that purports to show the reasons for the colonies seeking independence? Equally important, since Jefferson showed the document for corrections, additions and deletions to the other members of the committee, especially Franklin and Adams, why did they refrain from adding "property" to the Declaration? Neither of them was shy in making other changes. They appear on the original draft. Even stranger was the fact that among all the delegates, from all of the colonies, not a voice was raised to ask what had happened to the word property. Was it implied in the phrase "the pursuit of happiness," or was it omitted for a more fundamental reason? All of the colonies had received the charters for the lands they occupied from Kings of England or Britain. Their governors and the governors' officials were all appointed by the Crown. They had the right of veto over legislation passed by the colonies. In other words, they were the Crown's colonies, in effect, the property of the Crown. Did not the Crown, with its funds, buy out the original proprietors? If the colonies had originally been owned by the proprietors by virtue of their investment in planting these colonies, from which they expected to get a return on their investment, how did that change when the Crown became the colonies' landlord? There were other factors that had to be considered. If the Crown did not consider the colonies to be its possessions, why then would it expend an enormous amount of money and manpower to defeat the French in the French and Indian War? Why did the colonies welcome this participation by the Crown if they did not fundamentally believe that it was the obligation of England to protect its possessions? Then there is the matter of the Glorious Revolution, which stripped the King of his power to tax English citizens without the approval of Parliament. This was the basis for the complaint of the colonists: no taxation without representation. It was on this piece of legislation that the colonists based their complaint. It was their assumption that the individual Assemblies in the colonies had acquired the same rights as the British Parliament. To the colonists, their Assemblies were co-equal with Parliament, and therefore the same restrictions that had been placed on the King in Britain were applicable to the colonists. This was the crux of the difference between the colonists and the Parliament. As British citizens the same restrictions that had been placed on the Crown by the Glorious Revolution redounded to their Assemblies as well. It mattered not that it was Parliament that was levying the taxation and not the Crown; it was the principle that counted.

Could it be that the pursuit of happiness was a euphemism that would allow the colonies to get around the thorny question of property? There is no doubt that the words Jefferson used in his preamble to the Declaration of Independence, while an enormous improvement as far as the use of language is concerned, followed along the lines of those penned by George Mason in his preamble to the Virginia Bill of Rights. Since Mason's preamble applied to Virginia, the basic rights of property had to be included. Jefferson, however, had to skirt the issue of property since all the colonies owed their charters to the various Kings of England and Britain. It was these charters that delineated the boundaries of the various colonies. Jefferson therefore took the tack of listing all the injuries the King had imposed on his colonies as justification for their seeking their independence. This does not make the Declaration of Independence any less meaningful. There is no doubt that the colonies had a sufficient number of grievances with the conduct of Parliament and the King. Certainly, the stationing of troops in their midst as an effort to intimidate them was reason enough to incite the colonists to rebellion. This intimidation was followed with an attempt to subjugate them by the use of force, which provided more than an excuse to declare one's independence. That the Parliament and the King had treated them on the same level of contempt as they did the exploited Irish was intolerable. This was the nub of the conflict. To the Parliament and the King, the colonists were spoiled brats who only took what the Empire could offer in terms of safety without feeling that they were obliged to give anything in return. What the Parliament and the

King failed to comprehend was that distance did not make the heart grow fonder, but rather that it created a huge chasm between the two countries. By passing the Stamp Act, the Parliament had set the stage for the unification of these disparate states, which had their own economies and evinced little or no interest in what was taking place in the neighboring states, to say nothing of those colonies far more distant. Until the passage of the Stamp Act there was no reason for the colonies to act in unity. With its repeal, the colonies settled back into their isolation. Then came the Townshend Acts and Lord North's effort to salvage the fortunes of the East India Company with its culmination in the Boston Tea Party; suddenly these disparate states realized that they had a common interest which transcended their individual lives. The British Parliament, through its stupidity, had created the outline of a nation which the Declaration of Independence turned into a reality.

While the Second Continental Congress during the month of June was gradually working its way towards proclaiming the thirteen colonies to be a united nation, Washington, after the departure of the British troops from Boston and their temporary movement to Halifax, waiting for reinforcements from the mother country, was busy trying to create an Army that would defend the colonies from the expected British return to the mainland. To say that this would prove to be a difficult task would be an understatement. A large number of the original forces that had comprised the Continental Army had finished their temporary terms of enlistment; now that the British were out of the country, the members of the Continental Army were prepared to return home and resume their lives. Washington found himself a prisoner of a problem that would plague him throughout the course of the war. Unlike European nations with their standing armies and their professional officer corps, America was entirely dependent upon volunteers; the individual states were expected to provide the volunteers for this national army. Initially, from the New England states, there was no shortage of volunteers. But once the British Army had been forced to evacuate Boston, as far as most of the volunteers were concerned, their period of enlistment was over; they had completed their service to the cause. An incentive for these veterans to reenlist for further service would require a bonus either from the individual states or from Congress. Once Congress had enacted the legislation creating a national Army, as far as the states were concerned it was incumbent upon Congress to supply the necessary funds. This was the crux of the dilemma facing Washington throughout the war. Under the Articles of Confederation, which was the law that bound the thirteen colonies together, Congress could not levy taxes on the states. Instead, it was dependent upon contributions from each of the states to fund the war. Without the means to tax, Congress was forced to print its own money. At this stage of the conflict, with Congress yet to have enacted the Declaration of Independence that would signal a definitive break with Great Britain,

Congress balked at the idea of supplying Washington with funds for the reenlistment of those soldiers who had completed their terms of enlistment. Despite this and other obstacles, by the end of June Washington's Army was ready to march to New York where the British invasion was expected. It was 220 miles from Cambridge, where the Army had been assembled, to New York. For everyone from Washington on down, the experience was novel. This was not Concord or Breed's Hill or even the invasion of Canada. For the first time American troops led by American officers would take the field against a professional British Army reputed to be among the best in the world.

With the American Army finally in New York, prepared to meet the British invasion, back in Philadelphia the struggle led by John Adams and Richard Henry Lee to get a majority of the colonists to vote for the Declaration of Independence was entering its final stages. Maryland, which had been vacillating, finally decided to vote positively. A delegate from Delaware was rushed from his wife's sickbed to break a tie. Edward Rutledge of South Carolina suddenly decided to oppose ratification and was only brought back into the positive column when he agreed to bring his delegates along, provided that Pennsylvania was brought in to sign the document. That was achieved when two of the delegates abstained from voting and a three-to-two majority approved of the Declaration. Only New York, where the Continental Army was to fight its first major battle, refused to sign, waiting until July 19, before the Assembly finally instructed its delegates to support the Declaration. Observed in the light of these facts, it appears to be almost a miracle that the colonies finally were able to reach an agreement that committed them to the path of secession and freedom.

Any serious account of the revolutionary war has to focus on how the British managed to lose rather than how the Americans won the war. Furthermore, to recount all the skirmishes that took place between the British and the Americans over the six years the war lasted is meaningless. Four battles decided the fate of the war — Saratoga, Brandywine and Paoli, and the final one, Yorktown. In the case of Brandywine, British General Howe allowed Washington's Army to escape to Valley Forge after inflicting a series of defeats on it at the battles of Paoli and Germantown, which left the American Army in total disarray to the extent that had Howe pursued it, the remnant left would have disintegrated and fled for their lives. Instead, Howe assumed the war was over since he had captured and occupied Philadelphia, the capital of the nation, and forced its Congress to flee. Instead, we read in our history books of the hardships endured by the troops at Valley Forge, and how a fighting force emerged from its trials and tribulations, now trained in the art of soldiering by a German émigré, Baron Von Steuben, and with its recovery, a prolonged war that lasted until 1781 with the surrender of General Cornwallis at Yorktown.

At almost the same time Washington's Army was suffering from one defeat after another, an American Army under the command of General Horatio Gates had forced the surrender of a British Army force commanded by General John Burgoyne. It was this ignominious defeat of Burgoyne's troops that convinced France that the Americans were capable of winning the war and led to a Franco–American alliance that enabled the Americans to pursue a lengthy war culminating in the surrender of General Cornwallis to a combined force of French and Americans at Yorktown. What remains somewhat of a mystery is how one British Army could readily defeat the major forces Washington had at his disposal while another British Army facing a far smaller number of men and without the cadre of officers available to Washington was forced to capitulate? The answer will come as a shock. The cause for Burgoyne's defeat and surrender was a woman, the wife of the captain of his quartermaster corps, whose favors and delights he sought and received. Nor was her acquiescence and that of her husband unusual in the British Army. There were many routes to promotion and this was one.

Lord George Germain, the minister in London who devised the strategy for the conduct of the war, intended to cut off the New England states from the others so that George Washington could receive no reinforcements. Once they had been severed, they would be dealt with later. Burgoyne was to lead an Army of British and Hessian troops down from Canada, and after seizing Fort Ticonderoga, sail down Lake Champlain and then Lake George so his Army could avoid a trek through the wilderness. But if Burgoyne followed those plans, his tryst would be brief. So instead, informed by his Indian guides that his Army would encounter no problems if it moved by land, he followed their advice. In moving his Army by land rather than by water, he faced one serious problem. Since the overland route would take longer, he would have to depend upon the local inhabitants for food and forage for his horses. While some of the colonists were hostile and placed impediments on the route his Indian allies had prescribed, and while it slowed down his advance, he had no concern. Most of the farmers were willing to sell him supplies since he paid for them in specie. Then the unexpected happened. One of his Indian allies raped and murdered the wife of one of the settlers who had been supplying his Army. This placed Burgoyne in an untenable position. If he punished the offender, his Indian allies would desert him and leave his Army in the wilderness; if he demurred, he'd lose the support of the settlers who were supplying his Army with the necessities. The General opted for the Indians, and learned that the colonials would rather destroy their crops than sell them to the British. Desperate for supplies, he sent a large detachment of Hessians to raid some of the farms in nearby New Hampshire. Warned of their approach, Captain John Sparks, the hero of Breed's Hill, whose troops had turned back the elite of Howe's Army when they tried to turn the flank of the Americans, organized a group of volunteers to attack. Half the Hessians were killed, wounded or taken prisoner, and those who made it back to camp returned empty handed. Burgoyne who had been counting on his cavalry in the expected battle with the Americans now had to use the starving horses to feed his troops.

Having emerged from the wilderness, he now faced the American forces led by General Horatio Gates. In the eighteenth century, military strategy meant turning the flank of the enemy and getting behind his lines, and, in the resulting pincer movement, create panic and havoc leading to the enemy's defeat and surrender. The only risk is in failure to turn the flank. Then, a counterattack by the defenders can lead to a disaster if they overrun the attacker and turn his flank.

Battles are not fought on chessboards, and great generals act from instinct. General Horatio Gates' strategy, if he had any, was to have the Americans hold their position and prevent the British from advancing further. He maintained a reserve force under General Arnold to insure that there were no breaches in the American lines. Arnold was anything but a conventional military man. His concept of war was to defeat the enemy. Observing that Colonel Daniel Morgan and his Virginia sharpshooters had prevented the British from turning the Americans' flank, he threw his reserves in support of Morgan's men, which prevented the British from turning the American flank and broke the back of the attackers, placing them on the defensive.

Dressed down in front of the other officers by General Gates for having disobeyed orders, the impetuous Arnold resigned his commission and planned to leave the Army. When the battle resumed the following day, he joined the forces of Morgan as a private and despite his wound led the charge that turned the British flank, which in turn forced Burgoyne to ask the terms for a surrender of his Army. Gates, flush with a victory he had played no role in achieving, insisted on an unconditional surrender. Burgoyne refused.

At that moment the Americans captured a messenger sent by General Clinton announcing that his Army was on its way and would join up with Burgoyne's forces in a few days. Gates changed his terms; the surrender would no longer be unconditional, but would allow the troops to be repatriated and the officers to retain their arms. Burgoyne after agreeing to these new terms learned from another messenger, dispatched by Clinton, that his Army was only a few days away. Burgoyne consulted with his officers to determine if they were prepared to continue fighting; he was informed that having given his word as an officer and gentleman, he could not renege. Once back in Britain, the humiliated Burgoyne requested a court martial and trial, and was turned down.

As for the enlisted men who were supposed to be repatriated, Congress overrode Gates' decision and they became prisoners of war. On the basis of that victory, France entered the war on the side of the Americans, and thanks to their financial and military support, America was able to sustain a war that lasted another four years. Absent from this account of the battle of Saratoga was a failure in communications between Lord Germain and General Howe, commander-in-chief of the British land forces in America. According to Howe, Germain was vague in assigning the specific time for Clinton to leave New York City to join his forces with those of Burgoyne. Nor was Burgoyne aware of when Clinton was supposed to join him, since the Americans had strung chains across the Hudson River to prevent Clinton's ships from using the river. Despite the "what ifs," the blame for Britain's defeat rests on the shoulders of Howe and Burgoyne

The battle at Yorktown, which ended the war and brought independence, could not have been won without the French fleet and French engineers and sappers who knew how to conduct a siege. There was a final touch of irony to the battle of Saratoga. Arnold, the hero of the day, would later turn traitor and fight on the side of the British. And Gates, whom Congress assumed was responsible for the victory of Saratoga, later disgraced himself by fleeing from the battlefield, leaving his troops and officers behind when they were sent south to defeat the British.

CHAPTER 5. THE TORTUOUS PATH TO A NEW NATION

The surrender of Cornwallis did not mean the end of hostilities as far as George III was concerned. He refused to accept the demission of Lord North and vowed to continue the war. Since Parliament controlled the nation's purse strings, the King's fulminations were for naught and he was forced to accept a ministry determined to end the war. The man chosen to officially end the war and begin peace negotiations was Lord Rockingham who, in his previous role as Prime Minister, had convinced Parliament to rescind the Stamp Act.

When he died unexpectedly, he was replaced by the Earl of Shelburne, who also was pro-American. Congress decided to send four more commissioners to negotiate the peace treaty with Britain, informing all that any peace treaty signed would have to conform to the terms of America's alliance with France. The men chosen for this role were John Adams, currently in Holland negotiating a loan with the Dutch, which would enable the American government to function; Henry Laurens, who had been captured at sea and kept in the Tower of London for 14 months before being released; John Jay, and Thomas Jefferson (who declined because of the death of his wife). Of the four, John Jay was a latecomer to the cause, having refused to sign the Declaration of Independence. But when Jay learned that the French Foreign Minister was engaged in secret discussions with the British, without informing his colleagues he journeyed to London to begin negotiations himself. Jay believed that once a peace treaty was signed with the Americans, the British would be in a better bargaining position with the French, whom they feared far more than the Americans.

Jay's judgment proved to be accurate and most of the American objectives were included in the peace treaty. The New England states were granted fishing rights off the coast of Newfoundland with the proviso that the fish could be dried on British land; all the territory behind the Appalachian Mountains extending to the Mississippi River; free access to the river; and finally, cession of Canada. When Shelburne presented these one-sided terms to Parliament, he was censored and replaced by Lord North and Charles Fox (who had been pro-American before the outbreak of hostilities). In the final agreement, ratified by the British in January 1783, the United States guaranteed the repayment of the debts owed to British merchants, and it was left to the individual states to settle with the Loyalists whose properties had been confiscated. The only major sticking point was Spain's refusal to allow free use of New Orleans, and adjudication of the northern boundaries separating the United States from Canada.

The successful peace negotiations, which more than doubled the size of the nation, did nothing to resolve the fundamental problem facing what purported to be a unified nation. The Articles of Confederation, finally agreed to by all 13 states in 1781, still failed to provide for majority rule. As had been the case during the war, any state could veto the legislation agreed to by the other 12 states. A prime example was the proposal to impose a five percent tax on all merchandise imported into this country, which was vetoed by Rhode Island because it would impose a hardship on its smuggling business. Shortly after, Virginia rejected it as well, and it was a dead letter. Without a source of income, the government could not meet any of its obligations, especially to officers or the enlisted men who had served throughout the war. While the war was being waged, half pay for life was guaranteed to the officers, and land grants in the territories to enlisted men. When the officers threatened to revolt, only Washington was able to prevail upon them to have a little patience. Their patience was rewarded, upon their discharge from military service, with certificates for three months of back pay for officers and 40 cents for enlisted men. As in any long conflict, the public had enough of war and anything associated with it. Thus, the public was in an uproar when Henry Knox and other officers formed the society of Cincinnatus, named after the Roman general who following his triumphs had put down his sword and returned to the plough. Although the funds raised were to be used to support the widows and orphans of officers who had died in the service, and Washington was its first president, people were outraged because future membership in the society was limited to the oldest son and members wore a distinctive ribbon. The objection was not as pretended, that the officers intended to establish a military clique within a republican society, but that it highlighted the paucity of men who had volunteered to serve their country. To pacify the public uproar, the funds raised were turned over to the state legislatures for distribution to the widows and orphans.

As had been the case following the end of the French and Indian War, an economic depression overwhelmed the states and the federal government as well. This time, however, it wasn't due to the withdrawal of specie from the economy but rather the valueless paper currency issued by the states and Congress. To add to the nation's miseries, property had been damaged by the British and Hessians. Following their initial victories in the Southern states, the British had removed thousands of Negro slaves who were sent to work on the sugar islands of Barbados and Jamaica. Not only was their replacement expensive, but few if any people possessed the currency to acquire them. As a result there was a sharp decline in the sale of commodities for export. In certain areas of New Jersey, the Hessians had stolen everything they could. The British Navy had bombarded and set fire to the coastal cities of New England, and once the British departed New York City, its wartime economy vanished with nothing to replace it. Some of the states were attempting to restore the value of their currency through taxation; on the federal level, nothing was being done.

Even the Northwestern territories, which had been acquired through the peace treaty, had yet to be resolved. The roadblock was that a half dozen states laid claim to these lands on the basis of their charters from different kings. It was Virginia, the oldest state with the first charter, which broke this impasse by agreeing to release its claim if the others would follow suit. While Maryland agreed to relinquish its claim, the Northern states which also had legitimate claims on these lands only agreed to relinquish their claims provided slavery was prohibited in any territory north of the Ohio River. Based on these accords, in 1784 Congress enacted the first version of the Northwest Ordinance in which these lands would be divided into states which eventually would be equal in power to the original 13 states. While Jefferson's proposal to limit the size of these states was agreed upon, that would be the extent of the legislation enacted, although efforts were made in 1785 and 1786 to no avail. One thing was obvious: the petty jealousies between the states were preventing Congress from agreeing to any meaningful legislation as long as one state could prevent the rule of the majority.

Of the many myths that surround American history, one of the most egregious is that which credits James Madison as the father of the Constitution. It all began over a 100-year quarrel between Virginia and Maryland over fishing rights in the Potomac River. On learning of this imbroglio, Washington suggested to James Madison who had served as a delegate to the Continental Congress that he contact a counterpart in Maryland and resolve the senseless dispute. As a result of this settlement, a similar discord between Pennsylvania and Delaware over fishing rights in Chesapeake Bay was settled. Supposedly it was these two thorny problems that led to the need for a Constitutional Convention to resolve differences between the states. Nothing could be further from the facts. The bones of contention were not between the states but between the US and Great Britain. Under the peace treaty, the northern borders between Canada and this country had yet to be defined. British troops were still in these areas and supposedly inciting the local tribes against settlers moving into these vacant lands. There were reports of massacres, and when the American minister to London lodged a protest, there was no central government to back him up. The 13 states were a body without a head. The only organization that had represented them was the Continental Army, and it had been disbanded once the British troops left New York City. Washington's major concern was that unless a central government was established, Britain's economic policies would divide the colonies and that the long and costly war had been fought in vain. It was under these circumstances that Washington suggested to Madison and Alexander Hamilton (his aide de camp during the war) that a letter should be sent to each of the state legislatures inviting them to send delegates to a convention whose purpose was to draw up a constitution for the 13 states.

Make no mistake, the states that sent delegates to Philadelphia in May 1787 were not responding to Madison or Hamilton but to Washington, whom they unanimously elected president of the convention. Once elected, Washington laid down the basic rule: All discussions which took place at the convention had to be kept secret, or the meeting would fail. It is a tribute to Washington that during the three and a half months of arguments and disagreements among the delegates, including those who came and left, not a word of what was taking place was released to the press. More than anything else, it was this secrecy that enabled the delegates to draw up a constitution. Nor should this be surprising. The men chosen to represent the interests of their states were all members of the establishment. Either they owned large plantations with slaves or they were successful lawyers, doctors or businessmen; they all had personal financial stakes in whatever document was agreed upon. Almost all of them understood that the Articles of Confederation no longer served the interests of their state, but they were equally concerned with what would replace it. All of them were patriots who had supported the revolution but their principal loyalty was to their state

The first item on the agenda was whether to work within the existing framework of the Articles of Confederation or create a new document. The consensus was that since all the states present possessed their own constitution, any document developed should follow along the same lines. Since Edmund Randolph of Virginia had a plan ready for discussion, it was the first proposal on the agenda. His plan called for two legislative bodies — a House where all bills of appropriation would originate, whose members would be elected by the populace, and a Senate which would be elected by members of the state legislatures. The configuration of both bodies of Congress would be based on proportional representation, giving the larger states an advantage over the smaller states. The reaction of the smaller states, as would be expected, was to threaten to leave the meeting and return home. This resulted in Randolph's proposal being tabled for the moment while the next item on the agenda was discussed, the type of government envisaged. Obviously, the government most familiar to the delegates was that of Great Britain, stripped of its King and hereditary nobility. Imitating Britain did not sit well with most delegates and other options were put on the table. It was only when Charles Pinckney of South Carolina addressed the delegates that the subject was put on track. The United States, he began, is unlike Britain or any other nation; it is not a society in which wealth and privilege dominate the rest of the population, nor does it possess a large underclass of the desperately poor. He continued: it is a middle class society where upward mobility is open to all; we are not constricted in terms of land but have an entire continent in front of us, which will be occupied by our children and grandchildren. It is because our potential for growth is unique that we would have to invent our own form of government, he concluded.

While Pinckney's speech resonated with the delegates, it did nothing to resolve the question of representation in the Senate. The representatives from the smaller states were prepared to leave the convention if membership in the Senate was based on proportional representation. Once again it was Charles Pinckney who stepped into the breach by informing the larger states that if they gave ground on equal representation in the Senate, that concession would eliminate any other objections the smaller states might have. Of course, that was nonsense once the issue of slavery came on the agenda. It was not the institution that came under attack, since slavery existed in the Northern states as well as those in the South, but the efforts of the Southern states to have slaves included as part of their population. Doing so would increase the number of representatives they could send to the House, since representation in that body was to be proportional to a state's population. Their argument for including slaves was that they had to be housed, clothed and fed in the same way as indentured servants, who were considered part of the population. Since there were six states that depended on slavery for their economies, if there was to be a constitution a compromise would have to be made. How the figure of counting slaves as three fifths of a white was arrived at remains a mystery. What was clear, however, was that the issue of slavery was dividing the nation. The Northwest Ordinance passed by the old Congress, which opened the territories north of the Ohio River to be admitted as states with the same privileges as the original 13, had been ratified by the Northern states only because it contained the proviso that slavery would be banned. The other major dispute over slavery was whether to have further importation of slaves banned. In this instance there was a sharp division between the Northern and Southern slave states. Virginia and Maryland supported the ban because their growing slave population was more than sufficient to meet their economic needs. As a matter of fact, their rate of propagation was so high that there were more slaves in Virginia than in the Carolinas and Georgia combined. There also was a touch of greed in their opposition. Without any further imports not only would the value of their slave population increase but they could make a fancy profit by selling off their excess slaves in the Carolinas and Georgia. Once again the threat of packing up bags and leaving the convention resulted in a compromise. The slave trade would be extended for another 20 years, at which point Congress could ban it.

Once the issues of slavery had been resolved the delegates had to tackle such basics as: the chief executive and his role in the government as well as the duration of his term in office; the length of terms for members of the House and Senate; and the methods of election as well as the role of the courts and the judiciary. While it was assumed that Washington would be the first president, the limitations on the power of his office had to take into account those who would follow him. What the delegates were seeking was a balance of power between the man who would be chief executive of the nation and commander-in-chief of the armed forces, chief law officer, and the Congress. Whether by design or inadvertently they managed to stumble upon the basic concept of the Constitution, a series of checks and balances between the three branches of government: the executive, the legislative and the judicial. While the president could command the armed forces, only Congress could declare war; while the president could veto legislation, a two-thirds majority in both Houses of Congress could override his veto. Having circumscribed the power of the Congress and the executive and decided in favor of a four-year renewable term for the president, the next major conflict among the delegates was the role of the Supreme Court. The principal objection was that its authority superseded that of the state courts, and in its interpretation of the Constitution it could overrule both the executive and the legislative branches of the government. Given that enormous power, some restraints had to be placed upon its decisions. In its interpretation of the Constitution its decisions could be overridden by a two-thirds majority in both Houses of Congress along with three fourths of the states. Furthermore, while the president could appoint the Justices, they had to be approved by two thirds of the Senate. However, the delegates agreed that the Justices could serve as long as they desired or until they expired.

The document forged together by these delegates was designed to prevent the nation from falling into one of the two extremes – an aristocracy or a democracy. The election of the president by popular vote would insure against an aristocracy emerging; on the other hand, the fact that the president was elected by electors who were free to cast their votes as they pleased would prevent the emergence of a dictator who might appeal to the baser instincts of the public. While the chief executive could negotiate treaties, it took a two-thirds vote by the Senate to ratify them. For these delegates, all members of the establishment in their states, the Senate was to be the bulwark against any excesses committed by the executive branch or the House. For this reason the term of office of senators was six years, compared to two years for members of the House and four years for the chief ex-ecutive. Furthermore, a senator would be appointed to office by a vote of members of his state legislature, rather than by the public, under the assumption that men elected to state legislatures would be men of property. Still on the agenda was whether the Constitution should provide for a Bill of Rights. This concept was championed by George Mason, the author of the Virginia Bill of Rights, which had been incorporated into the Constitutions of four other states; to its support-ers, it was viewed as the sine qua non for the Constitution. However, after three months of deliberation in the extreme summer heat of Philadelphia, the majority of delegates were exhausted and anxious to return home. Since all the states had some version of a Bill of Rights, the motion for its inclusion was overridden. The time had come to take a vote on the Constitution. It was only then that Benjamin Franklin offered his opinion, which reflected the attitude of the majority of the delegates: "There are several parts of this Constitution which I do not at present approve...It...astonishes me...to find this system approaching so near to perfection as it does." Of the 55 delegates who were instrumental in drafting the Constitu-tion, 39 signed it. While some left Philadelphia before the signing on September 17, 1787, others did not approve of the final document. Three who voted against its ratification, Edmund Randolph and George Mason of Virginia and Elbridge Gerry of Massachusetts, did so because it failed to include a Bill of Rights.

The Constitution had two hurdles to pass before it could take effect. It had to be approved by three fourths of the states. And the Congress established under the Articles of Confederation had to be dissolved. The three-quarter mark was reached when New Hampshire became the ninth state to ratify the Constitu-tion, on June 21, 1788. The Continental Congress then put the Constitution into effect on July 8, 1788 by setting dates for national elections, and dissolved itself officially in March 1789.

At the same time that the delegates were in Philadelphia drafting the Consti-tution, the existing Congress was prepared to put the final changes on the pro-posed Northwest Ordinance at last. Under the legislation finally ratified no fewer than three and no more than five states could be created out of these territories. It also reaffirmed that the new states would have the same rights and privileges as the original 13 states. Also specified was the necessary number of citizens in-habiting the circumscribed acreage before it could be considered to be a state. Prior to reaching that number, a governor would be appointed to represent the interests of the proposed state. An arbitrary figure of ownership of 50 acres was the criteria established for citizenship. These figures would be applied not only to states carved out of the Northwest Territories but to Southern states as well.

In light of the delegates fear and opposition to a democracy, ratification of the Constitution would not be left to a referendum among the population but was to be decided in the state legislatures by their elected representatives. As Pinckney had predicted, most of the small states were among the first to ratify the document, with Delaware being the first, on December 7, 1787. The real struggle for confirmation would take place in the three largest states, Virginia, New York and Massachusetts. A fundamental objection to the document in those states was relinquishing some of their autonomy. Some also objected because it lacked a Bill of Rights; others because it ceded too much power to the Supreme Court. To support ratification of the Constitution, a series of articles were written by Madison, Hamilton and John Jay, which have come to be known as the *Federalist Papers*. However, these had little impact on the decisions arrived at by the individual legislatures since there were an equal number of pamphlets published in opposition. In Massachusetts, ratification passed by a slim majority thanks to pressure from John and Sam Adams. The objections voiced by some members of the legislature were difficult to answer. All the delegates at the convention were members of the establishment. The majority of the state's population — the independent farmers, artisans and mechanics — had no input into the document. In Virginia the opposition was led by Patrick Henry and would have succeeded had not Edmund Randolph switched his position in response to New Hampshire's vote to ratify, which met the established three fourths of the states necessary to put the Constitution into effect and form a government. Under those circumstances, Virginia had no alternative but to cast its lot with the new nation. What is even more remarkable about the opposition was that George Washington had put his prestige behind its ratification. New York followed shortly behind Virginia; only pressure from the commercial interests forced it to reverse its original decision, which had been negative. Rhode Island, which refused to send any delegates to the Convention, was the last state to ratify – on May 29, 1790.

A major reason for Virginia's opposition to the Constitution was the absence of a Bill of Rights. Many leaders in that state were determined to have it included once the new Congress met. When James Madison sought election as a representative in the first Congress, the supporters of the amendment opposed him; the candidate they wanted was James Monroe, who unlike Madison had fought in the war and carried a bullet in his shoulder thanks to the British. Madison, desperate to be a member of the new government, promised his constituents that if elected he would introduce legislation to amend the Constitution to include a Bill of Rights. Knowing he would never be reelected if he did not honor his pledge, Madison kept his word. Today, Madison is known as the Father of the Constitution when in fact that credit belongs to George Washington. Madison's major contribution was that during the discussions among the delegates, he kept copious notes of the proceedings; we are dependent upon the notes he took to describe how the Constitution was fashioned.

CHAPTER 6. A NATION IN TRANSITION

While the Constitution was specific about the powers of the president and the way he should be elected, there was no mention of how he should be nominated or selected since everyone assumed that Washington would be the nation's first president. The question remains: who chose John Adams to be his vice president? The only plausible answer is George Washington, which poses a second question. Why John Adams? While Washington chaired the Constitutional Convention, he never voiced any opinion or made a suggestion, according to the notes taken by Madison. However, Washington was an astute listener, and the sharp differences between the Northern and Southern delegates became clear. Since his principal objective was to keep the nation united, he determined that after he had served his term, the presidency should go to a Northerner. In his mind, no man was more qualified for that position than John Adams. Washington followed the same policy in selecting his key Cabinet officers. For Secretary of State, he named Thomas Jefferson, who had just returned from France where he had served as American minister to our ally; for Secretary of Treasury, his former aide de camp, Alexander Hamilton. While Jefferson had been the author of the Declaration of Independence and had served as Governor of Virginia, Hamilton's only claim to fame was that he had authored some of the *Federalist Papers*. On the other hand, Washington had total confidence in Hamilton's ability.

The members of the state legislatures that had voted to ratify the Constitution were unprepared to cope with the reality of a Congress where a simple majority of the members of both chambers could enact legislation injurious to a state's economic and political interests. While all of them understood that the import duties they formerly collected would now be collected by the federal government to pay for its operations, they were unprepared for other duties designed to raise additional revenues. The first to feel the pain were the New England states when a tax was levied on the importation of molasses, the base for producing rum, the national alcoholic beverage; when Pennsylvania sought a tariff to protect its nascent iron industry, the Southern states objected because they could buy it cheaper in England; and when a head tax of $10 was place on every imported slave, South Carolina threatened to secede. The biggest uproar, however, was over the federal court system established by the Constitution. Not only did the state courts have to contend with a Supreme Court which would consist of one Chief Justice and five Associate Justices, but there were federal district courts and circuit courts. Lawyers in particular objected since they had established a cozy relationship with the judges in state courts.

In the second year of the existence of Congress, the administration decided to address the major problem facing the nation — the funding for the debts owed its allies; those of the Second Continental Congress, and those of the individual states. About $12 million was owed to France, Holland and Spain; $42.5 million for the paper certificates issued by the old Congress to pay off the officers and servicemen who served during the war, and $21 million in paper money issued by the states. When Hamilton presented his fiscal budget for the year, which called for the government to assume all these debts at par value and to lump all these debts into one bill of $75 million, with Congress assuming the responsibility for its repayment, its members went into a state of shock. While Congress was prepared to assume the payment of interest and principal to its foreign creditors, it balked at the nation assuming at par value the debts of the old Congress, when they had been sold to speculators and now were valued at ten cents on the dollar. Even more disturbing was his proposal to assume the debts of all the states, when there was a sharp difference in the amount of debt owed by each state. Although Jefferson was Secretary of State and a member of the administration, he led the opposition to Hamilton's policy. Jefferson's concept for the new government differed from that of Washington and Hamilton. Fundamentally, Jefferson was a romantic while Hamilton and Washington were pragmatists. Jefferson's concept for the government was a loose federation of states that were preeminent except when it came to national security. To the manor born, he never developed a concept of money, and despite his munificent salary during his eight years as president, when he died his heirs had to pay off the debts he had accumulated. Despite the opposition he rallied behind him, Washington's support for Hamilton's policies carried the day.

Only Hamilton's proposal for a private National Bank, which would house all the revenues coming into the national treasury, gave Jefferson the leverage to secure enough congressional votes to block him. The opposition was predicated, first, on the fact that since it was a private institution, Congress would have no jurisdiction over its policies; second, since most of its capitalization would come from Northerners, they would have a dominant voice in the bank's lending policies. But the peg that Jefferson hung his hat on was that there was nothing in the Constitution that called for a private bank. Viewing the Bank as the capstone for the nation's finances, Hamilton traded Northern votes for the contested location of the nation's capital for Southern votes for the Bank – that is, the North wanted the establishment of the Bank, and got it, and the South achieved having the Capital moved from Philadelphia to the banks of the Potomac. One proviso was insisted upon by Jefferson: the charter of the Bank of the United States, which opened its doors in December 1791 in Philadelphia, was limited to 20 years, at which time it would have to be renewed by Congress. Hamilton's plan to have the nation's finances on a sound footing was realized just half an hour after the Bank opened. The initial capitalization was to be $10 million, with $8 million available to the public and $2 million held by the government (purchased by a loan from the Bank). The final item on the agenda of the first Congress was a Bill of Rights, promised to four states if they ratified the Constitution. True to his promise, Madison introduced the legislation. But, 16 other amendments to the Constitution were added to the proposed legislation, which would have made a shamble of the original document. While most were approved by the House, all of them were rejected by the Senate.

The last thing the new government needed was to be caught in the middle of a life and death struggle between its former ally France and its former enemy Britain. Only the policy of neutrality laid down by George Washington prevented a disaster. He alone understood the fragility of this new government. The overwhelming majority of the American public embraced the French Revolution, especially in its early stages when Lafayette appeared to be playing a central role, but the President's concern was to focus on America's interest. When the *Girondist* party dispatched its envoy Citizen Edmond-Charles Genet to involve this country in France's war with Great Britain, he was feted in every city. However, Washington turned down his request for repayment of a loan not yet due and for French ships to be permitted to use American ports as part of France's war effort, reminding Genet that America's treaty of alliance was with the Old Regime and not the current government. Above all, the President was a pragmatist whose sole concern was the future of this country. Genet's effort to arouse public opinion against Washington backfired, and Genet lost his credibility among the American public.

It was not only the success of the French revolutionary armies against the combined effort of the European monarchs to restore the Old Regime that brought Britain into their partnership but the fear that the ideas and concepts of the French Revolution might spread to their country. What led the members of Parliament to vote funds for war was not the act of regicide but that the revolutionary governments had stripped the church and nobility of their inherited properties. To prevent the ideas and ideals of the revolution from crossing the Channel, Britain joined the alliance. While America assured the British that its policy was one of neutrality, its definition of neutrality differed from that of Britain and France. To America, it meant free trade with both adversaries, allowing its merchants to profit from the ongoing war. To Britain, control of the seas was its major weapon against the revolutionary forces, and it intended to use it despite protests from the American government. The war cry to initiate hostilities against Great Britain was universal, although the reasons for this sentiment were varied — the Northern states because British policy affected their commerce with France; the Southern states because they sympathized with the aspirations of the French. Washington understood the futility of declaring war. Not only could the British Navy impose a blockade on American ports, cutting off shipping to the West and East Indies as well as to South America, but its warships could bombard America's coastal cities as it had done during the Revolutionary War. It was about this time that Jefferson tendered his resignation. Opposed to the foreign and domestic policies of the administration, he recognized that as long as Washington was president there was no possibility of changing them. Instead of remaining impotent, Jefferson would lay the groundwork to build an opposition to these policies. Since those who espoused his views referred to themselves as Democratic-Republicans, the assumption was made that the supporters of Washington's and Hamilton's policies were members of the Federalist Party. The problem with that syllogism was that there was no Federalist Party. There were no more ardent Federalists than Madison and Jefferson. John Adams and Hamilton were Federalists who opposed each other when it came to policy. Unlike the Democrat-Republicans, who developed a political organization along with a propaganda machine, the only platform of those who deemed themselves to be Federalists was a wish to be elected. With Adams' failure to be elected for a second term, the ephemeral Federalist Party disappeared from the political scene as a serious contender. Historians were the ones who breathed life into this corpse by doting it a political party.

In 1794, the United States faced a real threat of war with Great Britain, which Washington was determined to avoid. He dispatched John Jay to London to negotiate with the British. The problem facing Jay was he had no quid pro quo to offer the British. The only threat the US posed was an invasion of Canada, and since America had no standing Army and was certain to meet stiff opposition from the Loyalists who had fled to Canada, it really posed no danger to Britain's interests. Jay's bargaining position was made worse by America's failure to live up to the peace treaty. Americans had yet to repay all the debt owed to British merchants, and no efforts had been made by the states to reimburse Loyalists for their confiscated properties. But these delinquencies had nothing to do with the terms the British offered Jay. They were designed to humiliate the fledgling republic, merely eliminating Britain's control of Northwest posts and granting the US "most favored nation" status. Had Washington revealed the terms at that time, he believed the public outcry might have led Congress to declare war against Britain. Since Congress wouldn't be in session for another four months, it enabled him to convince the necessary two thirds of the Senate to ratify the treaty except for the prohibition on exports shipped to Europe. When the Democrat-Republicans in the House, where they had a majority, insisted that Washington reveal the contents of the treaty so they could vote it up or down, Washington refused, referring them to the Constitution, which stipulated that only the Senate could approve treaties. Furious, at first, Congress refused to appropriate the funds necessary to implement the treaty. Eventually, cooler heads prevailed and the funds were allocated. This was the first Constitutional crisis, and it revealed why the document had been designed to restrict most major decisions exclusively to the Senate. It also exposed the inherent power in the presidency. By the end of Washington's second term, the white knight on the horse who had led the states to their independence, was referred to in the press as King George and a dictator. Only later did Americans appreciate Washington's policy of avoiding war at all cost.

No one could question John Adams' patriotism or the major role he played prior, during and after the Revolutionary War. Had he not been suffused with his self importance, his one-term presidency might have turned out differently. What infuriated him during the eight years he waited in the wings to become president was Washington's reliance on Hamilton for the direction the nation should follow. Even after Hamilton resigned from the Cabinet, the President still depended on his former aide de camp for advice and counsel. In a moment of anger and frustration, Adams referred to Hamilton as the bastard son of a Scottish peddler. Hamilton took umbrage, and when he selected Thomas Pinckney of South Carolina as his vice president, convinced some or the electors in that state to abstain from voting for Adams so Pinckney would become president. News of Hamilton's plot must have leaked out, resulting in New England electors withholding their votes for Pinckney. As a result, Jefferson, running for the presidency on the Democrat-Republican ticket, received the second largest number of votes and became vice president. Upon learning this news, he pleaded ill health and retired to Monticello. The animus between Adams and Hamilton was no different than that between Jefferson and Hamilton. Both men believed they should have had Washington's ear in determining domestic and foreign policies. Neither man understood the symbiotic relation that existed between the General and his aide de camp, since neither had chosen to join the Army. Hamilton was Washington's only confidante and sounding board. As a result Washington came to depend upon Hamilton's judgment which must have proved to be reliable.

Adams' presidency was challenged at the onset not by domestic politics but by stupidity committed by the new French government in power. Having defeated the Royalist armies assembled against them, the French Directory, which replaced Robespierre, took on an attitude of arrogance towards the United States. When James Monroe, US minister to France, raised no objections, Washington recalled him and replaced him with Charles Cotesworth Pinckney. By the time he arrived in Paris to present his papers, Adams was the president and had to cope with the refusal of the head of the Directory to receive Pinckney. Before taking precipitous action against this diplomatic slap in the face, Adams consulted both Houses of Congress to receive their support. Adams then decided to send three men, Pinckney, John Marshall and Elbridge Gerry, a staunch Republican and supporter of Jefferson, as envoys extraordinary and ministers plenipotentiary.

Instead of formal negotiations taking place when the envoys arrived in Paris, Pinckney, who had awaited the arrival of the others, was called to a meeting with a Major Montmorency, who informed him of the following: before a meeting could take place, certain remarks in Washington's farewell address would have to be publicly repudiated by the former president; a generous bribe would have to be paid to members of the Directory, and a substantial loan would have to be promised to France. The Major had been informed of these terms by the private secretary to Talleyrand, the Directory's foreign minister. As a parting gesture, the Major threatened the delegates with arrest if they didn't agree to these terms. A few days later a man who identified himself only as Y, reiterated the demands made by the Major and added that Adams also would have to retract some objectionable references to the Directory. He continued: "I will not disguise from you that these satisfactions having been made, the essential parts of the treaty remain to be adjusted. You must pay money. You must pay a great deal of money."

The reaction of the American envoys was one of outrage as was that of Adams when he finally received their communication. Once again he spoke of war, and once again he was dissuaded by members of his Cabinet who convinced him that the country was ill prepared for such an event. The message that Adams did send to Congress merely stated that he saw "no ground of expectation that the objects of their mission can be accomplished on terms compatible with the safety, honor or essential interests of this nation." To Jefferson, the romantic Francophile, Adams' report of the failed mission didn't make sense. Even though one of the ministers who had signed onto the report, Elbridge Gerry, was an ardent Republican, Jefferson and his supporters both within and outside of Congress attacked the probity of Adams in a campaign in the press. So intense was their vilification of the President that Adams decided to release the report. While Jefferson's reaction was to blame the delegates, what came to be known as the XYZ affair infuriated the general public, including avid Republicans. Using the famous slogan "millions for defense but not one cent for tribute," money was raised to build warships to protect American shipping against French privateers.

Shortly after, Lieutenant Stephen Decatur on one of these new warships would capture a French privateer ship and sail it into Philadelphia's harbor. Adams, reveling in his new popularity, lost his perspective. He had raised taxes to create a Navy when the nation had yet to declare war. Moreover, he was receiving conflicting information about the attitude of the French government. He had no idea that the corrupt government of Count Barras had been overthrown and a quasi-dictatorship established under General Napoleon Bonaparte with Talleyrand continuing to serve as foreign minister. All he knew was that his administration and person were continually under attack by the Republican press. He also viewed the growing strength of the Republicans as a direct result of unfettered immigration. Taking advantage of his popularity, he had Congress enact the Alien and Sedition laws. Among other restrictions, they required 14 years of residence in the United States before becoming a citizen, and imposed fines or prison sentences on any person or newspaper that criticized the President or members of his Cabinet. It mattered not to Adams or to members of Congress that the Sedition Act violated the First Amendment to the Constitution, which guaranteed freedom of speech and the press. Of far more significance were the responses to this legislation written by Jefferson and Madison respectively in the Virginia and Kentucky Resolutions, which did more than imply that under certain conditions a state possessed the right to secede from the Union. These resolutions were used later to justify secession.

Meanwhile, with the presidential election of 1800 being imminent, Adams turned his attention to American–French relations. Having received a communication from William Vans Murray, the young American diplomat to Holland, that he had been contacted by Talleyrand who wanted to normalize relations with the United States, Adams decided to explore that possibility. Since Murray was considered inexperienced, Adams sent along Chief Justice Ellsworth Oliver and William Davies of North Carolina to conduct the negotiations. Under Napoleon, Talleyrand followed his instructions and a peace treaty was negotiated that treated both nations as equals. The treaty arrived too late, and Adams was defeated by Jefferson in the electoral count. When the Constitution was drawn up, no thought had been given to the emergence of political parties or to a separate vote for the president and vice president. No consideration had been given to the possibility of a tie vote since it was assumed that only two men would be vying for the presidency and that the man with the most votes would become the president. In the election of 1800, Jefferson and Aaron Burr received the same number of electoral votes. The Republicans had assumed that Jefferson would become the president, with Burr elected as vice president, but Burr refused to accept the lesser position because of the electoral vote tie. He ignored the fact that the majority of the Republican votes had come from the Southern states and focused instead on the fact that it was his presence on the ticket that enabled both candidates to carry the critical votes of New York and in turn, to achieve victory. What the Constitution did state was that in the event of a tie, the decision as to who would be president would be decided in the House of Representatives. Since the majority of the House membership supported Adams in the election, they preferred to see the results left in limbo. It was only after 35 ballots that Hamilton persuaded two of the electors to abstain from voting on the thirty-sixth ballot, giving Jefferson the majority at last. Hamilton did not maneuver Jefferson into the presidency because he supported Jefferson's politics or policies; rather, Hamilton had a visceral distrust of Burr, which later would be borne out.

Jefferson was a federalist except when it came to the US Supreme Court. His opposition was more emotional than rational since its jurisdiction was limited to interpreting the laws set down in the Constitution. The case that would establish the authority of the court occurred at the onset of his administration. Prior to leaving office, Adams had appointed a man named Marbury and three other men as Justices of the Peace for Washington, the nation's capital. The papers were signed by the Secretary of State but never delivered to the men. When Madison took office as Secretary of State, he refused to turn over the papers to the men appointed by Adams, instead filling their positions with loyal Republicans. Marbury appealed to the Supreme Court where John Marshall had been appointed Chief Justice. In his opinion Marshall stated that while an injustice had been done to the men, the Supreme Court had no jurisdiction since it did not refer to a law in the Constitution. The long-lasting implication of *Marbury vs. Madison* was hidden in the obverse: any law that impinged on what was specifically stated in the Constitution came under the jurisdiction of the Supreme Court, and its verdicts became the law of the land. From then on, those appointed to the Supreme Court would decide what laws enacted by the states, decisions made by lower courts or actions of individuals were or weren't in violation of the laws set down in the Constitution.

The highpoint of Jefferson's first term was the acquisition of the territories associated with the Louisiana Purchase for three cents an acre, which doubled the size of the United States. Neither Jefferson nor the negotiators in Paris had anything to do with the decision. As a matter of fact, in the early negotiations, the President sought only the port of New Orleans and if possible western Florida. It was Napoleon who insisted that the US acquire the whole enchilada for $15 million. An explanation for his motivation may be found in his declaration: "This accession of territory affirms forever the power of the United States, and I have given England a maritime rival who sooner or later will humble her pride." While it was Hamilton's fiscal policy that enabled the US to float the $15 million loan on the foreign markets, Jefferson deserves all the credit for sending his personal secretary Captain Meriwether Lewis, along with William Clark, to explore and chart the new territories acquired. In tracing the course of the Missouri River to discover its source, the two explorers catalogued all the flora and fauna along their route as well as the various Indian tribes and their customs, and revealed the existence of the Rocky Mountains. It was their decision to reach the Pacific Ocean, however, that proved to be the most important legacy of their exploration as it enabled the US to lay claim to the land variously called the Oregon Territory and Oregon Country.

To recount the adventurous life of Aaron Burr and place it in some kind of perspective would require a novelist, and Gore Vidal's work managed to achieve that goal. Following the loss of the presidency to Jefferson, instead of assuming his role as vice president, Burr attempted to create a new nation by tying the economic fortunes of New York to the New England states, with Burr as president. In order to attain that end, Burr attempted to align his political fortunes with those of the Federalists, the party in opposition to the one that had just elected him vice president. To Burr, switching political parties was the same as changing one's shirt. As a first step to his scheme, he would run for governor of New York on the Federalist ticket, even though he was still serving as the vice president who had been elected as a Republican-Democrat. Hamilton, who had been instrumental in seeing that Jefferson not Burr became president, sent a letter to a fellow Federalist alerting him to Burr's plan. For Burr, this seeming innocuous letter served as an excuse to challenge Hamilton to a duel. While Hamilton fired his pistol in the air, Burr aimed and succeeded in killing his opponent. Charged with first degree murder, before fleeing to the West, he attempted to persuade the British minister to this country to have Britain back him financially in a scheme to establish a new nation carved out of the Louisiana Purchase. Having failed to persuade the British, he set out for the West, which was under the control of the American Army commanded by General Wilkinson. Burr's efforts to involve the General in his scheme failed, and eventually Burr was caught and placed on trial, charged with treason. Since the prosecution lacked a confirming witness, Burr escaped the death penalty. Afraid he might be tried again, he fled to England; when the British refused him asylum, he fled to Sweden. Eventually he returned to this country, married a wealthy widow and died a poor man.

Jefferson's second term started out in a blaze of glory and ended in a disaster. The disappearance of the imaginary Federalist Party enabled Jefferson to receive virtually all the electoral votes. Given this mandate, the President was in a position to initiate any policy that would benefit the interests of the United States. Foremost on his agenda was addressing the continued threat posed to American commerce in the Mediterranean by the Barbary pirates. Unless a bribe was paid, they would capture unarmed American ships and seize the crew; unless a ransom was paid, the pirates would sell the crew into slavery. With the fleet of warships, whose development began under Adams, now ready for active duty, and with the addition of the Marines trained to engage in land warfare, the free-wheeling corsairs were temporarily driven from the sea and their land outposts destroyed by the Marines. While the public gloried in these victories, a far more serious threat to American commerce awaited action from the President. Prior to the 1802 temporary peace treaty of Amiens, when the Napoleonic wars were being waged on the Continent as well as on sea, neutral US ships had enjoyed enormous profits from shipping silver to Spain from Mexico and Peru and other commodities from their Caribbean possessions to France and Holland. It was Britain's decision to renew the war with Napoleon in May 1803 that destroyed the glory of Jefferson's presidency and lead this country to undertake a war it couldn't win.

With the renewal of the war American ships returned to transshipping merchandise from foreign colonies to the parent nation. Britain now waging war against France alone, decided to end this practice. First it established a naval blockade of all European ports occupied by France; next it issued its Orders of Council that would treat American ships transporting merchandise to any country under French control as brigands, which would be treated accordingly. What Jefferson and the American public were unwilling to understand was that Britain, single handedly, was engaged in an all-out war with Napoleonic France. Then a British warship disabled an American frigate outside of Norfolk harbor, killing several US sailors, wounding many more, and seizing seamen it claimed were British citizens; Jefferson lodged a protest through his foreign minister, James Monroe. When Monroe's complaint was brushed aside, in retaliation Jefferson asked Congress to enact a non-importation agreement. This was watered down when Southerners complained it would interfere with the sale of cotton and pointed out that British imports were providing the treasury with $5.5 million, almost half of the government's revenues. It was the Berlin Decree, however, issued by Napoleon in 1807 following his conquest of Prussia that led Jefferson to take actions he later regretted. Under its terms, Napoleon decreed Europe to be a French fortress and any ships entering its ports would be seized along with their cargoes. Furious at what he believed to be a betrayal by a friendly nation, he ordered an embargo placed on all American shipping, naively assuming it would bring Britain and France to their senses. Napoleon's response was to seize the cargoes on all American ships in ports under his control while informing the American minister that his actions were helping reinforce the President's embargo.

Jefferson now was determined to enforce the embargo even if it destroyed the US economy. To prevent ships from pretending they were engaged in coastal trade, he doubled the bond they had to post. When that failed, he banned all ships of any tonnage from leaving any port. Furious that some ships might escape, he pushed through Congress the Force Act, which allowed custom agents to search and seize any ships engaged in illegal trade. The country was in an economic depression. In the Northern cities unemployment was rampant; in the Southern states the debtor laws were removed from the books because of the spate of bankruptcies. When there was a shortage of flour in a city, special permission had to be granted before a ship could bring in relief. Even though the Sedition laws had been revoked, Jefferson had editors jailed who criticized his policy. In March 1809, Congress replaced the Embargo Act with the Non-Intercourse Act which prohibited trading with both France and the United Kingdom. Jefferson's last act as president was to sign this legislation.

CHAPTER 8. THE WAR OF 1812

Signing the Non-Intercourse Act may have been Jefferson's last official act as president, but for the next 16 years he would be America's version of Cardinal Richelieu, the man behind the throne who controlled his two puppets, Presidents Madison and Monroe. Although the latter went so far as to build his home next to that of Jefferson, Madison was far more dependent upon the man he considered to be his mentor. With the passage of the Non-Intercourse Act, which forbade trade only with Britain and France, American ships came out of mothballs and if nothing else inter-coastal trade among the colonies was resumed allowing southern cotton producers to ship cotton to the growing number of textile mills in New England. In that sense the embargo was a blessing; it allowed for the growth and expansion of domestic manufacturing. A year after the enactment of the Non-Intercourse legislation it was apparent to members of Congress that it had accomplished nothing in terms of altering the attitudes of Britain and France. American ships seeking to trade with other nations still were subject to attacks by British and French marauders, so a second bill was passed in 1810, known as Macon's Bill No. 2. It not only removed the restrictions on trading with Britain and France but added a new twist. Whichever of the two nations lifted the Orders of Council, allowing free trade with the United States, the other would have 90 days to reciprocate or an embargo would replace free trade. The revised legislation was as meaningless as the original until events in Spain challenged Napoleon's rule over that nation. In 1808 Napoleon installed his older brother, Joseph, as King of Spain as part of his overall strategy in waging the war against Britain. With Spain under his control this would enable his Army to capture Portugal, thereby isolating Britain from any contact with the continent. The revolt of the Spanish oligarchy and church against the liberal reforms of Joseph coupled with the British liberation of Portugal with its armed forces, was the first sign of a crack in Napoleon's fortress Europe. Neither Madison nor Congress was aware of the Peninsula War or Napoleon's plan to invade Russia. So when Napoleon cynically announced in 1811 that he was lifting his Orders in Council, the revised Non-Intercourse Act automatically kicked in. Britain now had 90 days to follow suit or an embargo would be placed on British merchandise. There was no mention in the revised Act of declaring war. But when members of the House were apprised of Napoleon's lifting of the embargo, instead of allowing Britain the original 90 days to respond and remove its Orders of Council, the time limit was reduced to 60 days. Even though the Senate argued that 90 days was in the legislation in a joint meeting of the two bodies, the House version prevailed.

Caught up in the war hysteria that seemed to grip the nation, Madison called on Congress to declare a state of war despite the fact that Britain's Orders in Council had been lifted prior to the specified time period of 90 days. Critics later would blame Madison's decision on the propaganda war waged by the War Hawks in the House. Little thought was given to the decision or to the events taking place in Europe or to the fact that the US was totally unprepared to wage a land war, much less a sea war against the most powerful navy in the world. It was a mystery how much input Jefferson had in the decision. Instead, all the blame was placed on the War Hawks in Congress. In declaring war, Congress assumed that by seizing Canada it would force Britain to come to terms — or better yet, it would add the territory to the United States. With British troops still engaged in the Peninsula War in Spain, the Americans experienced no opposition. Overlooked in these calculations was this country's lack of an army. Except for victories achieved by the Navy on the Great Lakes, the war waged against Canada resulted in one disaster after another. While West Point did supply able junior officers, the recruits under their command were worthless as were the generals who conducted operations. The campaign's sole accomplishment was to burn to the ground the temporary capital of Canada, today's Ottawa.

The Americans had been able to seize the initiative as long as Britain was engaged in a war on the Continent. The defeat and eventual route of Napoleon's Grand Army in Russia released British troops to fight in America. The US had started an unnecessary war; now the problem was how to extricate itself without incurring a penalty for having invaded Canada and destroyed British warships. A delegation of five leading Americans met with their British counterparts in Ghent. The British terms were harsh: an Indian buffer region in the Ohio Valley separating the US from Canada; demilitarization of the Great Lakes; the withdrawing of the US–Canadian border to the advantage of the British. In case the Americans misunderstood the weakness of their bargaining position, Foreign Secretary George Canning ordered Admiral Sir Thomas Cochrane to teach the Americans the meaning of sea power. Part of his fleet was sent north where they bombarded seaport towns and occupied parts of Maine and Nantucket, but the principal goal of Cochrane was to bring war home to the Americans so they would never forget it. After sacking Havre de Grace in Maryland and Hampton in Virginia, his fleet sailed up the Potomac River with the intention of attacking the nation's capital, Washington. The hastily organized militia fled at the sight of the hardened veterans of the Peninsula campaign, as did Madison and his Cabinet. The British set fire to the President's mansion, the Navy Yard and the Treasury building on the first day. On the following day, the War Department, some private houses and the official newspaper were attacked. But for the occurrence of some thunder storms, the nation's capital would have been burned to the ground. Having encountered no resistance, Cochrane decided that Baltimore should be the next target, and if the military situation continued on its current course, Philadelphia and New York should be next. Guarding Baltimore from invasion by sea was Fort McHenry; protecting it from the British, taking the route by land, was the local militia reinforced by contingents from Virginia and Pennsylvania. It was a lucky sniper's bullet that saved the day by killing Major General Robert Ross, who had led the assault on the capital. Colonel Edward Brooke, next in command, took over and proceeded to follow the usual plan of outflanking the Americans on the left, which his forces easily accomplished. Realizing the threat the maneuver posed to the center, the Americans broke the battle line, and there was a mad retreat, leaving the city of Baltimore open for destruction. In the end, Baltimore was saved by the timidity of Brooke who was reluctant to endure further casualties. As for Fort McHenry, by sinking ships in the harbor, it prevented the large British warships from moving into the range where their big guns would be effective. Instead the Admiral resorted to small ships armed with rockets with delayed fuses to penetrate the wall of the fort. It was purely by chance that a young lawyer, Francis Scott Key, found himself in the fort watching the rockets explode all around its walls. To describe his experience, he penned a poem that was published in several newspapers. One of the editors titled his poem: *The Star Spangled Banner*; with the addition of a British melody, it became our national anthem.

Meanwhile, the peace negotiations taking place at Ghent were at a standstill, the Americans categorically rejecting the British terms. Had Britain not just emerged from its two-decade war against France, the American negotiators would have been told "take it or leave it" and the conflict would have continued. Almost 20 years of continual warfare, however, had resulted in an enormous debt, which had to be paid off with increased taxes. Furthermore, the toll on British industries that had been cut off not only from its lucrative American market but from Europe as well had resulted in massive unemployment and manufacturers forced out of business. The Prime Minister, Lord Liverpool, was anxious to resolve the impasse; not being a military man, he asked the advice of the Duke of

Wellington, the war hero who had defeated the forces of Napoleon in the war of the Spanish Peninsula. Wellington's advice was to make peace with the Americans. His rationale was logical. The US is a country with a vast undeveloped frontier. Given those conditions, the war would go on interminably, with both sides the losers and no winners. In the long run, it would be better to make peace with the Americans, leaving the status quo in place. It was Wellington's endorsement that silenced the British War Hawks. On December 24, 1814, a peace treaty was signed.

When the Duke of Wellington referred to the US as a frontier nation, he was not speaking of the original thirteen colonies but of its vast interior still in the process of being settled. Nor was he referring to the 500 million acres acquired through the Louisiana Purchase, which had yet to be settled. The frontier was that area between the Appalachian Mountains and the Mississippi River where the growing white population still wrestled with the native Amerindian tribes for control of the lands that they had occupied since time immemorial. The struggle was uneven not only because it pitted an advanced civilization against a primitive one but because the whites were united in their purpose while the various Indian tribes were incapable of forming a united front against a common enemy. Pontiac had tried, at the conclusion of the French and Indian War, but he was unable to keep the alliances together. Shawnee leader Tecumseh's efforts to unite the southern and northern tribes in a common cause failed as well. Meanwhile, colonists from the New England states, New York, and Pennsylvania, had streamed into Ohio in such numbers that not only was it admitted as a state but its population soon exceeded that of Massachusetts. From Ohio, the migrants moved into what became known as the Indiana territory. Madison had appointed General William Henry Harrison as temporary governor, and Harrison in a sign of good will had purchased three million acres of land for $10,000 plus an annual fee of $2,500. At three tenths of a cent an acre, it was a better deal than the Louisiana Purchase. A great deal of alcohol helped consummate the deal. No thought was given to where the Indians who occupied these lands might move or how they would cope with those tribes currently occupying the lands they would attempt to settle. As far as the Americans were concerned, it was a clean business deal. While Tecumseh was attempting to rally the southern tribe of Creeks and Choctaws to his alliance, his younger brother, known as "the Prophet," attempted to launch a preemptive attack on Harrison and his military forces. The Prophet was not stupid. He told his warriors to fire first at the officers because once they were dead or wounded, there would be confusion in the ranks, the Americans would panic, and the Indians would triumph. The principal target to be killed was Harrison; had he not changed horses with another officer, he would have been killed. With Harrison quite alive, he rallied his forces and the Indians were slaughtered.

Although the battle was fought near Chillicothe, Ohio, the Indian name for the Indiana site was Tippecanoe; Harrison became a national hero.

It wasn't until Andrew Jackson's amazing victory over the British at the battle of New Orleans that another American general would supersede Harrison as a victorious leader. Unlike Harrison, a Virginian whose father had been a signatory to the Declaration of Independence, Jackson was a man of the frontier. In many ways his career parallels that of Aaron Burr. Both men were fearless adventurers who viewed themselves as men of destiny. From his duels Jackson carried a bullet next to his heart as well as in his shoulder and arm. Both men were ruthless and vindictive. As a touch of irony, they had met when Burr was attempting to establish a separate nation from the Louisiana Purchase; Jackson had sold him some boats and even considered joining up with him. Fortunately for Jackson, his name never surfaced during Burr's trial for treason. Jackson's rise in politics was meteoric. Asked by a friend of his youth, who had been appointed a judge for the western district, to become prosecuting attorney for the district, Jackson joined the judge in Nashville, Tennessee, population 300. Given his position he became a prominent figure in the growing town, so that when Tennessee was admitted as a state, he was the first man to be elected to the House of Representatives. Shortly after, he was appointed a senator when one of the incumbents was accused of treacherous dealings with the Spanish and resigned his seat. Jackson resigned that seat to become a Supreme Court judge in Tennessee because it paid the second highest salary. He also married a woman whom he believed to be divorced but who actually wasn't. Finally, like most successful Westerners, he speculated in lands which left him heavily in debt. Determined to succeed, he resigned his judgeship and set out to become an entrepreneur. With 400 acres and some slaves he became a player in the cotton market. He also acquired a cotton gin machine, which he leased out to smaller farmers, and a famous Arabian stallion which he rented to sire horses. A wealthy man by Western standards, he built a large house which he named The Hermitage and settled down to the life of a country gentleman who entertained lavishly.

Prior to the battle of New Orleans, Jackson's claim to fame as a military commander was developed during the war he waged against the Creek Indians. Unlike the northern Indian tribes who were hunters and gatherers, the Creeks tended to be sedentary and adopted the lifestyle of the white settlers. They lived in houses rather than tepees, dressed like whites, owned and cultivated lands, and even acquired slaves. A certain percentage, however, especially among the young, viewed this mimicry as a betrayal of their heritage. Some had been indoctrinated by Tecumseh in his effort to have them form an alliance with the northern tribes; others had been influenced by the British in Canada and in western Alabama and Florida, who provided them with guns and ammunition. It was these anti-America young braves called Red Sticks who were responsible for the massacre of 250 men, women and children barricaded in Fort Mims whose gates had been left wide open. Jackson, who had yet to acquire a military reputation, viewed this incident as an opportunity to achieve battlefield fame. While he had no problem raising troops to wage war against the Red Sticks (he amassed 3,300 men), he was unable to engage them in a fixed battle where they could be destroyed. It was his friend and military strategist, John Coffee, who devised the plan to entrap and defeat them. Forging an alliance with friendly Creeks, he located the Red Stick force of 800-plus warriors. Coffee's Creek allies were the ones who stole the canoes the Red Sticks had left in the river in the event they needed to escape. Coffee and his men were the ones who attacked from the rear while Jackson, his arm in a sling from a wound he had suffered from a duel, directed the cannon fire from the front. Jackson did offer them the opportunity to surrender but they fought until virtually all were killed. While Jackson had yet to exhibit his prowess as a military leader he was an astute politician. Jackson's peace terms were ruthless and vindictive. All 30,000 Creeks would have to vacate their lands and move across the Mississippi River. Three fifths of Alabama and one third of Georgia would have to be evacuated by the 30,000 Creeks who had lived there to make room for white squatters. All their entreaties were in vain. The lands they had cultivated and the houses they had built were to be left behind. Their departure was the federal government's gain since 23 million acres of uncontested land now became its property and could be put up for sale. Madison, who used the pulpit of his presidency to counsel his fellow citizens to treat the Amerindians fairly, rewarded Jackson by commissioning him a major general in the US Army, with the responsibility for the defense of the Southwest which included Louisiana, now a state, as well as the territories of Alabama and Mississippi.

A fleet admiral in the British Navy tended to view himself as independent of his nation's political leaders since on the sea he was master of that domain. Admiral Cochrane had received no instructions or orders to capture New Orleans. His only motivation was greed and his reasoning logical. Because of Britain's naval blockade the warehouses of the city would be crammed with merchandise. If the city was captured by dint of a seaborne invasion, then he would receive the largest percentage of that merchandise for his personal profit; if by land, the fruits of victory would go to the commanding general. That simple fact when combined with some bad luck explains the horrendous defeat suffered by the British at the battle of New Orleans. When the British fleet of 50 warships was spotted entering the Gulf of Mexico, Jackson rightly assumed the invasion would be through Mobile, Alabama. Once landed there, they could march overland to Vicksburg, Mississippi and from there descend upon New Orleans. A naval invasion was difficult because the city was surrounded by small lakes. Admiral Cochrane's larger warships could not traverse the lakes, and the lighter ships he ordered had never arrived. The last place on earth where British troops were trained to engage in a battle was a bayou. Yet that was where the battle of New Orleans was fought, with the resulting disaster. Granted that bad luck and British stupidity played the major role in the American victory, and if the battle had continued the British would have routed the Americans. Nevertheless, the fact that Andrew Jackson, a politician whose only previous military experience had been limited to fighting 800 Creek Indians in an ambush prepared by his friend, had been able to establish a defensive line capable of inflicting 2,500 casualties on crack British officers and soldiers (who had defeated some of the best troops and officers of Napoleon's Army in Spain) was a tribute to Jackson's ingenuity. Jackson was no more of a military strategist than Washington, but like the General, he understood the strengths and weaknesses of the frontier men he led. Admiral Cochrane, now with his tail between his legs, did pursue the logical strategy of a land invasion through Mobile, but shortly after he succeeded in taking the fort there, news of the peace treaty put an end to military operations.

CHAPTER 9. AMERICA SHEDS ITS ADOLESCENCE

The Democrat-Republican Congress, which had propelled the nation into an unnecessary war, also was determined to undo as much as it could of Hamiltonian economics. Its major target was the Bank of the United States; when its 20-year charter came up for renewal in 1811, it was discontinued and was replaced by state banks. In 1811, when these state banks were chartered, there were only 88. But, by 1816, their number had multiplied to 208. Acquiring a charter proved to be quite easy. Having no stockholders other than the founders and a few friends and political cronies, they were overly generous in their loans, most of which were for land speculation. Moreover, instead of the paper currency being backed by one third specie, most of them ignored good banking procedures. The end of the war altered the economy of the nation. While Southern states profited from the cotton and tobacco stored in warehouses, the New England cotton mills now had to compete with cheap British imports; the same held true for iron manufacturers in Pennsylvania. At the same time, land speculation had outgrown the number of buyers. Smaller banks, which had borrowed from the larger Eastern banks, were called in to make good on the money they had borrowed. Without any regulation, the banking system collapsed. There was only one solution if the economy was to function. Holding its nose, in 1816 Congress re-chartered the Bank of the United States, now dubbed the Second Bank of the United States. It also imposed tariffs to protect nascent industries. As a result of the economic depression, there was a mass migration to the still sparsely occupied territories. Louisiana had been admitted as a state in 1812, and by 1819 four new states had been added to the Union: in the South, Alabama and Mississippi; in the North, Indiana and Illinois. The rationale for the development of these territories into states differed. The Southern states were driven by the quest for new lands to produce cotton, a money-making product; the Northern states needed to accommodate the continual flow of immigrants seeking lands to farm. Although there was little difference in the birth rate between the two regions, the overwhelming majority of immigrants were settling in the Northern states. There were two reasons for this discrepancy. Since the large ports were in the Northern states, most of the immigrants disembarked there; the other was the presence of slavery in the Southern states. Most slaves were forced to toil in the fields, but a notable number were artisans and mechanics — Monticello was built and rebuilt by Jefferson's slaves. In the Northern states, artisans and mechanics could earn a living because they had no such competition.

The demand for cotton pushed settlers to cross over the Mississippi River and acquire lands in Missouri. What began as a trickle grew into a flood. As its population continued to grow, the demands for statehood became louder. The acting governor and legislature petitioned Congress for admission as a slave state since slaves were a necessary component for the cultivation of cotton. As important as cotton was in the growth of Missouri, so was Robert Fulton's invention of the steamboat in 1807. The ability of ships to move up river as well as down river accelerated the growth of those villages along the major waterways, the Ohio and Mississippi Rivers, into towns and then cities. St. Louis, because of its unique location as the junction point between the Ohio and Mississippi rivers, also contributed to the state's increasing population.

Since the northern part of Massachusetts (Maine) also had petitioned for admission as a state, maintaining the parity between slave and non-slave states, the petition easily passed the Senate. In the House, however, it was blocked. The hang up was the clause in the Constitution that allowed the slave states to count the Negro as three fifths of a white citizen. While all the Northern states but Connecticut had abolished slavery, the Negro still wasn't considered a citizen and couldn't vote. To the 84 newly elected members of Congress in 1820, 56 were from Northern states because most immigrants had settled there, and they had the voting power to prevent the admission of Missouri. The issue was not slavery but why the Southern states were entitled to an advantage over the Northern states. It was Jesse Thomas, the senator from Illinois, who devised the Missouri Compromise, with a dividing line of 36°30' latitude as the separation point between slave and non-slave states, with the exception of the proposed state of Missouri. In the end, it was House Speaker Henry Clay who brought about the Compromise by using his power to assign committee chairmanships.

While the US was recovering from the economic depression that followed the end of the war and had succeeded with the re-chartering of the Second Bank of the United States, Europe was attempting to grope with the post-Napoleonic period, following Napoleon's final exile to St. Helena. What Europe needed after 25 years of continuous war was peace, and the two men determined to maintain it were Czar Alexander of Russia and Prince Klemens von Metternich, the Foreign Minister of the Austrian Empire. The latter ostensibly was responsible for setting the stage for the various alliances among the five strongest powers: Prussia, Great Britain and France, as well as Russia and Austria. These alliances helped to maintain a balance of power on the Continent, which lasted throughout the century. The only nation in post-Napoleonic Europe unable to adjust to the newly created order of peace and harmony was Spain. When Napoleon placed his oldest brother, Joseph, on the throne of Spain, Mexico, Argentina and Venezuela had declared their independence from Spain. With the end of the war in 1815, the population of eastern and western Florida appealed to the US for recognition. Having barely recovered from one war, the Monroe administration was loath to begin a war with Spain, so those clamoring for independence were placed under the jurisdiction of Governor Claiborne of Louisiana. Very little thought had been given to the acquisition of Florida. Beside Spanish garrisons stationed at St. Augustine and Pensacola, Seminole Indians were the only inhabitants outside of alligators. Not all of the Creek Indians whom Jackson had forced to abandon their homes and move across the Mississippi had followed his instructions. Some had moved into northern Florida, settling alongside of the Seminoles. There is no doubt that the Monroe government sought the acquisition of Florida, or why would it have constructed a fort in northeastern Florida? While moving a contingent of soldiers with their wives and children to the fort, a pretext was found for its addition to US territory. Attacked by Indians, believed to be Creeks and Seminoles, the entire party was slaughtered. Upon receiving this news, Monroe ordered General Edmund Gaines in eastern Florida and General Jackson in the western section of Florida to punish the Seminoles but avoid attacking the Spanish. Jackson later would claim he never received that part of the instructions and captured the Spanish fort at Pensacola. With this *fait accompli*, negotiations began with the Spanish government for the acquisition of eastern and western Florida which included territory extending to the Rio Grande River. Monroe overruled his Secretary of State, John Quincy Adams, and ordered him to settle for lands only as far as the Sabine River. Monroe feared Congress never would approve the Missouri Compromise if there was a potential for Texas to be admitted as a slave state. Florida was acquired officially in 1821 when the treaty between Spain and the US finally was ratified by the Spanish Cortes. The cost to the US was $5 million, most of which Spain owed to American citizens.

It was during Monroe's first term that Russia advanced across the Bering Straits and took possession of Alaska. With this new territory as a jumping off board, it laid claim to all the maritime fishing rights as far as San Francisco. Adams, who had earlier served as Minister to Russia, filed an objection, informing Russia and Britain that US territory extended to the latitude of 54 degrees and

40 minutes, and that Russia was infringing on American territorial rights. Russia not only backed down but apologized.

What is known today as the Monroe Doctrine was neither a doctrine nor a declaration but part of President Monroe's State of the Union address. All Monroe stated was that the United States would look unfavorably on any effort by European powers to establish colonies in the American hemisphere. This concern stemmed from the declaration of independence from Spain by Mexico, Argentina and Venezuela when Napoleon seized Spain and established his brother Joseph on the throne. With the defeat of Napoleon, Ferdinand was restored to his throne as King of Spain. While the Spanish people had resented the imposition of a foreign ruler, they were unwilling to accept the restrictive policies of Ferdinand now that he had recovered his throne. Rebellions broke out in Spain and in the Spanish possession, the Kingdom of the Two Sicilies, as well. The alliance of strong European nations called on Louis XVIII to restore Ferdinand to his throne, while Austrian troops quelled the insurrection in the Two Sicilies. Czar Alexander had experienced a revolt of his own personal guard, and he viewed these rebellions as an effort to destroy Metternich's peace. He offered to send 15,000 troops to restore the Spanish possessions in the Americas, and Louis XVII, in turn, volunteered members of the extended Bourbon family as rulers of Spain's rebellious colonies. Immediately, Britain warned France that any effort on its part to meddle in the affairs of South American would be a *casus belli*. It was then that George Canning, Britain's Foreign Minister, suggested that the United States and Britain should issue a joint statement. Since Britain had yet to recognize the newly created republics while the US already had exchanged ministers, Adams and Monroe decided to eschew the role of little brother. That was the rationale for Monroe's statement in his State of the Union address. The US would not play second fiddle to Britain. Moreover, the President's statement was vague enough to allow the United States to take over Mexico without appearing overly hypocritical.

By the first quarter of the nineteenth century, this country had undergone a radical change in the distribution of its population and its economy. The westward movement of its people was altering the demographics of the nation. In the 1820 census, Ohio now had a population of 561,000 as compared to 516,000 for Massachusetts which had experienced a gain of 65,000. Indiana now had 154,000 and Illinois, only recently admitted as a state, 55,000. The same population movement was taking place in the South. Kentucky already had a larger white population than any of the original 13 states. Only North Carolina came close, with 419,000 whites. The white population of Tennessee, which was 340,000, was greater than the population of South Carolina or Georgia, respectively 237,000 and 190,000. Along with the change in population there was an alteration in the economy. People had left Massachusetts because all the lands were occupied.

Given the state's abundance of water power, manufacturing replaced agriculture. Tanning industries cropped up in Maine for the production of footwear. The textile industry, which started in Lowell, Massachusetts, now had spread to other nearby cities. Manufacturers sought tariffs to protect their nascent industries while those engaged in producing agricultural commodities opposed them. The completion of the Erie Canal in 1823 opened an agricultural market for the states of the Northwest. The idyllic United States of Jefferson with the happy yeoman tending his soil and livestock was vanishing. American exports in the year 1825 totaled $100 million; $67 million were in agricultural products such as cotton and tobacco; $24 million in re-exports, and $8 million in silver. The economy of the United States was about to enter a new stage: the Industrial Revolution was knocking at its door.

The 1824 presidential election did more than mark the end of the Jeffersonian dynasty where his ideas and ideals had been passed down through his acolytes. The nation was showing signs of being divided into different economic interests. Of the five men who sought the presidential nomination of the Democrat-Republican party, two were from the Southwest (Henry Clay from Kentucky and Andrew Jackson from Tennessee), two from the Southeast (John Calhoun from South Carolina and William Crawford from Georgia) and only one from the North, John Quincy Adams from Massachusetts. Monroe had abstained from endorsing any of them since three were members of his Cabinet. With five candidates running for the presidency, it was obvious that no one could attain a sufficient number of electoral votes to attain the necessary majority. At the last minute, Calhoun decided to run unopposed for the vice presidency on the premise that Crawford, who recently had suffered a heart attack, would win the election and not live out his term. It could be considered cynical but Calhoun was enough of a realist to understand that was his best bet. When the electoral votes were counted, Jackson had 99, Adams 84, Crawford 41, and Clay 37. In the popular vote, however, Jackson, with his national reputation, was the unquestionable winner. As a result of the conflict for the presidency between Jefferson and Burr, a Constitutional amendment specified that only the top three candidates would be eligible for the final vote; each state would have one vote in the House, and the victor would have to attain a majority. Since Clay had the least number of votes, he was dropped from the final choice. On the other hand, as the former Speaker of the House who had decided committee assignments, Clay was owed markers by a large number of Congressmen. His personal choice would have been Crawford whose political views coincided with his own, but given Crawford's state of health and with Calhoun a "states' righter" likely to inherit the presidency, he was left with a choice between Jackson and Adams, neither of whom appealed to him in terms of their personality or political views. Adams was a difficult man for an easygoing Westerner to swallow. His dour Puritan personality, his self righteousness, and his seeming contempt for the great unwashed masses hardly made him palatable. On the positive side, however, there was his knowledge of foreign affairs, a requisite for any president. Clay's judgment of Jackson was based on his record as governor of Florida, when he had shown himself to be rash and impetuous in his dealings with the Spanish and Indians. While all three candidates had courted him, over the objections of the radical wing of the party, he lined up 13 votes to give Adams the presidency. Every politician commits blunders, but when Clay accepted Adams offer to become his Secretary of State, the Cabinet post considered to be next in line to the presidency, Clay had sealed any chance of ever attaining the nomination. Although Clay and Adams denied there was any quid pro quo, no one believed either man. Ironically, although always a bridesmaid and never a bride, except for the eight years of Jackson's presidency, Clay was the greatest political figure who dominated American politics prior to the outbreak of the War Between the States.

The use of the term *The War Between the States*, used by the Confederate government, rather than the accepted term of *Civil War*, is not without reason, and has nothing in common with the rationale for its use by the Confederacy. The Confederate states based their justification for secession on the Kentucky and Virginia Resolutions written respectively by Jefferson and Madison in response to the Alien and Sedition Acts passed under the administration of John Adams. Both pieces of legislation violated the Constitution — the former violating the right of states to determine what constitutes citizenship; the latter, far more grievous, since it violated the First Amendment to the Constitution which guaranteed freedom of speech and the press. Furthermore, both Acts expired two years after their enactment. In fact, the four-year conflict did not meet the standards associated with a civil war. A civil war, such as the one which took place in England in the seventeenth century or in Spain during the twentieth century, constitutes an effort by one segment of the population to overthrow the existing government. The seven states of the Deep South who comprised the original Confederate government had no such aspirations. Their goal was to live peacefully side by side with their former government. The Constitution they developed was almost a replica of the one they had abandoned. The rationale for their secession was to protect their economic interests, which they believed were jeopardized by the policies of their former government. The issue was neither that of slavery, since to change the Constitution required an approval of three fourths of the states, nor the extension of slavery into the territories, another red herring. The economic issue which led them to secede was that of tariffs, and the political one was their inability to prevent the imposition of tariffs. The first indication that this nation was divided by economic interests was not the Missouri Compromise but the ratification of the Constitution. The delegates from the Carolinas and Georgia had threatened to leave the convention unless the Negro slave was counted as three fifths of a white male and the importation of slaves was extended for another 20 years. Long before cotton had become King and these men and their descendants had become prisoners of a single-crop economy, the establishment in these states viewed itself as a minority that had to protect its economic interests from the majority. The war wasn't fought over the immorality of slavery but over the potential threat to the Northern economy of an independent nation existing side by side with the other states. Given the close ties of the seven Confederate states with British cotton mills, British imports would have supplanted American manufactured merchandise, posing a threat to the North's economy. Where a Civil War did occur was in the Border States, which had developed a mixed economy. Even Lincoln's contention that the act of secession was in violation of the Constitution because it hadn't been approved by a referendum was fallacious since none of the states that ratified the Constitution had submitted the document to a referendum. While there was opposition to secession among the establishment of the seven states, once it was approved by the majority, its fiercest opponents rallied to the cause and never posed an opposition. Finally, the only reason why it developed into a civil war in the Border States was geography. The only way the war could be prosecuted against the seven states of the Confederacy was through the Border States, and when Lincoln called on them to federalize their militia and prosecute the war against the seceding states, they refused, with the exception of Kentucky. Virginia alone cast its vote through a referendum. Placed in its actual perspective, Lincoln launched a preemptive war to force the seven Confederate states to return to the Union. This is why what some refer to as a civil war, others, including this author, refer to as a War Between the States.

In the 1824 election neither the issue of tariffs nor slavery was on the table. It would be eight years before the first Abolitionist tract would appear in Massachusetts and seven years before Congress would enact a tariff bill that a year later would lead South Carolina to threaten to secede from the Union. But there was discontent among the Western states in both the North and the South concerning the policies of the Democrat-Republican party with regard to internal improvements. Despite the growing population of the Western states, political power still resided in the original 13 states along the Atlantic coast. With access to the sea, they were able to trade with one another. While cities located along the Ohio and Mississippi Rivers had access to New Orleans, and those in the Northwest had access to the Great Lakes and with the completion of the Erie Canal to the port of New York, those cities located in the interior of those states were at an economic disadvantage because their roads were inadequate. In their view it was up to the federal government to invest in building the roads that would improve their economies. To the settlers and their elected politicians, it mattered for naught that their attitude did not reflect the basic principles of Jeffersonian democracy, which adhered to the concept that the government that governs best is that which governs least. In other words, if a state requires roads, let the taxpayers of the state pay for them.

To expect that President John Quincy Adams would concern himself with their needs was to expect the impossible. Above all, Adams had never been a politician. His election to public office in Massachusetts was a direct result of being John Adams' son, as was his appointment to various ministerial posts in Europe. It was not that he lacked talent or ability, having been eminently successful as Monroe's Secretary of State in his dealings with Russia and Britain. In fact he played a major role in the concept behind the Monroe Doctrine. Foreign affairs, however, were not domestic politics. There was the question of the recently admitted Western states, which had taken no part in the framing of the Constitution and had been absorbed into the original compact without any voice in determining the role of the federal government. Along with their needs and demands was the conflict between the manufacturing and commercial interests of the Northeastern states as opposed to the Southern states, whose economies were geared to the production of one or more commodities. John Quincy Adams, the cosmopolitan intellectual who was fluent in many languages, was the last man to bring these diverse groups within the population together. His first State of the Union address to Congress was a disaster. Instead of touting the amazing progress this country had made in its relatively brief history, he referred to its deficiencies when compared to European nations. He called for a national university and an astronomical observatory, both of which existed in advanced societies. To the radical wing of the party, these remarks were heretical. Those nations were monarchies; the US was a democratic republic. By the time he got around to discussing the nation's needs for roads and canals, he had lost his audience. Having submitted his proposals, it was now up to Congress to enact the necessary legislation. The only power in the hands of the President was the veto. Nor could he use the press as a bully pulpit since the role of the press, aside from the government's paid organ, was to deride and mock the President and members of Congress. There were other problems Adams had to contend with. While the House was controlled by moderate Republicans, the legislative body that had given him the presidency, the Senate, was in the hands of the radical Republicans who were convinced the election had been stolen from Jackson. Adams was oblivious to this political reality, assuming like his father that the office of the presidency carried such prestige that it was above petty politics. He soon learned otherwise. His immediate problem was he lacked a minister to London when there were serious problems between the nations over borders ranging from Maine to Oregon, as well as the territories around Michigan. In addition, the British still prohibited American ships to trade with British colonies in the West Indies, and continued impressments of American seamen. (In general, the word "impressment" refers to the act of coercing someone into government service; specifically, in the early nineteenth century, Royal Navy ships halted US vessels ostensibly to search for British deserters, frequently "impressing" US naturalized citizens into service in the Navy.) Dealing with all this was a tall order, and making it more difficult was that Canning, the British foreign minister, had not forgotten how he had been re-buffed when Adams was Secretary of State. Finally, the only minister to London palatable to the radical Republicans in the Senate was Albert Gallatin, the Swiss-born Secretary of the Treasury in Jefferson's Cabinet, who only agreed to accept the position if he had carte blanche in the discussions, which Adams, given his background, would never allow.

The principal areas of contention were the final borders of Maine and the Oregon territory. At the conclusion of the meetings, nothing was resolved other than a tentative agreement over the disputed Oregon territory. This pact left the border at the 49th parallel in the middle of the Columbia River for another ten years, with both sides having fishing and maritime rights, and granted America the right to construct forts in the territory to protect against difficulties with the Indians. The territorial dispute, which wouldn't be resolved until 1850, under the Polk administration, was a victory for the Americans since the 49th parallel included two thirds of what is now the state of Washington. The only definitive agreement by the British was to accept the $1.2 million debt it owed to the own-ers of slaves who had been removed during the Revolutionary War.

It was Adams moral probity and self-righteousness that accounts in a large part for his failure to be reelected. His refusal to replace any appointed govern-ment officials with moderate Republicans was largely responsible for the loss of the House to radical Republicans, which enabled them to appoint the Speaker of the House and control all legislation. There was nothing he could do to prevent his vice president, Calhoun, from working for the election of Jackson in 1828, but he could have replaced his postmaster general who was using the power of politi-cal appointments to undermine Adams' reelection. While Clay and other mem-bers of his Cabinet pleaded with him to replace his postmaster general, Adams remained impervious to their entreaties. Adams considered his role as president to be that of a statesman rather than a politician. The campaign to replace him as president began immediately after the 1826 congressional elections. His nem-esis in the Senate was Martin Van Buren, who would lead the attack against the president. Van Buren was known as the "Little Magician" because of the rapidity with which he built a personal political base in the Empire State; after two terms in the New York State Senate, he joined the US Senate. He was the first major political figure to announce his support of political parties viewing them as the essence of democracy. Moreover, he was a man of deeds not words. Before he left for Washington, he developed a political base in New York known as the "Albany Regency," which enabled him to control politics at home while he was serving in Washington. Van Buren was convinced that the surest and quickest way to the presidency was to ride the coat tails of Jackson. First he had to get him elected. Knowing the New England states would support Adams, Van Buren focused his efforts on the states of the South by enlisting the support of Calhoun and Craw-ford. Given Jackson's war record, his amazing victory at New Orleans, Van Buren knew Jackson would have the support of the Western states. In 1828, Van Buren resigned his seat in the Senate to run for governor of New York. Once elected, he insured that the majority of electoral votes went to Jackson. It was while he was a US senator that Van Buren worked to sandbag the political future of Adams. He was a leading force among the radical Republicans in the composition of the Tariff of Abominations, which included levying duties on imported molasses and wool, both designed to hurt the manufacturing interests in New England. But the real purpose of the tariff bill was to defeat the concept of tariffs once and forever. To the amazement and dismay of the radical Republicans, their plan backfired and the legislation narrowly passed both Houses of Congress and was signed into law by Adams. Van Buren and the radical Republicans had misread the Pres-ident. Although the New England states had supported Adams in his run for the presidency, Massachusetts had deprived him of his Senate seat when he affiliated himself with the Republican Party. Furthermore, like his father, he was an Anglo-phobe and sought for the United States to escape from its dependency on British imports. To him, raising the tariffs was a step in the right direction.

Historians have excoriated Adams for his failure to use the inherent power of the presidency to uphold the Constitution. The first case was the imprison-ment of a free Negro employed on a British ship that had discharged its cargo in Charleston, South Carolina. When he was jailed by the authorities, under an or-dinance which prohibited any free Negro from entering the state on the pretence he might incite Negro slaves to rebel, Great Britain launched a protest as did At-torney General William Wirt, and the federal courts declared the law unconsti-tutional. The authorities responded by stating that the actions of the legislature took precedence over the Constitution. Once the Negro's room and board had been paid, he was released to the British ship.

In 1832, however, when South Carolina threatened to secede over the issue of the tariffs, President Jackson threatened to raise an Army and hang the leaders of the insurrection. South Carolina backed down. Adams forgot he had taken a presidential oath to defend and protect the Constitution. A somewhat similar sit-uation arose in Georgia — this time with the governor attempting to defraud the remnants of the Creek tribes. When Adams ordered General Gaines to maintain the peace and adjudicate the affair, Georgia's Governor George Troup threatened to raise an Army of 10,000 men armed with bayonets to prevent federal interfer-ence. The threat was hollow, but Adams backed down. These incidents enabled the radical Republicans to hang the label of an effete Easterner backed by money interests on Adams, in the 1828 presidential campaign. Van Buren, knowing that the Southern states never would support a New Englander, used the Tariff of Abominations to obtain votes in the Northern states. It was a no-holds-barred campaign, with the press accusing each side of the worst crimes. The better political organization of the radical Republicans determined the outcome. When the final vote was tabulated, Jackson won the popular vote by 647,276 to 508,064 for Adams. In the Electoral College, Jackson had 178 votes compared to Adams' 83, or fewer electoral votes than he had in 1824.

Chapter 10. The Emergence of Political Parties

Jackson's perception of the presidency differed dramatically from that of his predecessors. Where the Constitution had given the president the role of Commander-in-Chief of the armed forces, Jackson often viewed the position of chief executive extending to the legislative and judicial branches of government as well. Once he had made up his mind as to what was right or wrong, or what he considered just or fair, he let nothing stand in his way. This attitude prevailed in domestic and foreign affairs, and to people he considered his friends as well. Jackson had spent his adult life on the frontier and that had shaped his values and his prejudices. To him a man's honor took precedence over his life; he walked around with a bullet lodged next to his heart, the result of a duel when he was challenged by the one of the best marksman in Tennessee. He even gave his opponent the privilege of firing first, before Jackson shot the marksman to death. He viewed the Amerindians as being incapable of being assimilated into America because their value system focused on the tribe rather than the individual. Thus he felt no compunction when he ordered 30,000 Creeks, who believed they had assimilated by aping the American mode of dress and habits, to abandon the 23 million acres they had cultivated and leave everything behind and cross over to the western side of the Mississippi River. His attitude was the same towards Negroes and slavery. To him, they were an inferior race, and slavery was destined to be their plight. When members of the militia attached to his Army disobeyed orders, he had six of them summarily shot as an example to others. Accused of being a cold blooded murderer, he ignored the criticisms. The only reason why he has been doted as being the father of the Democratic party, when he and every other citizen considered themselves to be Democrat-Republicans (the party founded by Jefferson), is because his policies led to the formation of an opposition party, the

Whigs. Even the view of him as the champion of the common man is based largely on what happened following his inauguration when the White House was open for all his supporters and hordes of the great unwashed masses trampled through its rooms with their muddy boots. By Western standards, Jackson was a wealthy man, and Heritage, the large house he had constructed, was designed to reflect his affluence. He and his wife were lavish entertainers, but those invited to Heritage were only members of the establishment – no "common men."

Jackson was loyal to his friends and political allies. To acknowledge efforts on his behalf, he appointed Martin Van Buren as his Secretary of State, the Cabinet position usually reserved for the successor to the presidency. The other Cabinet posts were meaningless to him since he intended to follow his own agenda, but he also realized the political necessity of rewarding supporters from other states who had contributed to his election. In addition, he felt it incumbent to find a place in the Cabinet for his personal friends, in particular John Eaton. Since he knew he would be criticized if he chose two men from his home state of Tennessee for political plums he arbitrarily selected John Eaton because he knew him longer. Jackson's wife, Rachel had died just prior to his election. During the campaign when mudslinging at an opponent was considered normal, the opposition press had attacked Jackson as an adulterer, among other charges. In fact he was, since at the time he married Rachel, her divorce had yet to be finalized. Quite naturally Jackson was very sensitive on this subject, and while he had no recourse to the slanders in the press, it remained a sore point with him.

John Eaton also was a widower and when he arrived in Washington he took up residence in a boarding house, where he made the acquaintance of Polly Timberlake, a widow living in the same house. Unbeknownst to Eaton, or perhaps he didn't care, Polly had a reputation for extending her favors to other boarders. In a small city like Washington, where gossip was the basic amusement, Polly Timberlake was considered to be a prostitute. Whether Eaton was aware of her reputation is immaterial; he married her and now she was Mrs. Eaton, the wife of a member of Jackson's Cabinet. In the Western states, whom a man married was his own business. Washington, however, was culturally a Southern city, sandwiched between Virginia and Maryland, and whom one married was a reflection on the individual. When the wives of the other members of his Cabinet refused to associate with her, Jackson took it as a personal slur on his own marriage to his late wife. Showing his well-known temper, he resolved the problem by forcing all the members of his Cabinet to turn in their resignations, and he formed a new one. While the President had eliminated the friction within his Cabinet, there remained the long-term question as to who should succeed him in the White House after his two terms in office. Van Buren as Secretary of State had been viewed as his successor; now that he had been forced to resign, Vice President Calhoun pictured himself as the heir apparent. While the two men were probably equal in intelligence and ability, and both espoused the same political views as the President, Van Buren was a more astute politician, and in turn, far more devious and clever than Calhoun. Jackson's rise to fame and to the presidency was a result of his military victories, first over the Creek Indians and then New Orleans. If there was a taint on his military record, it was that he had disobeyed President Monroe's orders and attacked the Spanish garrison at Pensacola, Florida, opening the door to a possible war with Spain. When charged, Jackson's excuse was that he had never received the President's order. As far as he was personally concerned, he should have been praised for his action since the defeat of the Spanish led eventually to the ceding of Florida to the United States. At that time, Calhoun had been Secretary of War in Monroe's Cabinet, and he had called for Jackson's immediate dismissal and a court martial. Monroe, of course, was too astute a politician to level charges against the general who had defeated the British at New Orleans. During the 1828 presidential campaign, Van Buren had sent a friend, Colonel James Hamilton to Nashville as a further effort to cement his relations with Jackson. From there, the Colonel moved on to Georgia in the hope of getting the support of William H. Crawford, one of his opponents in the 1824 presidential campaign. While there, he met Governor John Forsyth who informed the Colonel that the breach between William Crawford and Jackson was based on Jackson's assumption that it was Crawford, the Secretary of the Treasury, who had sought the General's scalp when he disobeyed orders and attacked the Spanish garrison at Pensacola. The Governor then informed the Colonel that it was not Crawford but Calhoun who as Secretary of War had transmitted Monroe's instructions. Upon learning this invaluable piece of information, Van Buren asked Hamilton to have Crawford write him a letter confirming who was responsible. It was this letter, along with Calhoun's position on nullification, which scotched the possibility of Calhoun succeeding him to the presidency. Van Buren, astute enough to realize that the finger of guilt would be pointed at him, resigned as Secretary of State while Jackson, afraid the story might find its way into the press and sully his name and reputation, once again called for the resignation of all members of his Cabinet. This time instead of reappointing Van Buren as Secretary of State, he named him Minister to Britain. John Calhoun, a very astute politician, was capable of reading the tea leaves. When Van Buren's name came up for confirmation by the Senate, he was able to line up enough senators so the final vote resulted in a tie, leaving the deciding vote in his hands as president pro-tem of the Senate. Calhoun had his revenge when he voted against Van Buren's confirmation.

Jackson's approach to foreign affairs differed dramatically from any of his predecessors. He viewed the US not only as the equal of any European country but as far superior because of the liberties and freedom its people enjoyed. The first example of his tough no-nonsense attitude towards foreign nations was when the rulers of Naples refused to pay for damages owed Americans from previous wars and brushed aside all diplomatic protests. Instead of the usual pussyfooting, which had characterized American diplomacy, he sent an American warship into the harbor at Naples and had the Captain issue an ultimatum. Either American claims were satisfied immediately or the city would be reduced to ashes. The threat produced immediate results, with all US claims satisfied. While every previous president had failed to open up the British West Indies, closed to American commerce since the Revolutionary War, his Minister succeeded. The instruction given to American ministers to foreign nations was to be tough when America's claims were justified. As a result, the US demand for $2 million in reparations owed by Denmark was paid. Reparations also were received from the Spanish government for the depredations done to American shipping during the revolt of the Spanish colonies in South America. There was more than a touch of irony in Jackson's policy when it came to free trade. The New England states, which had supported Adams in the presidential campaign, now were reaping the benefits. Jackson was successful in establishing reciprocal trade relations with Russia, and he also was partially successful in negotiating trade relations with countries in Asia. His most notable success, however, came about in his dealings with France, our former ally. With the demise of the last Bourbon regime and its replacement by the so-called Second Republic under Louis Philippe of the House of Orleans, the government had agreed to make good on damages done to American ships under Napoleon's Berlin and Milan decrees. While the sum involved had been agreed upon, the Chamber of Deputies had refused to allocate the funds. At first, the government claimed it was an oversight that soon would be rectified, but when the Chamber did vote, the measure was defeated. There were a number of reasons why this rejection became a *cause célèbre*. There was no disagreement over the amount to be paid; the government had agreed to reimburse the United States 25 million francs in nine installments with interest. It became obvious that the government was playing games when it informed Edward Livingston, our minister to France, that the decision of the Chamber was not final and that the money would be paid eventually but that it wouldn't come up for a vote until the following December. When Jackson received the news he became furious. In his State of the Union address to Congress, he told the members that if the money was not paid, the US would take the necessary action to collect it by seizing French property in this country. Jackson also added in his speech to Congress that when a similar situation had arisen between France and Portugal, property seizure was the method the French government had used to collect its debt. The reaction of the French government and the Francophiles in this country was one of horror. How could Jackson do this to a former ally that had been largely responsible for the country gaining its independence? To Jackson, however, a debt was a debt. The French recalled their minister and offered to give his papers back to Livingston, who refused to accept them. To some, Jackson's message presaged war, and members of Congress sought to have him retract them. Jackson, however, refused to budge. When the French government realized he was serious and intended to do what he had stated in his State of the Union address, the Chamber of Deputies approved the payment, while adding an amendment that the president should offer some expression of apology for the language he had used. Jackson refused to retract a word and in the face of this impasse, with Holland threatening to invade Belgium and the Spanish regime tottering, Great Britain intervened and managed to smooth France's ruffled feathers. While the Francophiles found Jackson's language intemperate and believed that he should have apologized, the overwhelming majority of Americans were ecstatic. Jackson had shown that the US was a country not to be trifled with, even by such a powerful nation like France.

If foreign nations had learned not to trifle with this President, some members of the American establishment failed to understand his resolute nature. Unlike Adams, who failed to act when the South Carolina legislature thumbed its nose at the Constitution, Jackson responded immediately when that legislative body threatened to secede from the Union. At issue was the Tariff of Abominations, which raised the duty on British imports to the point where it was damaging some of the state's economic interests. Because British exports to the US were decreased, the British were forced to reduce their imports of cotton from the United States, which hurt the South. In addition, the South found itself paying more for manufactured goods because the tariff raised the price of imported goods to the point where they were even more expensive than goods manufactured in the United States, most of which were produced in the North. Whether South Carolinians actually intended to secede or were hoping to pressure other cotton producing states to join them was immaterial to Jackson, as was the debate in the Senate as to the justification for nullification — legislation passed by the South Carolina legislature declaring that the tariff were unconstitutional. First the President moved to have all custom duties paid in ports outside of the state; then he ordered the port in Charleston to be reinforced with officers and soldiers from the US Army. The reaction of the state's governor was to call up the militia, along with a call for all men between the ages of 18 and 45 to be ready for military action. In the face of this impending crisis, Henry Clay, the author of the Missouri Compromise, called a private meeting with Calhoun. Meanwhile, Jackson lined up his congressional supporters to enact the Force bill, which authorized the president to bring military action against any state in rebellion against the Union. Clay and certainly Calhoun recognized that if it came to a showdown, South Carolina would be the loser, so they worked out a compromise bill, where over a period of several years the tariffs gradually would be reduced to 20 percent ad valorem. The new bill actually was less favorable to South Carolina's economic interests than the original bill Congress had been working on to reduce excessive tariffs. At the same time, Jackson's Force bill was passed, and to prove his attitude towards the concept of nullification, Jackson signed the Force bill first.

What made the Jackson presidency unique was his interpretation of the powers of his office. There is no better example than his decision to destroy the Second Bank of the United States. Jackson's fundamental opposition to the Bank's existence was that it was a private rather than a public facility. To him it was criminal that the revenues of this country should enrich private individuals rather than be devoted to the public weal. The rationale for instituting a private rather than a public bank was that the Constitution made no mention of a federal bank. Of course, the Constitution also excluded the acquisition of territory from a foreign country, and that did not stop Jefferson and Congress or the Supreme Court from purchasing the Louisiana Territory. Hamilton's decision to launch a private rather than a public bank was based on physical and practical constraints rather than on the impediment posed by the Constitution. The number of people who possessed the necessary specie to fund a bank was limited, and it was highly unlikely that they would entrust their capital to a public institution given that, based on the previous record of the Congress, there would be little or no prospect of making a reasonable return on their investment.

Since the new government lacked the funds to begin a bank, Hamilton had no alternative for securing the nation's finances. Aside from the fact that it was a private institution and had among its stockholders the British bank Baring Brothers, the President was convinced that because it was headquartered in Philadelphia, it favored Northeastern interests in granting its loans, even though the Bank had branches in all the states. He also was aware that a great number of members of Congress were stockholders and had a vested interest in preserving the Bank and would fight any effort to replace it. As he had proved already, once Jackson made up his mind nothing could stand in his way.

With the Bank's 20-year charter coming up for renewal in 1836, in 1835 Congress enacted legislation that would renew the charter for another 20 years. Jackson's veto of the legislation came as a bombshell to the members of Congress. The Bank's constitutionality having been established by the Supreme Court in the case of *McCulloch vs. Maryland*, the only explanation for his veto was that Jackson deemed himself superior to both the legislative and the judicial branches of government. In fact, the reasoning of Chief Justice John Marshall was subject to question. Marshall's decision in the case, where the state of Maryland had imposed a tax on a branch of the Bank, was based on the premise that the Constitution had been ratified by the people of this country and not by the states. Therefore, the federal government took precedence over states' rights. It was the same argument Jackson had used in opposing the nullification of the Constitution by South Carolina. For the people of the United States to have ratified the Constitution would have required a referendum, as would be the case in 1861 when Virginia voted to secede from the Union. In the case of the Constitution, it was ratified by a majority of elected representatives who supposedly reflected the views of their constituents, which was the same as if their states had ratified it. In fact, it wasn't put to a referendum because the representatives doubted it would be approved.

Having defeated the Bank's renewal, since Congress was unable to obtain the two-thirds majority necessary to override Jackson's veto, his next move was to attack it while it still was a functioning institution. To achieve this goal he sent his assistant, Amos Kendall, to sound out various state banks to determine whether they would be receptive to receiving government deposits. Kendall was successful in lining up banks in New York, Baltimore and Philadelphia. With their adherence, he now instructed his Secretary of the Treasury William Duane to funnel all new revenues coming into the government coffers to the state banks and to use only the Second Bank of the United States to make disbursements. By this action, the assets of the Bank would be reduced. Duane, who alone possessed the authority to make the transfers, categorically refused. When he refused to resign, Jackson fired him, setting up another storm with Congress. Since the Senate's approval was required for each member of the president's Cabinet, it assumed the same approval was required for the dismissal of Cabinet members. Jackson paid no attention to Congress's remonstrations and appointed Roger Taney to replace Duane and carry out the transfer of the funds coming into the Treasury to the newly appointed state banks. Beginning in October, all new deposits were transferred to the seven state banks Kendall had selected. As the new Secretary of the Treasury, Taney monitored the banks and oversaw the expansion of their number to 22; by the end of Jackson's second term, there were 90 sanctioned banks. Nicholas Biddle, the head of the Second Bank of the United States, recognized Jackson's squeeze play and fought back. His only weapon was to limit loans and curtail the supply of money to business. The repercussions were felt immediately. With the retraction of loans, some businesses collapsed; men were thrown out of work, and the business community was up in arms. A delegation called on Jackson protesting his action. Jackson's response was that he had no means of rectifying the shortage of money but that Biddle did. As business began to retract, the recession deepened and the ranks of the Republicans split, in particular in the Senate. In an unprecedented action, the majority of the senators voted to censure the President. The vote, the first of its kind in the nation's history, not only devastated Jackson but presaged a division within the Republican Party that could not be repaired. Clay, Calhoun and Daniel Webster represented different economic interests; their coming together to defame the President signaled a community of economic interests between the North and the West. Calhoun's adhesion was based on his anger over Jackson's handling of South Carolina's nullification. If the senators who had voted for censure believed it would alter Jackson's position on the Bank, they were mistaken. Having initiated the fight, he had no intention of ending it until his opponent was dead. To the President, it was a duel of wills, not guns. But he did answer the rebuke by declaring in a public statement that the President represented the people and was solely responsible to them. In part it was sour grapes but it also reflected his thinking. He not only was opposed to the Electoral College but believed senators should be elected by popular vote. To his opponents, a man like Jackson was the sort of individual the Founding Fathers had in mind when they wrote the Constitution — a dictator capable of swaying the emotions of the masses and attaining absolute power.

In essence, the war over the Bank was a personal struggle between the President and Biddle. If the Panic had continued or if any of the newly appointed deposit banks had been thrown into bankruptcy, Biddle would have won. But the Panic began to ease as the newly appointed banks began to issue loans to business; it was still undecided who would emerge the victor until Biddle committed a fatal error. A series of bonds had been floated by the state of Pennsylvania, where the Bank was chartered, and the issue failed to be sold. The Governor and the members of the state legislature placed the blame on Biddle. While everyone entered the blame game, the death blow to the Bank was delivered by James Polk, chairman of the powerful Ways and Means committee in the House. First, the House voted that the Bank should not be re-chartered; then, it voted not to restore the deposits to the Bank, and finally, it voted that the state banks should continue to act as repositories for the deposits of Federal funds. Without the Senate signing off on these bills, they were meaningless. When a committee was authorized to investigate the business affairs of the Bank to determine whether it had deliberately brought on the financial Panic, it struck pay dirt. When the members of the committee arrived in Philadelphia armed with a subpoena to have Biddle open the Bank's books and its correspondence, and Biddle refused to comply, the committee returned to Washington determined to cite him for contempt. The fact that the citation never was enforced only proved how many Congressmen had used the Bank for their personal affairs.

With the business community gradually adjusting to borrowing from the state banks, the financial Panic eased, and with no government deposits entering the Second Bank of the United States, it was apparent that it didn't have much longer to survive. It was then that Jackson proposed to Congress a series of reforms for the currency and banking system. These included that the selection of state deposit banks be left in the hands of the Secretary of Treasury; that he be permitted to remove deposits from any bank after submitting his reasons to Congress; that the banks submit monthly reports of their condition; that the government have the right to examine the books and records of the banks; and finally, that the ratio of gold to silver should be pegged at 16 to 1. Jackson also recommended that the banks should no longer issue bank notes in small denominations, so that specie would serve as the common agent for most transactions, with bank notes left entirely to the commercial sector. It was a broad and sweeping program, but most of his recommendations never became law, except for the currency ratio of gold to silver. The influx of Federal funds into the state deposit banks did stimulate the economy, but without proper controls, this initiative would soon run amuck. Meanwhile, as a result of the Tariff of Abominations, the flow of income coming into the national treasury escalated to the point where by the end of his term Jackson could announce that the national debt had been paid off, and that there was a surplus in the Treasury of $21 million, which should be divided among the states in accordance with their representation in Congress. On the negative side was the explosion in the sale of lands backed by nothing more than paper currency. By the year 1836, this figure had reached $25 million a year. That was only the beginning. It soon accelerated to the point where it was estimated that this figure was running at a rate of $5 million a month. The situation was a repeat of what had occurred between 1811 and 1815 when the Congress was forced to renew the charter of the Bank of the United States. There were too many state banks to be overseen by the Treasury, and once on their own, with the steady influx of Federal funds into their coffers, greed replaced judgment. Jackson was furious. He had assumed, wrongly, that given their new opportunity, the state banks would act responsibly. Waiting for Congress to adjourn, he issued his Specie Circular forbidding the general land office from accepting paper as payment for public lands. Unfortunately, his reaction turned out to be a little late and failed to stop the panic of 1837. The last item on Jackson's agenda before he vacated the presidency was Texas. Actually it had never left his mind. He was still angry with John Quincy Adams, Monroe's Secretary of State, over his negotiations with Spain concerning the acquisition of Florida because Adams left the border of the new territory at the Sabine River rather than the Rio Grande. Two years later, in 1821, Mexico's freedom from Spain was ratified and Texas was included as part of the new independent country. While Mexico welcomed the emigration of white settlers to its province, and they soon began to pour in, there was a hitch. Mexico did not recognize slavery, so the whites who migrated to the new region were obliged to classify their slaves as indentured servants. Within the next decade, what started as a trickle soon became a flood, and the number of whites in this province of Mexico increased by the thousands. Meanwhile the original (Mexican) Republican government, which had granted relative autonomy to the various provinces that made up the state of Mexico, was overthrown, and a military dictatorship under Antonio Lopez de Santa Anna was established.

By 1836 there were more than 30,000 white settlers in Texas, outnumbering the local Mexican population by more than four to one, and they were clamoring for independence. Santa Anna, on the other hand, was determined to centralize all the provinces and had no intention of granting independence to the white settlers. Given the disparity between the white and Hispanic populations in Texas, and Santa Anna's obduracy on the subject of independence, it was inevitable that an armed conflict would occur. The first battle took place outside San Antonio where several hundred Texan forces and their families were garrisoned in a Franciscan mission, the Alamo. Opposing them, Santa Anna had sent several thousand troops to besiege the settlers. Sam Houston, who was in command of the Texas Army, had committed a terrible military blunder. After a long siege, the mission house was invaded and all the defenders put to the sword, including the legendary James Bowie and Davy Crocket; however, the women and children were spared. With the war cry of "Remember the Alamo," Sam Houston organized a new Army of Texans, and despite being heavily outnumbered by Santa Anna's Army of 6,000, the Texans not only won the battle of San Jacinto but took Santa Anna prisoner. With this victory, the Texans declared their independence and waited for recognition by the United States. A great number of sorry explanations have been offered by various historians as to why Jackson, who had been so desperate to annex Texas, especially given the fact that Sam Houston was a close friend from Nashville, did not react immediately. Instead, upon the suggestion of his Vice President Van Buren, the President dispatched a shady character, Anthony Butler, to negotiate with the then existing Mexican government for the purchase of the territory. Butler, who was obviously a schemer looking to line his own pockets, returned with one scheme after another, all of which involved bribing officials who would then sign the necessary papers. Disobeying the orders of Secretary of State Forsyth, pretending that his mission was strictly in the hands of Jackson, dispatching his letters in clear English rather than using the codes employed by people representing the American government in foreign lands, Butler achieved nothing, other than to confuse the situation. All during this period of time the Texans were still waiting for recognition of their independence. Two incidents further confused an already murky situation. The first involved a ship of the American Navy that pulled into the harbor at Tampico in order to acquire some fresh water. The Mexican officials, obviously a little irked at the capture of Santa Anna and his being held prisoner, refused the Captain's request. When the news of the incident was reported to Jackson, he lost his temper and advised the ship's Captain to present an ultimatum: either the Mexican authorities would accede to the Captain's request or he would level the ship's guns at the city and destroy Tampico. Upon notification of this threat, the Mexicans backed down. The second event was stranger yet. In an effort to gain recognition for the newly liberated state of Texas, Sam Houston decided to dispatch his prisoner, Santa Anna, to Washington to meet with the President. Here was a prisoner of war, whose troops had massacred all the Americans at the battle of the Alamo, welcomed and feted at the White House. Ostensibly, Jackson was trying to convince Santa Anna to consummate a deal whereby the United States for a sum of money would be able to purchase not only Texas but also the entire state of California as far north as San Francisco. Nothing came out of the discussions, and Santa Anna was sent back to Vera Cruz on an American Navy ship.

The reason supposedly given for Jackson's failure to recognize the state of Texas once it had defeated Santa Anna's Army and announced its independence was political. Jackson was determined to have Van Buren succeed him as president, and the recognition of Texas as an independent state certainly meant that once the new state had sufficient population, it would petition Congress to be admitted to the Union. The addition of another slave state would not sit well with the Northern states, where Van Buren needed the necessary electoral votes to win the election. Jackson, of course, had alienated a number of Southern states with his threat to South Carolina and the passage of the Force Bill, which threatened military action against the state if it refused to rescind its notification of Nullification. But the election was decided in November and still Jackson made no move to call for recognition. Since the political excuse no longer held water, the only possible reason for Jackson's timidity was that the new Senate, where his adherents now would have a majority, would not be seated until March. Given that the sitting Senate was the same Senate that had censured him and refused to accept Roger Taney as Secretary of the Treasury, there was a strong possibility that they would further embarrass Jackson by refusing to recognize the new state, and if not that, then turn down the appointment of whomsoever he would nominate as the representative to Texas, which was to be treated as a new country. Therefore, Jackson did wait until the last days of his presidency to call for the recognition of Texas. The new Senate ratified the recognition, and this was followed by the concord of the House of Representatives to allocate funds for the new *Chargé d'Affaires* assigned to Texas. It was only on the last day of Jackson's term in office that the Senate ratified his choice of Alcee La Branche to be the new *Chargé d'Affaires* and that the question of Texas was finally settled. Because he was such a strong president, who attempted and often succeeded in imposing his views on domestic and foreign affairs — up until then considered to be the province of Congress — Jackson sundered the Republican-Democratic party of Jefferson into two warring factions.

The once monolithic Democrat-Republican party divided itself into the Democratic Party (those who espoused Jackson's philosophy of government) and the Whigs (those who believed that the power of government resided largely with Congress and sought to expand the role of the federal government when it came to internal improvements). But even within the two major parties there were dissensions. The Deep South was becoming more and more concerned about the attempted distribution of anti-slavery literature through the mails. In response, Jackson proposed a law prohibiting the circulation through the mails of literature designed to bring on the insurrection of slaves. Since this proposal was obviously a flagrant attack on the First Amendment, which guaranteed freedom of speech and the press, the Southern representatives took a different tack, suggesting that postmasters be forbidden from delivering such literature when it was barred by state laws. Clay and Webster opposed the bill, and the result was a tie vote with Van Buren, hoping to retain some support in the South in the forthcoming presidential election, breaking the tie in his role as president of the Senate. But it was not only abolitionist pamphlets that were disturbing the Southern bloc. There had been the slave revolt in Virginia in 1831, which had led to the massacre of between 50 and 60 whites and raised the specter of the Southerners' greatest fear — that one day the slaves, who were steadily increasing in population, would rise up and slaughter their masters. Equally disturbing to the South was a petition to ban slavery in the District of Columbia. Although a compromise was reached, which stated that it was inexpedient to tamper with slavery in the District, for the Southerners this compromise did not resolve the problem since in the future, legislative bills banning slavery in the District might be introduced and passed.

As for the Whig party, it was actually a catch-all for those who were opposed to Jackson's domestic policies. In New York it attempted to make an alliance with the Equal Rights party, an offshoot of Robert Owens experimental community in Indiana, New Harmony. Of Owens socialistic ideals, only free education and temperance were adopted. The remainder of its programs was a composite of radical Jacksonian philosophy with general opposition to all banks; insistence that only hard currency was valid; and the call for direct elections and term limits for office holders. The Equal Rights party was subsequently referred to as the Locofocos, after a newly introduced sulfur match that they used in the midst of a brawl with Tammany Hall when the regulars turned out the lights; their presence on the political scene was limited to New York, Pennsylvania and Massachusetts. While the Locofocos had no impact on the national scene, the influence of this party was strong locally, and especially among the working class. As was the case with many fringe parties that would surface over the course of the nineteenth century, they disappeared into history books. The other party to emerge from what had been the old Democrat-Republican party, and which aligned itself with the Whigs, was the American party, later on to be known as the Know-Nothing party. Unlike the Locofocos, the American party grew in strength right up to 1860. Its philosophy was basically anti-immigrant, which meant anti-Irish in particular, and as a corollary, anti-Catholic. Most of its original membership was drawn from the large cities on the Eastern seaboard where the Irish competed with US-born Americans by providing cheaper labor.

The election of 1836 would reflect all the divisions that were taking place in the country now that the larger-than-life figure of Andrew Jackson no longer dominated politics. Martin Van Buren, the vice president, being Jackson's choice, was nominated, but his nomination was not universally accepted, with the legislatures of two states refusing to commit their delegates. On the Whig side, while Clay longed for the nomination, it went instead to General William Henry Harrison, the victor over the Indians in the battle of Tippecanoe. While on the whole the Jackson Republicans, now renamed Democrats, were better organized, there were major breaks in their ranks. Hugh White, at one time considered one of Jackson's closest friends in Tennessee, ran against Van Buren and captured his home state and that of Georgia. South Carolina voted for its own favorite son, Willie P. Mangum, as did Massachusetts for Daniel Webster. Harrison carried Ohio, Indiana, New Jersey and Vermont. Van Buren carried the rest of the states for a total of 170 electoral votes. The combined tally of the other candidates was 124 electoral votes. While Jackson's presidential choice had triumphed, he certainly had received no great mandate from the public, garnering little more than half the popular vote. In the Senate, the Democrats had a sizeable majority, but in the House the combination of conservative Southern Democrats now sitting side by side with radical Whigs would make governing difficult.

There has been much debate about the legacy of the Jackson era in American political life. In some ways Jackson's thinking about democracy was a forerunner of the evolution of this country from a Republic to a democracy. That was certainly true in his call for direct elections to the Senate, which finally became the law of the land in the twentieth century. Even more significant was his use of the Bully Pulpit to go over the heads of Congress and appeal directly to the people to establish his programs. In this sense he established a new and different role for the president in the area of domestic affairs. It would not be until Teddy Roosevelt assumed the office of the presidency that the power of the chief executive of the nation was used against the Congress, pushing the legislative branch in the direction that he believed the nation should follow. Jackson's great belief that all authority stemmed from the people, and that *vox populi* was *vox dei*, may have made for good theory but he honored it in the breach more than in the observance because his thinking did not mirror the thinking of the average citizen. The populace would rally around him in his effort to destroy the Second Bank of the United States but their reasoning was quite different from his. Jackson believed in hard currency, gold and silver as the basic specie; the people believed in soft currency, paper, and believed that it was the Bank that was restricting their potential purchasing power. Jackson sought a lean federal government with all physical improvements left in the hands of the states. That was not the viewpoint of the people; they cared not who provided the services available for their use. What Jackson had going for him was a charisma unknown to previous occupants of the White House. Washington was a father figure; Jackson was the dashing knight out to do battle against the entrenched and greedy financial aristocracy whom the people believed controlled the country. Jackson could be considered a "states' righter" but not in the usual sense of the term. (The usual sense carried the connotation that the federal government was a creation of the states, which gave them the right to nullify and even secede from the Union when the laws passed were not in accord with their beliefs.) In many ways, however, Jackson did not really comprehend the genius of the Constitution with its built-in checks and balances. Jackson was for abolishing the Electoral College and having the presidency determined by a popular vote, with the term of office limited to one term of either four or six years. Furthermore, he was in favor of applying the same standards to all federal judges including those on the Supreme Court. As an autocrat, Jackson was certain he knew what was best for the country. He viewed his role of president as analogous to that of a commanding general. He would listen to the advice of those who were part of his command, but in the final analysis, the judgment was his to make. To members of Congress and especially those in the Senate, Jackson was interpreting the Constitution to fit his desires, showing no regard for the express purposes of the document. Had he not had a loyal following among the radical Republicans in the House, he certainly would have been impeached by the Senate if the House had initiated the proceedings. It was perhaps a fitting end to his career that in the final days of his presidency, his former enemy in Tennessee, Thomas Benton, now a senator from Missouri, would lead a charge to have the Senate expunge the censure it had inflicted on the president. Despite the fierce opposition of Clay, Calhoun and Webster, the vote of censure was expunged, thanks to the addition of two new senators from the recently admitted state of Arkansas, and a change of votes by several others.

In the final analysis, was there actually an Age of Jackson that in some ways altered the basic direction of the country, or was his career merely an aberration on the American political scene that changed nothing (other than the establishment of today's Democratic party, of which he is credited as the founder)? For certain, he would be absolutely appalled that his party today is the champion of the federal government, poking its nose into the affairs of all the people and attempting to regulate their lives. But then again, like all of US presidents, he was a man of his times and nothing more. He was a champion of the people, provided they were white. He accepted slavery, and his only concern for the Amerindians was to move them out of the way. But above all, he was an American patriot. It mattered not that he was far less educated than Jefferson, Madison, Monroe or Adams. Unlike them, he was not an intellectual. He had gut feelings as to what was right or wrong, and he acted upon those feelings. This was reflected in his domestic agenda and in his dealings with foreign nations as well. It was this characteristic of the man that the average American of his day could understand and appreciate.

At the inauguration of Martin Van Buren, when the baton was passed from Jackson to his protégé, the intense feeling of the crowd for their former leader was made evident by the cheers and huzzahs and demonstrations of almost love.

Here was the first politician that the people had been able to identify with almost like a friend. As if to add a touch of irony to the event, Jackson had left office just in time to avoid the disaster of the financial panic of 1837. This panic would last for the better part of seven years, and four years later result in the election of a so-called Whig president who died shortly after taking office. There were a number of factors that played a role in this sharp economic downturn, which had its greatest initial impact on the large commercial centers of the nation, the cities, but which soon spread to encompass most of the nation. Before attacking what in those days were considered to be the root causes for the panic of 1837, it is important to understand the unique role the Bank played in the American economy. Because it was, relatively speaking, independent of the administration and Congress, it was free of any political pressure, with its only pressure being the need to satisfy its stockholders. By being independent of the government, it could act as a brake on any excessive or questionable loans made by any of its branches. While it is true that the Bank was not an instrument of the democracy, but a private corporation concerned only with its bottom line — as Jackson repeatedly emphasized in his attacks on the Bank — in looking out for its own interests, it was preventing any excesses within the nation's banking system. The big unanswered question, however, was not what he would find to replace the functions previously carried out by the Bank but in altering the financial structure of the nation, would the newly appointed state banks possess the requisite discipline demanded by stockholders in a private institution? Was Nicholas Biddle, chief operating officer of the Bank corrupt? Of course he was, as was later discovered when the books of the Bank were opened for inspection. Any monopoly in existence for 40 years, with no competition, almost axiomatically would tend to abuse its power. However, when all the legitimate objections to the Bank were peeled away, because it was a private corporation, accountable to its stockholders, it was forced to exercise some discipline in making loans. The Bank was headquartered in the Northeast, and while it had branches throughout the major states, the perception of the establishment in those states was that preference in loans was concentrated in the commercial areas of the country, namely the large cities in the Northeast at the expense of the agricultural interests. The term, agricultural interests, was a euphemism for those politicians deeply involved in land speculation. The United States was in the process of going through an economic transition from an almost totally agricultural economy to one that was mixed. The growth in population was creating new markets that previously didn't exist. Not only was the Industrial Revolution about to alter the previous economic world, but its most important child, the railroad, was about to transform the economy of the nation in ways never foreseen. The Northwest and the Northeast were about to be united by this engine of progress.

With the coffers of state banks that the administration had selected for deposits from the Treasury now swollen by the increased funds, as is the case with any functioning bank, the funds would not remain dormant but would be loaned out much as had been the case with the Bank of the United States. As a result of the government having taken possession of all the lands available after moving all the Indian tribes to the western banks of the Mississippi River, there now were millions of acres of lands open for either development or speculation. While the banks selected by the Treasury department to receive the funds from the custom duties collected were theoretically obliged to maintain a certain percentage of their reserves in hard currency, i.e., gold and silver, this expectation did not stop them from making loans on nothing more than paper notes, which in theory could be cashed in for hard currency. All those lands lying vacant waiting to be settled; all that potential wealth just waiting to fall into the hands of astute speculators; all the contacts between the good old boy politicians and the men who operated the banks, were a guaranteed prescription for inflation of property values, to be followed by a financial disaster. To get an idea of how rapidly this inflation occurred: in 1834, only a little more than $4 million would come into the federal Treasury from the sale of government lands. One year later, with the state banks now receiving the revenues that were coming in through Customs, the figure had jumped to almost $15 million; a year later, $24 million. As already noted, frightened by the oversubscription to purchase government lands using only paper currency, Jackson, while Congress was in recess, instituted the Specie Circular which mandated that all future land sales of government property could be consummated only with gold and silver. The government had realized, a little too late, that speculation was the driving force behind the enormous increase in sales. Nobody remembered the earlier event when the government had been obliged to return to federal ownership one third of the lands offered in the Northwest because there were no buyers.

The land grab was not fueled by individuals' intent on settling in these newly vacated territories but rather by speculators hoping to cash in and make an easy profit. Most of these speculators were members of the political establishment, much like the men selected to operate the state banks. In some instances, it may have been a case of collusion, which existed as well among members of Congress and Nicholas Biddle of the Second Bank of the United States; in other instances, it was the "good old boy" system of one hand washing the other. Now with the passage of the Specie Circular, which served to limit government land expansion, the designated banks turned to other avenues of the economy where there were no restrictions. Given this scenario, it is not strange that the initial rumblings of the panic and depression that would hit the US first showed its troublesome head in the commercial and manufacturing areas of the Northeast and Mid-Atlantic states where both of these forms of commerce were concentrated. Also significant was that the first seven banks selected to receive Treasury deposits all were from the Northeast — located in Baltimore, Philadelphia and New York. All of the foregoing is not to imply that these banks were frivolous with their newly acquired wealth whereas the Second Bank of the United States was judicious in its lending policies. The difference was twofold. First, the Bank had years of experience, which would certainly make it more knowledgeable as to the credit worthiness of potential customers as well as of those already carried on the books. The other factor was that the Bank had outside foreign investors, among them Baring Brothers, the leading private bank in England. Jackson railed about these outside investors, complaining that the dividends from the Bank were being dispensed outside this country and not being recycled into the American economy. However, Baring Brothers and other foreign investors were the ones able to pressure Nicholas Biddle to be cautious and circumspect when investing their monies.

With the end of the European wars, American trade had been able to expand at a prodigious rate, in particular with the growing exportation of cotton to feed the mills of Great Britain. But commerce is a two-edged sword. While the benefits surely outweighed the liabilities, when economic hardships fall on a nation's major trading partner, the consequences are soon felt. The British, like the Americans, also had experienced an enormous economic growth with the end of the Continental wars. However, whereas in the US the expansion had come with the expansion of land under cultivation, in England it had been in the arena of manufacturing. British mills were famous for their new high-speed spinning and weaving operations, which enabled them to produce cotton fabrics at a minimal cost, thereby giving them an advantage over the rest of the world. The problem was typical of early capitalism: over-expansion was followed by a sharp retraction as markets dried up. The Southern cotton planters felt it first as the price of cotton decreased from 17.5 cents a pound to 13.5 cents. The result was a diminution of the amount of hard currency coming into this country. Finally, where the Jackson administration had been cautious in selecting the first banks for its Treasury deposits, and tended to oversee them, the expansion of the number of banks receiving Treasury deposits had expanded from seven to 90 under the good Republican principles of spreading the Treasury largesse throughout the country. Again, in line with the Jackson principle of small federal government, the Treasury department was ill-equipped to determine either the lending practices of these additional banks or the actual state of their liquidity. The currency in circulation in 1834 had amounted to $124 million; in two years it had ballooned to $200 million, and too much of it was in paper money that could not be redeemed for specie. Some of the Western banks were lending out reams of paper money under the assumption that in return they would receive hard currency. Instead, they were paid back in paper currency which they would then recycle to new buyers. On paper, the Western banks were remarkably successful.

In reality, the percentage of hard currency to bank notes, which the banks were supposed to maintain at 35 percent specie, no longer reflected these numbers. Then Senator William C. Rives of Virginia, a Jackson man, desperate to come to the aid of the new deposit banks before they collapsed from an overdose of worthless paper, offered a solution in the final days of Jackson's term in office. Rives proposed that the Treasury Department be permitted to accept bank notes in larger denominations while maintaining a restrictive policy on issuing smaller bank notes. Both Houses of Congress joyfully fell in with this proposal to evade the restrictions on the use of bank notes and passed the legislation. Fortunately, in one of his last acts before leaving office, Jackson pocket vetoed the legislation. The simple fact was that there was not enough specie in the country to meet the greed of the speculators.

There were other factors that would add to the inflationary spiral that was driving the American economy. By 1836, the entire national debt had been paid off, leaving a surplus of $21 million in the Treasury. On the surface it would appear that the nation's economy had never been so healthy. While part of the surplus was a result of the higher tariffs on imported merchandise, the bulk of it was a result of government land sales, most of which had been paid for in relatively worthless bank notes. And, there were other factors responsible for the economic downturn in addition to the egregious issuance of bank paper to facilitate government land sales. Since one of the principles of Jackson democracy was that the Federal government should not be involved in Federal internal land improvements, but should leave that role to the individual states, the legislatures of the states had taken upon themselves the role of improving the means of transportation within their boundaries. Following the incredible success story of the Erie Canal, which had linked New York City with the Northwest region through the Great Lakes, thereby reducing freight costs dramatically, other states attempted to duplicate its formula. It was another instance of imitation not being the sincerest form of flattery but of imitation being blinded by success. It was true that the Erie project had paid off the excessive cost of the canal while producing huge profits for the state and its investors, but missing from the new ventures was the potential for such a success story. Overnight the magic formula for future prosperity was "canals;" soon it would be "railroads," with the states assuming responsibility for the loans. Hundreds of millions of dollars were provided by state banks hoping to cash in on this craze in imitation of the success of the Erie Canal. Moreover, the loans they floated were backed by guarantees from the state legislatures. In addition, loans were provided by these same state banks for roads and turnpikes, with the expectation that the tolls charged would more than reimburse the investors. In contrast to the Erie Canal, all the other efforts to duplicate its success proved to be unrealistic, leaving a number of banks carrying worthless paper. The one positive effect of these improved means of transportation was that they reduced the amount of time required to send information from one end of the country to another. Where it had taken 27 days for the news of the battle of New Orleans to reach New York, it now took but nine days for communication between the two cities. To send a letter or receive information on congressional doings, which previously had required four days, now could be accomplished in 15 hours, and even less with express mail.

All of these advances in transportation and communication, which helped link the various states and regions together, resulted in an enormous increase in the number of newspapers and Post Offices throughout the country; on the negative side, these advances added to the overall debt of the states and the nation. Nor was the loose use of available funds confined to the public sector. There was Wall Street which now had become a major factor in the growth of the nation. Wall Street, which owed its origins to a group of men engaged in commerce meeting under a tree on the street in 1792, had by 1817 evolved into a trading center for securities and bonds, with its own building, now called the New York Stock and Exchange. Despite Nicholas Biddle's complaints that the only reason to destroy the Second Bank of the United States was to move the financial center of the nation from Philadelphia to New York, and the Bank's demise certainly abetted this shift, the dominance of New York City actually was ordained because of its port facilities. By the 1820s, New York had surpassed Boston, Philadelphia and Baltimore as the leading port of entry for merchandise coming into the US from Europe. Its Custom House was the largest in the country, which is why Jackson's appointee to head it had been able to abscond with more than a million dollars before taking off for Europe. With the Hudson River flowing into the Atlantic Ocean, and now with the Erie Canal, merchandise from the Northwest was directly linked by waterways with the City. It is true that as long as the Second Bank of the United States was headquartered in Philadelphia, that city would remain a major financial center for the country, but with its disappearance, New York's financial markets, abetted by the presence of the New York Stock and Exchange, now became the financial center of the nation. Reinforcing the growth of New York as a financial power was the fact that the industrial growth of the nation was concentrated in the Northeast. New England was the center for the textile and footwear industries. Pennsylvania, from pre-revolutionary days, had been the leading producer of iron ore and the products fashioned from it, and also possessed a plentiful supply of coal as a fuel, as well as iron deposits.

Since manufacturing was in the hands of private individuals, the necessary ingredient for continued growth was capital. This was the role destined for Wall Street, along with floating bonds for state projects. As the commercial center of the nation, New York had access to excess capital, and the New York Stock and Exchange soon became the magnet for companies looking to expand. As long as the entire country was betting on the come, Wall Street flourished. But when the dizzying rate of expansion collapsed under the weight of excessive paper currency with no hard money to back it up, Wall Street, like so many banks and commercial houses in the City, collapsed. It was the cities located on the Eastern seaboard that felt the first impact of the panic of 1837. There was a rush among investors, and those who saved, to convert their paper assets into specie, and the banks were in no financial position to meet the demand. Faced with the prospect of bankruptcy, the banks closed their doors. Even the Savings banks, such as the Bowery and the Emigrant, which had catered to the average working man, witnessed a run on their capital, and the police had to be called in to prevent the depositors from breaking down the doors. Businesses with no access to cash closed their doors, expanding the numbers of unemployed. In Pennsylvania, the coal mines were shut down, adding to the general misery. Soup lines became the norm for a large majority of the population, and the wealthy were forced to sell their luxurious possessions for a fraction of their cost. The Locofoco political party, which consistently had harangued about the abuse of soft money, witnessed its political star rise while the public called on Congress and Van Buren to rectify the situation. What seems so bizarre when reading about the Panic of 1837 is that today, 170 years later, a similar scenario is being played out. The root cause was so simple and basic that it eluded everybody. It was the fundamental economic law of supply and demand. When supply exceeds demand, whether in finished cotton goods in England or unsold land or bonds and securities in the United States, the results are the same. Business wagers that demand will meet supply, and when it doesn't, investments have lost a major portion of their value and a crash results.

Only the independent farmer, who represented the majority of the nation and who was too immersed in coping with nature to speculate in grandiose schemes for instant wealth, was largely unaffected. But to the middle and upper middle class and the few who counted themselves as wealthy, the panic and the unforeseen depression that followed was a disaster. It proved to be even more so for their employees as one business after another went bankrupt or merely closed its doors. The effects rippled throughout the national economy. States that had issued bonds to pay for internal improvements, with the sharp decline in their value, either had to discontinue or greatly reduce planned projects. Manufacturers who had issued stocks to increase their capital and expand their operations reduced the ranks of their employees in order to be able to weather the storm. The same held true for the commercial sector. Even some plantation owners in the South, who had been caught up in the frenzy of land speculation, and who had borrowed money at usurious rates to acquire not only land but slaves as well, were forced to sell their holdings in order to survive. With the depression showing no signs of ameliorating and with the fear that it would leave the Treasury without the means to pay its expenses, Van Buren called for a special session of

Congress to meet at the end of September. After placing the blame for the economic woes of the nation on greedy speculators and bankers, he presented his remedies. He proposed passage of a law throwing into bankruptcy those banks that suspended payment in specie; postponement of the distribution of the surplus still in the Treasury in the event it was needed to cover estimated deficits for 1837; postponement of the payment of bonds posted for duties by the merchants of New York and other major trading cities; the issuance of Treasury notes to meet the immediate needs of the government; and finally, the passage of a law that would allow the government to keep its own receipts in its own Treasury vaults, thereby completely divorcing its fiscal operations from the nation's banks. His rationale for the last proposal (most of the others being temporary actions to forestall any immediate problems) was that it was not the function of the government to manage domestic or foreign exchange. He was opposed to a national Bank where private and public interests were involved. The expenses of the government should be limited to its needs, and its revenues to its expenses. He was opposed to a new national debt, and he favored limited government action when it came to commerce or the currency. In essence, what he proposed was that old bromide: "the government that governs least is the best form of government." For him, the general welfare clause of the Constitution was a platitude that had been inserted into the document. Van Buren's concept of government harked back to the days of Jefferson. Time and progress had left the idealist world of Jefferson behind. From 1810 to 1850, the percentage of the work force totally engaged in agriculture had declined from 84 percent to 56 percent. With Van Buren's plan on the table, now it was up to Congress to either pass or reject the proposed legislation. The first element to go by the wayside was the punitive action against the banks, quickly rejected by the House Judiciary committee. There were too many Congressmen who had vested interests in state banks. The Senate committee on finance, however, still dominated by the Democrats, authorized the following pieces of legislation: the first bill proposed that payment of the surplus would be postponed indefinitely; the second authorized the issuance of $10 million in Treasury notes bearing no more than six percent interest; they acceded to a six-month grace period for the payment of duty bonds; and finally, a bill was passed in committee that authorized an Independent Treasury which would divorce the government from all connections with the nation's banks and allow the federal government to control its own money. One by one, despite the objections of the Whigs led by Henry Clay, Congress approved most of the measures proposed by the president, with the exception of the Independent Treasury bill. Once again, it was the old case of shutting the barn door after the horse escaped.

In 1838 Congress repealed the Specie Circular, once again opening up the sale of government lands through means other than payment made in hard currency. The repeal provided a brief blip in the usual sorry economic news, but it was short lived. The fundamental problem of an oversupply and a lack of demand remained unsolved by passage of this measure. The land question was uppermost on the minds of the Western states. Unsold land did not provide any revenue for the states. What the West wanted was recognition of rights of squatters, provided they had improved the land, and a gradual reduction in the price of government land that still remained unsold after a number of years. The technical terms for these two measures were "preemption," in the case of squatters; and "graduation," in the case of the unsold lands. It was not a question that the squatters would possess the land gratis, but rather recognition that despite their initial illegal settlement of the lands, once they paid for their property, it was theirs in perpetuity. The preemption bill was finally approved by Congress, although the graduation was defeated. Nevertheless, with the passage of preemption, Van Buren was able to obtain a sufficient number of Western votes to have the Congress pass his Independent Treasury bill in 1840, making the Treasury independent of the banking system.

Midway through his first term in office, it became apparent to Van Buren and the Democratic Party regulars that the depression was turning the electorate away from supporting Democratic candidates and causing the voters to lean toward the Whigs. In his home state of New York, where the Democrats had once enjoyed a huge majority in the legislature, in the recent state election the Whigs were swept into office with an even larger majority. Only in the South and some parts of the Southwest were the Democrats still in control, and to a large degree, that was due to the emergence of the Abolitionist movement in Massachusetts in the 1830s. In the North where slavery had been abolished and in the Northwest, where under the Northwest Ordinance slavery had been prohibited north of the Ohio River, slavery per se was not an issue except for the advantage it gave to the slave states in gaining representation in the House of Representatives. As a political party, the Whigs did not represent an alternative to this injustice since the Whig party drew its supporters, not only from the Northeast and Northwest, but from the Southwest and Southeast as well, where the three-fifths rule allowed them to have increased representation in Congress. In other words, both political parties were satisfied with the status quo as far as slavery was concerned. Moreover, there was a practical reason for this indifference to the plight of the Negro. Between 1790 and 1860 the Negro population increased ten-fold, from 400,000 to four million. This increase, despite the high incidence of death among Negroes, could be traced to the growing importance of the Negro as valuable property, not only to the Southern economy but to Southern representation in the House of Representatives. Even before the mass emigration of the Irish as a result of the potato famine, it was clear that the majority of emigrants were opting for the Northeastern and Midwestern states.

To the slave owner his Negroes constituted a major part of his wealth. The Negro was an economic necessity not only for the operation of the large plantations but for those with medium-size land holdings and even for the small farmer who could afford to buy only one or two. Despite the belief in the North that slavery was confined to the Southern aristocracy, in reality 15 percent of land holders owned slaves. Most slave owners took good care of their slaves as they would any piece of valuable property. The real problem with slavery for the white Southerner was not that it was an inefficient use of labor. Rather, as the slave population aged and was no longer productive, the slaves still had to be fed, clothed and housed, which was an economic drain on the owner's resources. The fear of a slave revolt has been grossly exaggerated. During the four years of the war, when most Southern white males were absent, the slaves continued to labor in the fields and as house servants in the same manner as before. In truth, the continued toil of the slaves enabled the Confederacy to wage the four-year-long war. Because the Abolitionists were adamant in their denunciation of slavery, a form of paranoia developed in the South over the future of the Negro. Gag rules were established in the House and Senate, which forbade any discussion by Northern representatives of the question of abolishing the slave auctions in the District of Columbia. Pamphlets from the North attempting to promote freedom for the slaves were burned when they arrived in Southern post offices. As far as the Southern establishment was concerned, slavery was part of the Constitution, and until the Constitution was amended — an impossibility, since any amendment would require the approval of three fourths of the states — slavery was legal.

The position of the Southern states with regard to slavery was defined by John Calhoun in a series of resolutions that he presented to the Senate. Once again he reiterated the states' rights position; that the adoption of the Constitution was a result of the states acting "as free, independent and sovereign states"; that as a result they retained "exclusive and sole" control of their institutions where the Constitution had not specified otherwise; furthermore, interference by other states over their laws and customs was in effect dangerous to the entire concept of the Union; that it was the duty of the national government to safeguard the laws and institutions of the states; that domestic slavery was an important part of its institutions, and to attack it was a violation of the most solemn religious and moral obligations; that any attempt to abolish slavery in the District of Columbia or in the territories would constitute "a direct and dangerous attack" upon the institutions of the slave states; finally, any effort to limit the growth of slavery when it came to the annexation of new territories, in effect, would disenfranchise the slave states. The references to annexation and to the national government's obligation to safeguard state institutions were eliminated, but the other resolutions were passed the Senate. What is most remarkable about the Calhoun resolutions was their defensive nature. The Abolitionists might denounce slavery in their pamphlets and in the Sunday sermons from the pulpit, and later might liberate some of the slaves via an underground railway, but slavery was written into the Constitution. What then was the rationale for the Calhoun resolutions except paranoia? The answer is politics.

Following the defeat of John Adams and the beginnings of Jeffersonian democracy, the political power of the nation resided in the South. One Southern president succeeded another, and despite their numbers, Southerners tended to dominate the House and Senate. The explanation for this phenomenon, previously alluded to, was that the supporters of Jefferson's concept of government were drawn largely from the South. Since the so-called Federalists, or those who supported the policies enacted under Hamilton and Washington, no longer had a program to offer but were satisfied with the status quo, it was natural for any dissenters to gravitate towards those who espoused change. Once that political monopoly had been shattered, and the Whig party had emerged as a counterweight to the policies of Jackson, no longer could the South depend upon the other states to support the concept of slavery on the grounds of party unity. The emergence of an alternative political party presented an option for the voters. Calhoun's resolutions actually were a clarion call to all the slave states that they had a common interest which bound them politically in the face of potential political opposition. Ironically, the strength of the Whig party was concentrated largely in the slaveholding states in the West and not in the North or the Northwest.

Given the fact that the national depression remained unabated and that local elections reflected the increasing strength of the Whig party, the only matter to be resolved was who would be the Whig candidate for president. Henry Clay, because of his prominence on the national political scene, and his oratorical ability in the Senate chambers, was assumed to be the front runner. After all, he had been the unsuccessful presidential candidate running against the popular Jackson in 1832, and had been by-passed for Harrison in 1836. He, along with Daniel Webster, had been the leading Whig figures in the Congress. He had been instrumental in forging the Missouri Compromise and had arranged the compromise with Calhoun over the tariffs when the issue of South Carolina's nullification had come up in 1832. In addition, he had support in the North as well as the West and the South. When he arrived at the convention he had a plurality of the delegates, yet too many of them felt that his strength was in the Southern states which he would be unable to carry in the general election. The man who opposed his candidacy was Thurlow Weed of New York, who during Van Buren's absence as president, had risen to become political boss of that state. Also in the opposition corner was Daniel Webster, representing New England, who wanted the job for himself. Given Clay's plurality and his general popularity, the only way to defeat him was to rig the balloting for the nomination, which the anti-Clay forces proceeded to accomplish. The basic problem facing Clay was that as supposedly titular head of the Whig party, he was actually titular head, not of a party, but of a group of dissidents who for different reasons, depending upon whether they were from the North, South or West, found fault with the old republicanism of the Virginia dynasty of Jefferson, Madison and Monroe and were furious at Jackson's autocratic use of the presidency. Some of them were supporters of the Bank of the United States; others were opposed; some were "states' righters," as had been Calhoun, until he jumped ship; others defended the Union at all costs. In the South they were violently pro slavery, in the North and Northwest some were opposed to slavery, while others thought it to be relatively unimportant. In the West, the Whigs were for cheap land, preemption and graduation, as well as cheap money; in the Northeast, they were for hard currency. Nevertheless, it is important to bear in mind that similar schisms existed within the Democratic Party. What was different about 1840 was that the Democratic Party had lost its populist base in the North, the working class, as a result of the depression. The evolution of politics in this country was a mirror image of the evolution of the presidency. From Washington through Monroe, every one of the presidents elected played a major role in the founding of this country. Once that aura of legitimacy disappeared, those men who replaced them in the presidency could not fall back on these laurels. Except for Andrew Jackson, and to a lesser extent James Polk, the men who occupied the White House up until the War Between the States, not only were mediocre but had no agenda when they assumed office. The now Democratic party of Jackson had no more of an agenda than did the so-called Federalists who rallied around Hamilton and Washington. As the growth in the economies of the Northern and Western states began to diversify, no political figure emerged who either understood or was capable of directing the country as it went through its growing pains. The economy of this country had become too complex for any single person to grasp. Henry Clay, the most brilliant and dynamic politician of this period in American history, still was unable to comprehend the significance of the Industrial Revolution and the impact it was having on the future direction of this country. Daniel Webster, the greatest orator of his time, still was a parochial New Englander in his thinking.

As the country continued to grow both in terms of population and wealth, the idea of one party satisfying the diverse interests of different regions, each with different demands, no longer was possible. As a result, fringe political party's emerged in the North dedicated to special interests. At the same time, the growth of the cities in the North, in particular New York, now the largest in the country, created a new phenomenon, the political boss. The rise of the political boss differed from the usual political power elite in that their control over the electorate did not necessarily mean that they had direct control over the nominations for political office, as did the establishment, but rather that they were able to deliver the vote of the working class in the cities. The most formidable of these organizations was Tammany Hall in New York City, whose original strength was among the middle class but which soon came to represent the working class, whose numbers were in the tens of thousands. Its fundamental power lay in the charitable work for which the organization was renowned. With the influx of the Irish into the cities during the 1820s and 1830s, long before the great Irish emigration of the 1840s and 1850s, Tammany had been able to direct the vote to the Democratic Party, since in theory it represented the common man. However, with the depression of 1837 showing no sign of ameliorating and with tens of thousands of workers still unemployed, Tammany under the influence of Thurlow Weed rapidly shifted its allegiance to the Whig organization. Along with the soon to be famous William Seward, who was elected governor, New York changed its political bent from the Democratic column to that of the Whigs. In effect the largest state in the Union, which had been the springboard for Van Buren's prominence in the Democratic party and had helped elect Jackson, now was about to bring his dynasty in the state to an end. Firmly in power, and sensing that with the depression it was likely that the Whigs not only would control the new Congress but in all likelihood also capture the White House, to maintain its power Tammany would go with the assumed winner. At stake, of course, were all the privileges that went with the presidency. The problem for the New York leadership was that the leading candidate for the presidency in their party was Henry Clay. Clay, who had been defeated by Jackson in 1832 and had stepped aside for Harrison's nomination in 1836, was so certain that the Whigs would triumph given the state of the economy that he set out early on to insure his nomination by making peace with the Southern states.

Sensing that he would need their support if he was to nail down the nomination, he paid court to the Whig parties in the Deep South by promising them that he wasn't adamant about reestablishing the Bank of the United States; that it was he who had played the key role in reducing the tariffs; and that above all, he was a "states' rights" man. His due diligence paid off, and Virginia, Louisiana, Alabama, Mississippi and North Carolina all endorsed his candidacy. In addition, he could count on considerable strength in the Mid-Atlantic States, in parts of New England and in the West, where after all, he represented Kentucky. By the time of the convention, held in Harrisburg, Pa., he was by far the leading candidate with a plurality needed for the nomination. What he didn't realize was that there was a plot afoot to deny him the office that he assumed was his. The leaders behind the plot were Thurlow Weed and Governor William Seward of New York, Thaddeus Stevens of Pennsylvania and Daniel Webster of Massachusetts. They, too, believed that whoever the Whigs chose for president would be elected, but they had some doubts about Clay. For one thing, he was a slave owner, which would not sit well with people in New England and among the

Quakers. For another, it was felt that the South and the Southwest would have too much influence in a Clay administration. As the old saying goes, there are 43 reasons why people make certain decisions and then there is the real one. The others are merely conjecture. Whatever the reasons, they were determined to block his nomination. To do so required altering the normal system of balloting. Thus the conspirators conceived of a different approach to the usual method of selecting a candidate. In place of a simple majority, where all the votes from the delegates would be counted, they replaced it with a secret ballot in which each state would nominate three members, with a majority vote from the three delegates delivering the state's vote to the winner. No longer would delegate votes from the individual states be divided, but the winner would take all. It was a brilliant move, since in large states such as New York, Pennsylvania and Ohio, where Clay had many supporters, their ballots would be negated by the vote of the majority among the three chosen. There were three candidates for the nomination, Clay and Generals Harrison and Winfield Scott. Harrison was backed by Pennsylvania and Ohio, Scott by New York, and a smattering of New England states. At the end of the first ballot, Clay had 103, Harrison 95 and Scott 57. Then in the second balloting, Clay began to slip and Scott began to rise. Then, according to Robert Seager II, in his biography of John Tyler, *And Tyler Too*, Virginia with its 23 votes was considering dropping its support of Clay and turning its votes over to Scott. That would have resulted in a stampede for the General. It was at that moment that Thaddeus Stevens of Pennsylvania, an ardent supporter of Harrison, came upon a letter written by Scott in which his views on slavery were less than enthusiastic and showed it to the Virginia delegates, which nipped their defection in the bud. Whether there was such a letter or how Stevens managed to get hold of it remains one of those unsolved mysteries. Nevertheless, again according to Seager, Virginia then announced that its second choice, if it could not be Clay, was Harrison, and this turned the New York delegates around to vote for Harrison; a stampede followed. Whether this actually occurred or is apocryphal is unimportant. The reality is that it was the switch of the New York delegation that swung the vote to Harrison, who wound up with 148 votes to Clay's 90 and Scott's 16. Supposedly it was then that the convention turned to Tyler as the vice presidential candidate since none of the other potential candidates were interested in that position. Although Tyler was a reluctant candidate, the convention was enthusiastic about his joining the ticket assuming that he would balance the ticket as a Southerner and a "states' rights" man.

The results of the election, given the economic conditions of the country, were predictable. Forget all the trappings that the Whig establishment unleashed to promote Harrison's candidacy — the bands, the flags, the hard and soft cider, the allegations against Van Buren, the Democratic candidate. As the saying goes, a depression is a depression, and people voted with their wallets and empty stomachs. Almost 2,500,000 people went to the polls, and while Harrison's majority in terms of the popular vote was only 145,000, in terms of the electoral vote he carried 19 out of the 26 states. Far more important was the fact that the Whigs now had a majority in both Houses of Congress, which would enable them to pass whatever legislation the party might have on its agenda. The campaign itself was as frivolous as those launched by the Jackson Democrats, and neither Harrison nor Tyler would commit themselves to more than platitudes. What brought more people to the polls and moved them to decide for the Whigs was that the times called for a change. Any change was better than the status quo. At the inauguration, there were the usual huzzahs and celebrations along with the usual throng of office seekers, but the general mood of the country was focused on what the Whig Congress would do to alleviate the economic pain afflicting the country. Harrison, while campaigning had offered no nostrums, had promised to serve only one term if elected, and had emphasized that it was the role of Congress to decide on legislation. Harrison had just turned 68 when he assumed the presidency but his age had never been a factor in the campaign. As a matter of fact, he was in far better physical condition than Jackson, who suffered painfully from the bullets that were still lodged in his body. Yet, a month after his inauguration, Harrison was out in the rain, caught a cold that turned into pneumonia, and within a short period of time, the doctors called in to treat him managed to kill him off.

John Tyler, the vice president, was a relatively unknown man; for the first time in the history of this country, the vice president was elevated to the highest office without benefit of an election. Tyler was not unknown in his home state of Virginia. He had been a congressman, a senator and the governor. He had resigned his Senate seat when the Senate voted to expunge the censoring of Jackson and was locked in a battle with Senator Rives to regain his seat, which was resolved when he assumed the vice presidency, thereby retiring him from the deadlocked vote in the Virginia legislature. As a Virginian he endorsed the fundamental philosophy of Jefferson and the Democrat-Republican party, but what convinced him to leave the party and join the Whigs was his opposition to the high-handed tactics of Jackson. Except for this stance, no one was really sure of where he stood on any issues as he had followed in the footsteps of Harrison and had said nothing during the campaign. The attitude of the Whigs was that the depression, by itself, was sufficient for them to be elected to office. The Constitution did not specify what title Tyler should assume now that the president was dead — was he the vice president acting as president or should he actually assume the title of president? He decided early on to follow the latter course and set the precedent for future successions to the highest office. Henry Clay, still considered by most Whigs as the titular head of the party, reacted with a mixture of condescension and an effort to ingratiate himself with the new president. Harrison had come into office with the announcement that it was up to Congress to pass legislation and that his role would be minimal. Except for Daniel Webster, whom Harrison had appointed as Secretary of State for his efforts in the President's behalf, most of the other members of the Harrison Cabinet had been the choices of Henry Clay. Thus, at the very start of Tyler's term in office, the Cabinet in no way reflected his views. The natural assumption was that not having been elected to the office and having been offered the vice presidency because none of the other candidates desired by the convention would accept it, he would prove to be malleable and circumspect in his actions. At first, it appeared that he would create no waves as the Whig Congress immediately passed legislation eliminating the Independent Treasury created the year before; they were anxious to replace it with a national bank. To get around the Constitutional question of a national bank not being specified in the Constitution, the Bank would be incorporated in the District of Columbia, because the Constitution allowed Congress to legislate for the District. With the Constitutional question out of the way, a bill was introduced by Clay and his followers that called for a national Bank within the District, with branches in the various states. The Bank would have the authority to issue loans and to discount bills. With sizeable Whig majorities in both chambers, the bill readily passed and was forwarded to Tyler for his signature. To the utter surprise and indignation of Clay and his supporters, Tyler vetoed the bill on the grounds that it violated states' rights in that it infringed the right of the states to accept or reject a federal organism. To Tyler, the existence of a branch of the national Bank within a state would be serious competition to the existing state banks because of the enormous resources concentrated in the parent organization. Tyler was concerned that the local banking interests would find themselves non-competitive with the national Bank. Stung by the unexpected veto and determined to pass the legislation, a Congressman named John Minor Botts offered a compromise in a new bill, which once again passed both houses of Congress. Under the new bill, the states would have the right to reject a branch of the new Bank of the United States from entering their state by a vote of their legislature. However, if the legislature did not act, then a branch of the Bank could be established, and if later on a legislature objected, the Bank's charter could be annulled only by an act of Congress. The new legislation apparently satisfied the objections initially raised by Tyler. The states through their legislature could make the decision as to whether or not they would accept a branch of the national Bank. If they decided in the negative, there would be no branch. If, on the other hand, they decided to wait to see the effects that such a branch might have on their local banking system, then the decision no longer would be in their hands but in those of Congress.

Why Tyler vetoed the second bill, which met all of his initial demands, is subject to conjecture. To some, his purpose was simply to stick a finger in Clay's eye. To others, Tyler was upholding the preeminence of the states over the federal government, since the bill did not allow a state to revoke permission for a Bank of the United States branch if the state discovered that the branch was proving to be inimical to the interests of the state banks. In any, event it was ironic that Tyler, who had voted for the censure of Jackson by the Senate, because of the dictatorial powers that Tyler thought the President had used (and resigned from that body when the censure was expunged), was now behaving like Jackson. The resurrection of the Bank of the United States might not have lifted the country out of the depression, but it certainly would have been seen by the manufacturing and commercial elements within the society as a stabilizing force for the financial structure of the country. Needless to say, this incident only highlighted the serious divisions within the Whig party. Since there was no possibility of attaining the two-thirds majority in both Houses necessary to override the veto, there was the usual talk of amending the Constitution so that a simple majority would be sufficient. But that action also required a two-thirds majority as well as ratification by three quarters of the states.

This stalemate highlighted either the wisdom or the folly of the Founding Fathers, who had constructed a Constitution with checks and balances that could not be overturned by majority rule. This concept in the Constitution was un-Jeffersonian in that it required more than the angry voice of the crowd demanding that majority rule was King and forcing the minority to accept a simple majority's will. It was also very frustrating to Clay and his supporters because Harrison, the designated presidential choice, had voiced the opinion that if he was elected, the will of the Congress would be respected. Thus, except for dispensing with Van Buren's Treasury plan, the Whigs had done nothing to replace the failed system of moving the government's deposits from the customs duties into the coffers of the very corrupt state banks, which once again were charged with that function.

The second veto was too much for the Whigs, and the Cabinet that Tyler had inherited. They resigned en masse with the exception of Secretary of State Daniel Webster, who was in the process of negotiating a treaty with Great Britain that would finally decide the definitive border between the state of Maine and Canada. Negotiations had been carried on previously between the two contending parties, and an agreement had been reached in which both the US and Great Britain allowed the King of Netherlands to determine the final border. When his recommendations were submitted, the Senate refused to ratify the treaty. There were other problems as well during that time period, when a group of French Canadians, calling themselves the Sons of Liberty, attempted to involve the US in their quest for freedom from the British Crown. There was violence on both sides of the border, and once again arose the usual war cry by those living near the Canadian border to liberate Canada from British rule and to add it to the Union. The British sent in reinforcements, and there were armed clashes between the Americans and the British, and an Englishman was captured by the Americans and sentenced to death for the supposed murder of an American. There was talk of war between the two countries, and British Foreign Minister Lord Palmerston appeared to be intent on hostilities unless the British subject was released. Fortunately there was a change of government in Great Britain, and Lord Peel and Webster managed to arrive at a *modus vivendi*. The British prisoner who had been condemned to death was released a year later, and a permanent border between Maine and Canada was finally agreed upon. Under the new treaty between the two nations, Maine lost approximately 900 square miles of territory compared to the arrangement recommended by the King of the Netherlands. This time the Senate approved the treaty.

If the federal government was having serious problems coping with the growing national debt, the compromise plan worked out between Calhoun and Clay to reduce federal tariff to an *ad valorem* of 20 percent added to the woes not only of the federal government but of the individual states as well. During the boom years, the states had allocated large sums of money for internal improvements, betting on the premise that future revenues from state taxes would take care of the deficits. This expectation was particularly true in the West where the legislatures were counting on the sale of the government lands taken from the Indians. With the passage of the Specie Circular, which required payment in hard currency, coupled with the squatters seizing property they had yet to pay for, the deficits in the state treasuries kept accumulating. The federal government had not released the $21 million in excess Treasury funds accumulated in 1836, the year that the national debt had been paid off. To the states, once promised those funds, the fact that the government budget was no longer in balance and that the debt was once again increasing meant little. The states were desperate for money. The Whig Congress, with congressional elections coming up in the off year of 1842, was keenly aware that this could be a major issue in the forthcoming elections and was determined to act upon it. At the same time, with the national debt growing, disbursing these funds without increasing the revenue collected by the government from higher import duties would only exacerbate the growing federal deficit. To the Whig leadership in the Congress, the answer was simple. Disburse the funds to placate the states and increase the duties on imported merchandise to compensate for the funds released from the Treasury. To reduce the growing federal deficit, including that accumulated under Van Buren's administration which amounted to $17.5 million, plans to increase the Army and Navy had to be shelved. There was even a question of whether the federal government would be able to meet its payroll.

Tyler was well aware that with his vetoes of the bank bills, he was politically finished as the Whig candidate for the presidency in 1844. He not only had alienated Henry Clay but a majority of the party regulars. His Exchequer Plan for the nation's finances, which was a cross between the state deposit banks and a national bank, had been rejected. Whether he understood or cared that the disbursements of funds to the states would aid the Whig party in the forthcoming congressional elections was a moot point. He would sign the tariff bill to prevent the nation from a possible bankruptcy, but as far as disbursements to the states was concerned, he would use his power of the veto. The results were worse than expected. The Whig party had been elected in 1840 to bring the country out of its economic depression. In its two years in office, it had accomplished almost nothing to alleviate the economic woes of the nation; and, by raising the tariff, it had alienated the South. The Democrats took control of both houses of Congress by an even larger margin than had the Whigs in 1840. The Tyler administration had been a disaster for the party and for Tyler as president. But if Tyler's political career was a wreck, and his own personal pride at having occupied the highest office now consigned to one of total failure, he had one card left up his sleeve, Texas. After the battle of San Jacinto, when Sam Houston's Texas forces had defeated the Mexican Army and taken Santa Anna prisoner, the state had declared its independence from Mexico. After Santa Anna's visit to Washington and his meeting with President Jackson, who had sent him back to Mexico, the Mexicans refused to recognize the independence of Texas, still considering it to be a province of the Mexican state. Enter politics. Jackson, who desperately wanted to recognize Texas as a new state in the Union, realized that he would never be able to attain the two-thirds vote from the Senate in order to ratify the treaty, given his censure by the Senate. The problem was that Texas, unlike other states that were admitted to the Union, had declared itself an independent country, and as such, its admission as a foreign country required the two-thirds Senate approval, much as had been the case with Florida and the Louisiana Purchase. When Martin Van Buren succeeded Jackson as president, he faced the dual problems of Senate approval and holding onto the support of the Democrats in the North. With the admission of Michigan in 1837, the number of non-slave states equaled the number of slave states, 13 each. The addition of Texas would break that balance. The problem was not that the North was adamantly opposed to slavery but that it supported tariffs. And the key to the passage of any legislation was the Senate, where each state, no matter its size or population, had equal representation, two senators. Thus throughout Van Buren's administration, Texas was put on the back burner since the more important subject was how to deal with the depression. With the Whigs coming to power in 1840, the subject of Texas was not high on their priority list. Meanwhile, Sam Houston, elected president of the new republic, was frustrated by the indecision of the presidents and Congress. Texas might consider itself to be independent but that was not the view of the changing Mexican governments. Sam Houston made repeated calls on the government in Washington to supply his republic with military aid, but the Constitution forbade it. He made overtures to England in the hope that would galvanize the Congress, but the British government at that time saw no reason to become involved, facing as it did a similar depression and with the country involved at that time in the bitter controversy over the repeal of the Corn Laws. Equally important was the fact that Great Britain had abandoned slavery in all of its colonies whereas slavery was basic to the burgeoning economy of the Lone Star state.

To Tyler, a Southerner and a believer in slavery, adding Texas to the Union would more than make up for all the failures of his administration. With the Democrats now in control of both houses of Congress after the congressional elections of 1842, he believed that there was an opportunity to attain that goal. Unfortunately, not only Clay, the front-runner for the presidential nomination for the Whig party, but Van Buren, who it was assumed would head the Democratic ticket, both had pronounced themselves against the annexation of Texas and its admission as a state. The untimely death of Abel Upshur, Tyler's Secretary of State, as a result of an explosion on a naval ship, would bring John Calhoun into the Cabinet as Secretary of State. Not only was Calhoun pro slavery; he was adamant on the subject. His attitude towards the subject was no different than those of the Abolitionists in the sense that either side was ready to dissolve the Union of the States if the viewpoint of the other side prevailed.

To understand the attitude of Tyler with the approach of the presidential elections of 1844, it is necessary to observe the man as a failed politician who had deserted the policy of the Whig party by vetoing the return of the Bank of the United States, and as a result, was considered a *persona non grata* by the Whig party. He also possessed the hubris of a native of Virginia, a state that had bestowed on the nation four of its greatest presidents. It was assumed that he would serve out his term and fade into obscurity. But Tyler was not ready to throw in the towel. Ever an optimist, with an inflated opinion of his own self-worth, shrewdness and guile, he decided to use the Texas issue as a means of holding onto power by launching his own party. In his wildest dreams he envisioned the election being thrown into the House of Representatives, with the parties turning toward him as the compromise candidate ready to annex Texas; in his more sober moments he believed that he could put pressure on the Democratic party to come out for annexation by threatening to divide the Democratic vote in the North, thereby forcing the party to adopt his point of view. The key to the election, he believed, was New York, and by using his presidential power of political appointments, he hoped to gain the support of Tammany Hall.

To prove to the Democratic regulars how important he was to their success in the forthcoming election, he decided to hold the convention for his own, newly-created party, which consisted of a few cronies in Baltimore, at exactly the same time and in the same place as the Democratic convention. Concurrent with this artificial convention was the dismissal from office of the Whigs in New York, including such major positions as the head of the Custom House; instead, he appointed his in-laws to these positions, holding out to Tammany the plum of filling in the lower ranks with their partisans. Tyler was so wrapped up in his new intrigues that he forgot that he was a man without a party and with no standing in either of the two existing parties. Nevertheless, he was prepared to go along with this charade as if there were a possibility of his being returned to the presidency. When the Democratic convention opened in Baltimore, the natural assumption of the party regulars was that Van Buren, still titular head of the party, would be nominated. To his amazement and to that of most of the regular Democrats, Van Buren was unable to gain the two-thirds majority to be nominated. Once again, the heavy hand of the South was a roadblock to any Northern candidate who was not in total accord with the South's views. Furthermore, he had lost the election of 1840 to the Whigs and was considered to be used merchandise. With a deadlocked convention, and the Northwest touting the candidacy of Lewis Cass of Michigan and Pennsylvania touting that of James Buchanan, a compromise was finally reached after innumerable ballots. The convention decided upon James Polk, a relative unknown from Tennessee, whose only claim to fame was that he had been Speaker of the House; more importantly, he had the support of Andrew Jackson because of Polk's action as chairman of the House Ways and Means Committee, whose actions insured the demise of Nicholas Biddle. Polk ran on a platform of annexation of Texas; as a result, he dipped into some of the Southern support that was going to Clay. Tyler, still obsessed with his own importance as a sitting president, assuming that he would carry the all-important electoral votes of Virginia, offered the Democrats what he believed to be a reasonable deal. He would drop his candidacy, provided that those whom he had appointed to office, largely members of the new family into which he had married, would remain in their positions. Tyler was living in a dream world. Whatever influence he had in Virginia had been dissipated by his actions as president. The Democrats didn't even bother to respond.

The outcome of the presidential campaign would actually hinge upon three Northern states — New York, Pennsylvania and Ohio. Clay, in order to hold onto as many Southern votes as possible, had tempered his position on annexation. But what neither the Whigs nor the Democrats counted on was the emergence of a third party that would determine the election. The recently organized Liberty party was an anomaly. It supposed *raison d'être* was its opposition to slavery, yet the leading Abolitionists, William Lloyd Garrison and Timothy Dwight Weld, would take no part in it, believing instead that moral and religious suasion would convert the non-believers. Yet in 1840, Liberty party delegates from six states met in Albany, New York. Their platform called for the right of petition and freedom of speech. It blamed the depression on slavery and the financial control of the nation by the Southern aristocracy. In their first campaign they polled a little more than 6,000 votes, half of them from New York. In 1844, they returned to the political scene, nominating the same candidate for president, James G. Birney, a former slaveholder who had been converted by Timothy Weld. He had "seen the light" and recognized the evils of slavery. Unlike the other political candidates who straddled all the issues of annexation and tariffs, Birney's platform was consistent. He was opposed to slavery, banks and tariffs. The election was decided by less than one percent of the popular vote, with Polk's majority being less than 40,000 out of a total vote of about 2.7 million. The key to Clay's defeat was the Liberty party, which polled 15,800 votes in New York and 62,000 in total. Polk's margin of victory in the Empire state had been between 5,000 and 6,000. The same held true in Ohio, where Polk's margin was 4,000 and the Liberty party garnered 8,000 votes. Governor Seward would claim that Clay lost New York by his efforts to appease the South over Texas. Seward's assessment was wrong. The votes for the Liberty party were a reflection of the growing alienation of the working class in the cities with both political parties. It soon would manifest itself with the addition of other political parties intent on showing their dissatisfaction with the ruling elite.

With the election decided in favor of Polk, Tyler, anxious to promote his own part in the victory of the Democratic Party, based on his support of annexation, now urged Congress to act while he was still in office so he could take the credit. Late in January of 1845, before the new Congress and president would assume office, he pushed the House to pass a joint resolution for the admission of Texas as a state. The idea for this circumventing of the Constitution supposedly came to him from Jackson. Since the House realized that such unilateral action would be defeated in the Senate, they attached to it a proposal by Senator Thomas Hart Benton of Missouri, providing for its admission by negotiation between Texas and the United States. Benton later would claim that the only reason for the amendment was to leave the decision in the hands of the newly elected president, Polk, and that Polk would lean towards negotiation rather than direct annexation. The joint resolution in this alternative form barely passed the Senate, the vote being 27 to 25. Under the prodding of Tyler and Calhoun, the House agreed to amend its resolution to conform to that of the Senate. Tyler now had his 15 minutes of fame. Seizing only on the House proposal as one of the alternatives, and in his last days in office, Tyler sent an invitation to Texas to enter the Union. Lost in the debate was the fact that under the proposal the government of the US undertook to pay the $10 million debt of the new state. When Polk was sworn into the presidency he allowed Tyler's decision to stand. Temporarily, the South had won the day with the admission of the tie-breaking slave state, once the Mexican war had been won. In the meantime, it would increase its plurality in the Senate with the admission of Florida in 1845. For the moment the South believed that it had gained the upper hand in the politics of the country. It would soon learn otherwise.

CHAPTER 11. THE MEXICAN WAR

When American historians are asked to rate the various presidents in terms of how they influenced the history of this country, James Polk is given short shrift. There are a number of reasons for relegating the man and his presidency to a position of relative unimportance. First and foremost, he was a slaveholder (by itself not necessarily damning, since the Founding Fathers were as well), but what was unforgiveable was his advocacy for the expansion of slavery — which in the eyes of today's historians precluded him from holding any valued position in the nation's history. But regardless of Polk's views on slavery, his administration not only reshaped the map of the United States but set in motion the westward movement, aided by the discovery of gold in California. When Polk entered the White House in 1845, the economy was in transition while its political structure was still mired in the past. The sundering of Jefferson's Democrat-Republican party into Democrats and Whigs did not reflect the economic schism that was dividing the nation. The sundering was merely a revolt by some of the leading members of Congress in opposition to the autocratic role taken by Jackson. The Whigs came to power as a result of the depression that had devastated the economies of all the states. Unable to restore the national bank because of the unfortunate death of its presidential candidate and the senseless opposition of Tyler, the new party was unable to resolve the economic downturn opening the door for the Democrats once again to take control of Congress in the off-year elections. The basic problem facing the Whigs was their determination to be a national party at the same time that the economic interests of the North no longer were the same as those of the South. The Industrial Revolution which had altered the politics of Britain was about to have the same repercussions here.

Polk received the Democratic nomination for two reasons. He was in the forefront of those Southern politicians who viewed slavery as a necessity for the Southern economy; he also was determined to follow in Jackson's footsteps in his opposition to the national bank. On the domestic front he was going to reestablish the Treasury department as the sole repository for government funds; he was going to reduce the rate of tariffs in this country by making them more equitable than they were at the inception of his taking office; on the foreign front he was going to resolve the question of the border of Oregon with the British; finally, he was going to acquire the state of California along with the rest of the Southwest which bordered the new state of Texas. Not only did he attain all of these goals, but thanks to his efforts the United States acquired more acreage than the Louisiana Purchase and eliminated once and for all any conflicts with Great Britain over the boundaries of this country and Canada. The acquisitions of California and the Oregon territory set the stage for the full development of the West Coast and the establishment of this country as a major player in the Far East.

Polk's concept of Manifest Destiny was colored by his firm intention to increase the number of states allowing slavery. In that sense he was more prescient than any other Southern politician. Given the limitations placed on the expansion of slavery by the Missouri Compromise, the only territories open for slavery, even in theory, were south of the Mason–Dixon line, including Mexico's possessions in the Southwest and southern California. Nor did he initiate the Mexican War in a precipitous fashion to obtain his objectives. From the beginning of his administration, he had attempted to negotiate with the ever-changing Mexican governments to purchase those territories. Even while the war was being waged, he made one effort after another to purchase the Southwest and California from the Mexican government. However, there was no Mexican government other than a class of wealthy *hidalgos* presenting a thin veneer of a republic with a strong Army. In a game of musical chairs, they would use a general to seize power or a general would elevate himself to the office of president. In the meantime Mexico, of course, like most of South America, had abolished slavery, but ruled over its Indian population as though they were slaves.

The first and easiest problem on Polk's agenda was the boundary line between the Oregon territory and Canada. Polk paid no attention to the bellicosity of the "war hawks" with their "54–40 or fight." Since the temporary treaty had placed the boundary at the 49th parallel, that was the proposal that Edward Everett, the American minister to Britain, put forth. When the British still balked, Polk issued an ultimatum — take it or leave it. The Hudson Bay Company already had moved its headquarters outside the disputed territory and the United States had agreed to protect British citizens within the new territory as well as to provide access to the Columbia River for the Canadians. The British acquiesced and a treaty was signed and ratified by the Senate. The matter of the final boundary would be adjudicated in 1872. While these negotiations were taking place, most of Polk's attention was directed to the Mexican question and his ultimate goal of buying or seizing from Mexico the Southwest territories along with California.

Certain factors favored the Americans. The Mexican government had refused to pay $6 million in debt owed to American citizens, later reduced to $3.25 million; this was Polk's jumping off point for negotiations with the Mexican government. He commenced by offering that the US would assume these debts in exchange for the Mexican government ceding certain territories. The first step taken in this quid pro quo was to send along William Parrott — a man of dubious credentials but who had lived in Mexico for some years and who claimed to be familiar with the key Mexican leaders — to accompany the departing Mexican minister. On the basis of Parrott's report and the confirmation by the two American consuls in that country, Polk decided to send a minister plenipotentiary, John Slidell, to negotiate American claims.

Slidell was authorized by the President to offer various sums of money in exchange for the sought-after territories. The offers were: the assumption of the Mexican national debt in exchange for a boundary running from the mouth of the Rio Grande to its source and then north to the 42nd parallel; an additional $5 million for the balance of the New Mexico territory; $25 million for California as far south as Monterey, but only $20 million if the agreement only included the bay and harbor of San Francisco. Slidell had come to Mexico as a pitchman with a laundry list that treated the Mexican government, at best, with total contempt — not as a sovereign nation. He was the street hawker. Nor did the Mexican establishment misunderstand the implications of the Slidell mission. Mexican President Jose Joaquin de Herrera appealed to Britain and France to come to his aid, but his appeals fell on deaf ears.

Then a propaganda campaign against American imperialism was launched, and the Herrera government was toppled and replaced by that of General Mariano Paredes, whose slogan was, "No concessions to the US." Slidell reported to Secretary of State James Buchanan that the Herrera government had refused to receive him, and, given Paredes' stance, asserted that it was unlikely that Sidell would succeed any better with him. Slidell then withdrew from Mexico City to a city near Vera Cruz in case he had to be evacuated. Polk, more determined than ever, informed his Cabinet that aggressive measures might have to be taken against Mexico and that he would propose such measures to Congress. A new character appeared in this *opera buffa* in the person of Colonel A. J. Atocha, a friend and confidante of the disposed Santa Anna, now living in Havana. Santa Anna, through his emissary, proposed that he would favor a treaty between the United States and Mexico wherein the latter would cede all the territory east of the Rio Grande and north of the Colorado for the sum of $30 million. Santa Anna urged the use of military pressure and oddly enough was prepared to return to

Mexico to enforce this treaty. Polk was determined to have his way. He was not so gullible as to believe the words of Colonel Atocha and Santa Anna's proposition, but he was aware that if he continued to wait for success through negotiations, nothing would happen.

He ordered General Zachary Taylor, whose forces had been stationed at Corpus Christi, south of the Nuances River (which, as far as the Mexicans were concerned, was the boundary line of Texas) to advance with his forces to the Rio Grande. After a delay of two months because of inclement weather, Taylor and his Army of some 5,500 men arrived at the Rio Grande and began to construct a fort. Taylor announced that his presence there was only to protect American territory, and the Mexican general's reply was that he and his armed forces now were on Mexican territory since Mexico had never recognized the Rio Grande as the boundary line of the state of Texas. Strictly speaking, long before Texas attained its independence, the land between the Nuances River and the Rio Grande had belonged to a different Mexican province. It was Polk who had invented a new line of demarcation between this country and Mexico, and of course, the state of Texas was fully in accord with the position taken by the President.

Slidell's return to Washington confirmed the President's belief that the United States would be able to take the new territories only by force. While a majority of the Cabinet favored asking Congress for a declaration of war, a few members cautioned Polk that it would be difficult to get Congress to support a declaration of war without an incident of provocation to present as just cause. Then Polk got his lucky break. About 1,600 men from the Mexican Army crossed the Rio Grande, and a group of 67 scouts from Taylor's Army were ambushed and either killed or taken prisoner. Polk now had a *casus belli*. Polk's fear that a large group of Whigs might thwart his efforts and prevent a declaration of war proved groundless. By an overwhelming vote in both the House and the Senate, a declaration of war was approved, with the House voting for $10 million in war credits and the raising of an Army of 50,000 volunteers.

But when Zachary Taylor, commanding the American Army in the war against Mexico, achieved one victory after another, despite the fact that the Mexicans possessed far larger armies, the fame that began to accrue to him disturbed the President. Zack Taylor was neither a Democrat nor a Whig. As a matter of fact, he had never voted for any candidate. But now he was a hero to the American public in the same way that Andrew Jackson's heroics at New Orleans had elevated him to the presidency. Worse yet, the commanding general of all the American armies was Winfield Scott, who had all but attained the Whig presidential candidacy in 1840. At the same time that Taylor was ringing up one victory after another, Polk had ordered General Stephen W. Kearny to move from Fort Leavenworth in Kansas and attack the few Mexican forces defending Santa Fe. Having attained that object, meeting little or no resistance, he was then ordered to proceed to

California and link up with the American forces under Admiral Robert Stockton and John C. Fremont in the conquest of California. As in the case of Santa Fe, there was no resistance, since the approximately 6,000 Mexicans living there had no use for the ruling clique that had been appointed by the Mexican government. The naval forces under Stockton had little problem in seizing San Francisco, and the small armed American force organized by John Fremont, now aided by General Kearny's army, soon subdued Los Angeles.

Within no time at all, the Americans had conquered all of the Mexican territory that was to delineate the future boundaries of this country. Despite all of these conquests, including the successful campaigns of Taylor, who with his seizure of Monterey now controlled one third of Mexico, the bulk of the Mexican Army remained relatively intact, and the government showed no sign of admitting defeat. It was at this time that Polk began to consider his options. First he was concerned about the growing fame of Taylor who, after conquering the Mexican fortress of Monterey without the benefit of any siege guns, had moved further south to seize Saltillo. Polk was apprehensive that Taylor would continue his march south and finally end up in Mexico City, elevating him in the minds of the public to a position analogous to that of Jackson, and making Taylor a prime candidate for nomination as the Whig candidate for the presidency in 1848. He would have to cut Taylor down to size. Major General Winfield Scott, who was in overall command of the American Army and who was originally supposed to lead the American forces along the Rio Grande, but who had balked at leaving Washington since he was supposed to prepare the Army for the 50,000 volunteers that Congress had authorized, now was taken out of mothballs and ordered to lead an invasion force that would land at Vera Cruz and then proceed to Mexico City bringing the war to an end. Once again Polk was faced with the problem that Scott was a Whig and that if he succeeded and worked out the terms for peace, he would gain all the credit. To counteract this possibility, Polk came up with the idea of appointing Senator Benton, a Democrat, as a lieutenant general as well as a peace commissioner attached to Scott's Army; since he outranked Scott, Benton would dictate the terms, and the Democrats would win the laurels. But Polk's plan was defeated by a coalition of Whigs and Calhoun-led Southerners in the Senate. To supersede the commanding general of the US Army required a two-thirds vote of approval by the Senate.

There still remained the option of Santa Anna as a means of avoiding the Whigs taking credit for the success of the Mexican war. With that in mind, he sent an envoy to Havana to determine whether Santa Anna would, as Colonel Atocha had previously suggested, be willing to engage in peace talks with the Americans and to cede Mexican territories already occupied by the American forces for a sum of money. To sweeten the proposal, Polk promised that in the event Santa Anna regained power and concluded such an agreement, all American forces would vacate Mexico and his new government would not be charged with any wartime indemnities. Polk notified the American admiral blockading the Mexican coast to allow Santa Anna's return. Eight days later Santa Anna arrived at Vera Cruz to discover that the government of General Paredes had collapsed and that the way now was open for him to resume power. It is really irrelevant whether Santa Anna double-crossed Polk, or whether upon gaining Mexico City, Santa Anna realized that to remain in power he would have to continue the war. The fact is that Polk's supposed deal was off.

Meanwhile, Scott preparing for the Vera Cruz campaign, as commanding general of the Army, ordered Taylor to turn over most of his regulars to his expeditionary force. Both Taylor and Scott were aware that the overwhelming majority of the voluntary forces were almost impossible to discipline, looked askance at their regular Army officers and often threatened them. There was nothing unusual about their attitudes. The volunteers were drawn largely from either the unemployed or the under-employed with only a few joining for adventure. This had been the case in all previous wars, starting with the Revolutionary War. Unfortunately, the officer carrying Scott's order was ambushed and killed, and Santa Anna now was aware that Taylor's forces had been seriously depleted. The orders that finally reached Taylor were a copy of the original. Armed with this knowledge, Santa Anna immediately saw the opportunity to defeat Taylor's diminished forces, and not only to cement his position of power in Mexico but to alter the course of the war. With this in mind, Santa Anna assembled an Army of 18,000 men and prepared to attack Taylor's depleted Army at Buena Vista. With an advantage of four-to-one in manpower, Santa Anna assumed that he would be able to overwhelm Taylor's Army. The battle seesawed back and forth with at one time each Army in retreat, but at the end of the day the Americans held their positions. The casualties on both sides were enormous, with the Americans suffering almost half the casualties sustained in the entire Mexican operation, including Scott's successful march from Vera Cruz to the capital of Mexico City. But the Mexican casualties were even more horrendous, with more than 1,800 killed in comparison to 673 Americans killed. It was the officer corps, made up largely of West Pointers, who had saved the day. Santa Anna, with some of his Army prepared to desert, and having captured two American flags and three cannons, beat a retreat while claiming victory. Taylor was furious because he believed that had his regulars not been removed from his Army, he would have destroyed Santa Anna and brought the war to a conclusion. With the war now shifting to Vera Cruz, he asked permission to be relieved of his command. Polk's worst fears about a victorious general capturing the adulation of the American public were borne out when Taylor was mobbed by crowds upon his arrival in New Orleans.

Meanwhile, General Scott had landed his troops at Vera Cruz and began his march inland to the capital, Mexico City. There is no point in enumerating the various battles; it is enough to say that the Americans won them all and finally arrived in Mexico City. What is important to bear in mind is that both the campaign in the North led by Taylor and that of Scott proved to be the training grounds for the generals on both sides in the forthcoming War Between the States. On a more troubling note was the enormity of American casualties, not from the conflict but as a result of disease, in particular, yellow fever. Of the almost 14,000 casualties suffered by the Americans during the war, almost 12,000 could be related to one or more infectious diseases. In the glory of the victory and the expansion of the US to virtually its present-day borders (except for Hawaii and Alaska), the toll in lives lost appeared to be inordinate. Polk, naturally, remained more concerned with who would get credit once a peace treaty had been signed with Mexico. With Santa Anna no longer the friendly arbiter Polk had envisioned, and with Scott, a Whig, in command of the armed forces, a peace commissioner had to be attached to the General's headquarters who would dictate the terms. In Nicholas Trist, the chief clerk to Buchanan in the State Department, Polk thought he had found the perfect envoy. A Virginia Democrat who had married Jefferson's granddaughter, Trist was young, bright and honest. He was dispatched to Scott's headquarters with sealed instructions, which left the conduct of the war still in Scott's hands but deprived Scott of knowing what terms were admissible for the US to cease hostilities and bring about an end to the conflict. Scott was a little more than piqued at this slap in his face. Fortunately, Trist was immobilized for two months by one of the infectious diseases that were crippling the Army; upon his recovery, he made peace with the General. However, when Polk learned that Scott had captured Mexico City, he decided that the terms he had dictated to Trist were too liberal, and he sent word to Trist that he was being recalled. For some reason, more than likely because he was now under the influence of Scott, Trist ignored the recall and began negotiations with the Mexican plenipotentiaries who were authorized to make peace. Under the terms of the treaty, Mexico would cede all of California to a point just below San Diego; and, the entire New Mexican territory and the boundary of Texas would be fixed at the Rio Grande. According to Trist's instructions from Polk, for these Mexican territories the United States would pay Mexico $25 million. Trist, acting upon his own judgment, decided that $20 million would do the job, and the Mexicans accepted.

When Polk received the copy of the treaty negotiated by Trist, he was furious. Not only had Trist disobeyed orders by not returning when he was recalled, but he had left Polk with no room to maneuver for better terms, now that the capital city had been occupied. There was more than idle talk in the country of annexing all of Mexico. Some wanted to create an isthmus across Mexico, which would link the Atlantic with the Pacific. Polk favored both proposals, but his hands were tied. There was nothing he could do to change the terms negotiated by Trist. General Scott was well aware of the terms of the treaty, and if Polk did not submit it to the Senate for approval, there was more than a likely chance that the terms of the treaty would be leaked to the press. Finally, the cost of the war had been enormous, almost $100 million, without taking into account the $20 million payable to the Mexican government and the $3.25 million that the Treasury would assume as debts owed to American citizens. Perhaps even more important was the fact that it slowly began to leak out that gold had been discovered on Sutter's mill, just outside of today's California capital, Sacramento. This was in January 1848. Despite Polk's frustration, the treaty was submitted to the Senate, where it was overwhelmingly ratified, except for 12 Democrats who wanted to hold out for more land. In May 1848, the Mexican Congress ratified the treaty, and on July 4 of that year, Polk announced the treaty and the end of the Mexican War. The war was over and the news of the discovery of gold in California would send tens of thousands of men and women, by land and sea, to try their luck. Lost in all of this enthusiasm for peace and untold wealth (for the fortunate few) was the Wilmot Proviso. Repeatedly tacked onto bills that authorized the House of Representatives to provide funds for the prosecution of the war and payment for peace, this amendment categorically stated that in any of the new territories acquired, slavery would be forbidden. As many times as the House passed it, the Senate rejected it, but it was not going away.

It would be difficult if not impossible for almost any American today to understand the state of mind of the citizenry of this country following the successful conclusion of the Mexican War. The war that was promulgated and instigated by President Polk had ended with the United States having acquired all the territory outlined by the President in his first State of the Union message. A minority may have considered the price excessive in terms of the lives lost and the money expended, but for the majority of the population, the war did not have any impact on their personal lives. The rest of the country had gone about their business as usual. There was little or no opposition to the conflict other than from the pacifists and the politicians from the Whig side of the aisle, attempting to make political hay out of the conflict. The territory of the United States now stretched from sea to shining sea. Moreover, with the discovery of gold in California, it was obvious that there would be a flood of immigrants moving into the newly acquired territory. Hanging over this euphoria created by the war's successful conclusion and the discovery of gold loomed the dark cloud as to whether the new territories should be open or closed to slavery. This was not a moral question, as the Abolitionists believed, but a political one. Not long after President Polk made the formal announcement that the Mexican–American treaty had been ratified, the candidates for the presidency and vice presidency of the Democratic and Whig parties were chosen; and a third party, the Free Soil party, had emerged, which absorbed dissident Democrats and Whigs along with the remnants of the Liberty party. Now it was merely a matter of dividing up the spoils gained by the war. And that division centered on whether or not slavery would be permitted in the newly acquired territories. It was the Wilmot Proviso which banned slavery in the new territories that was creating a problem. Both political parties, the Democrats and the Whigs, had been formed by an alliance between the economic interests of the North and the South, and now both parties were coming apart by regional differences over the extension of slavery, as well as by the disposition of Western lands, by tariffs, and by hard versus soft currency. The fact that the Free Soil party, whose slogan was "free soil, free speech, free labor and free men," had chosen for its presidential candidate Martin Van Buren, the former Democratic president who was being supported by such Abolitionists as Seward and Salmon Chase, highlighted the disintegration of the usual alliances between the North and the South. It also served as a wakeup call to the Southern Democratic establishment. If the Democratic Party intended to maintain its role as the majority political party, it would have to court those Northern Democrats who supported their views on the issue of slavery. The presidential nomination would have to be tendered to a Northerner.

If the Democrats were beset by regional conflicts, the Whigs were even in worse shape. The Whig party had emerged as a viable political party as a result of the economic depression. Fixated on reestablishing the Bank of the United States and the use of federal funds for internal improvements, it achieved neither goal and since it had no solution to the economic woes besetting the nation, it lost control of Congress two years later. Since it had been created by dissidents from the Democrats, it too had its Northern and Southern wings, with the same economic differences. Not even Henry Clay, who believed he was the only man capable of bridging these differences, understood the fundamental cause for this division in the United States. The economy of the Southern states was static, exclusively tied to the production of agricultural commodities, which in turn were dependent upon slave labor. In the Northern states, the economy had become diversified. While agriculture still predominated, those engaged in it were self-supporting farmers rather than the Southern agricultural capitalists, whose fortunes were tied to a single product. The Northern economy was diversified; side by side with Northern farmers were manufacturing, commerce, finance and shipping. All the large cities and ports were located in the North. The continuous flow of immigrants arrived in this country through Northern ports and settled in that region. A number of reasons explain this disparity in population growth between the two sections of this country, such as the absence of transportation from North to South and climatic conditions, but the fundamental reason was the absence of economic opportunities in the Southern states. The massive flood of Irish immigrants who arrived in the US as a result of the potato famine was able to find employment because of the North's diverse economy. Some would find employment in the coal mines; others on the docks or as menial labor or household servants if they lacked a specific trade. The advent and growth of the railroads was a major avenue for employment. In the Southern economy, Negro slaves filled these roles. Fed by the Industrial Revolution and the influx of immigrants, the Northern economy was expanding and its wealth was increasing because of its economic diversification, while the Southern states continued along the same path that had developed from its earliest beginnings. Without the Southern export of cotton, the US would have had a negative trade balance, but it was Northern finance that was bankrolling the next year's cotton and tobacco crops. In the midst of the national euphoria following the military success and the discovery of gold, no one expected trouble to erupt so explosively as to divide this nation into two regions.

CHAPTER 12. THE COMING CRISIS

Although Polk easily could have been nominated and in all likelihood been re-elected by the end of his first term, he was a very sick man, dying June 6, 1849. The Southern wing of the Democratic Party, conscious of the growing animosity to-wards its dominance in selecting the presidential candidate, turned towards any Northerner who had opposed the Wilmot Proviso. All three candidates — Lewis Cass from Michigan, James Buchanan from Pennsylvania and Levi Woodbury from New Hampshire — filled the bill, but there was opposition to Buchanan from his home state, and it was felt that Lewis Cass, as a former general and the senator from Michigan, only would be able to carry the Midwest; Woodbury was relatively unknown, so the nomination went to Cass. The Whigs were caught in the dilemma of which Mexican war hero to choose, Taylor or Scott, but finally opted for Taylor, feeling that as a major slave holder, with more than 100 slaves, he would be able to carry the South. The presidential election of 1848 was unique in a number of ways. It was the first presidential election where all the states voted on the same day, November 7, 1848 — i.e., first Tuesday in November. It also was the first time that all the electors chosen by the states would be elected by a popular vote, with the exception of South Carolina where the legislature still appointed the electors. In the popular vote, Taylor won easily, capturing 47.3 percent as compared to Cass's 42.5 percent; the Electoral College vote credited Taylor with 163 and Cass with 127. As in the 1844 election, the swing state was New York, with the largest number of electoral votes. As the Whig party went down to defeat in 1844 by the Liberty party's capturing better than 15,000 votes in New York, which had cost Clay that election, so too did the 120,000 votes for Van Buren under the Free Soil ticket deprive Cass of victory. While Van Buren received no electoral votes, he did capture ten percent of the popular vote or

291,500, all of which came from Northern and Western states. This was a dramatic difference from the 23,000 votes received four years earlier when alienated voters cast their ballots for the candidate of the Liberty party, whose adherents now had joined the Free Soil party. While a certain percentage of the votes cast for him could be attributed to name recognition and the fact that he was a former president, there also was a portent to the general dissatisfaction of voters with both major political parties. Taylor, on the other hand, whose presidential campaign centered on platitudes, owed his election to a combination of votes from both Northern and Southern states. The unanswered question of the election still remained the future of the territories acquired through the war — whether they would admit or reject slavery remained in doubt.

When Taylor was sworn in as president in March 1849, the focus of the Southern establishment not only was directed towards the future of the new territories but also centered on the actions that would be taken by the new president, a Southerner who possessed 100 slaves. While most of the newly acquired territory was below the Mason–Dixon Line, and therefore open to slavery, the lands acquired were largely desert, unsuitable for the cultivation of cotton. But the real concern of the South was control of the Senate. The Senate was the great equalizer in determining political power. Most immigrants were settling into the North and Northwest so that their representation in the House of Representatives and in the Electoral College continued to increase. In the Senate, no matter what the size of the population, each state could elect only two members. What the Southern establishment was reluctant to acknowledge was that the combination of geography and the flood of new immigrants was irreversible. Not only were these newcomers increasing the population of existing states, they were pushing westward and settling in lands still sparsely settled. There was no hope of Oregon joining the coalition of slave states. It was so far north that it was assumed that it would join the Union as a free state. But there were California and the huge expanse of territory of New Mexico, incorporating some of Texas and stretching all the way to Santa Fe. The problem facing the South in the Senate was one of arithmetic. With the addition of Florida and Texas in 1845, the number of slave states equaled the number of non-slave states. But 1846 was to see the admission of Iowa, and two years later, Wisconsin, to be followed by Minnesota shortly after. Even if California sought and was granted admission as a slave state, the cards in the deck still were stacked against them. When in 1850, California opted to be admitted as a free state, the South's last vestige of hope vanished. All the remaining unoccupied or partially settled territories, which one day would become states and be admitted to the Union, were north of the Mason–Dixon line and climatically unsuited for the cultivation of cotton or tobacco. No longer a political force to be reckoned with in either the House or the Senate, the South's only hope was to maintain its alliance with the Northern and Western

Democrats, which would allow them to acquire the political power inherent in the presidency — the use of the veto.

The first item on the agenda of the newly elected president was the disposition of the newly acquired territories. California, thanks to the Gold Rush that began in 1848, witnessed an incredible growth rate within a year's time. Tens of thousands of Americans from every state and territory made fast track for the Golden State in an effort to acquire instant wealth. And wealth aplenty there was for the lucky few. Almost $2 billion worth of gold was extracted over a period of a few years — so much, that the Treasury department would set up a mint in the state. Within a year, enough settlers had arrived in California, coming by boat either around Cape Horn or crossing the Isthmus of Panama, or traversing the overland route, that their numbers had reached the point where California was eligible for statehood. Thousands, of course, would perish in making the journey, either from disease or from attacks by the Indians. Most never would strike the mother lode or would lose what they had acquired in gambling, but once they were there, the winners and losers, they discovered what millions have since — the state's marvelous climate and its fertile soil — and decided to remain there. Moreover, the lure of instant wealth was not restricted to Americans. Since gold is the universal precious metal, men arrived from Europe, and from Central and South America, and from China as well. Many who came to the Golden Bear state often were accompanied by their wives and children.

Despite the fact that most of California was geographically below the Mason–Dixon Line and open to slavery, there were no slaves and most of its recent population were Northerners. Nevertheless, once the number of residents had grown to the point of eligibility for statehood, Congress voted against its admission as a slave state. Still undecided was the territory out of which eventually three states would be carved — New Mexico, Arizona, and Nevada. Texas's claim that its territory extended up to Santa Fe also had to be resolved. Since most of these lands were part of the great desert, which extended as far west as southern California and as far north as Colorado, without the concept of irrigation and the diversion of the Colorado river, the territory hardly seemed promising for the growth of cotton and the need for slaves. Thus, except for Texas, which already had established itself as a slave state, the winning of the Mexican War did nothing to enhance the prospects for the advancement of Southern slavery.

To Zachary Taylor, the question of whether a state should admit or ban slavery was very simple and logical. It would be up to the settlers of the state to decide. To the Southerners, the answer also was logical and simple. The Missouri Compromise of 1820 had established a line of demarcation as to which states should be free and which could admit slavery. It had been set at 36°30' latitude, and it should apply to the newly acquired lands. If one followed that train of thought, then all the territories acquired by the US as a result of the final peace treaty with Mexico, except for the extreme northern tip of California, should be open to slavery. Into this divisive breach between the two sides stepped Henry Clay, newly returned to the Senate after an absence of seven years, and while he himself was a slave holder, had arrived at the decision that slavery was inimical to the future development of this country. Clay, as was the case with every other politician, had no idea how to deal with the problem of slavery. Like most of the leaders of his generation, except for those on the large Southern plantations who needed their slave labor for economic survival, he would have preferred that the slaves be returned to Africa. His attitude was no different than that of Lincoln. Slavery should be contained within the existing slave states, and then gradually it would die off. Why or how it would die off neither one of them had the answer. Clay, now over 70, not only was past his prime but was a very sick man with incipient tuberculosis. He, representing the West, along with Calhoun, representing the South, and Webster, representing New England, not only were the best orators in Congress but had dominated the political scene over the past 30 years, along with Jackson. Once again Clay believed that he could step into the breach and resolve the sectional differences with a compromise, as he had accomplished with the case of Missouri, and later with Calhoun over Nullification. In January 1850, Clay offered to the Senate eight propositions for their consideration. The first called for the admission of California without any mention of slavery; the second provided for organization of territorial governments for New Mexico without any congressional restriction or condition on the subject of slavery, since the institution did not exist under Mexican law and was not likely to be introduced; the third and fourth dealt with the final boundary of Texas and the assumption by the United States of the Texas debt, on the condition that Texas relinquish to the US any claim that it might have to any part of New Mexico. These two resolutions, he added, must be taken together. The fifth declared it inexpedient to abolish slavery in the District of Columbia without the consent of Maryland and the people living in the District and without just compensation for the owners; the sixth called for the abolition of the slave trade in the District, forbidding the sale of slaves or their transportation to other markets; the seventh called for a stricter Fugitive Slave Law; the eighth stated that Congress had no power to interfere in the interstate slave trade, leaving it to the particular laws of the states involved.

When he had finished Clay announced that he would make his formal presentation to the Senate on the following Tuesday, thereby allowing all the senators the time to study his propositions. What Clay had set out to do was to make a nice Christmas package that would satisfy all sides of the equation. Nor were the eight propositions all of his making. He had consulted with other members of Congress before arriving at his presentation. What Clay was attempting to accomplish was an omnibus bill — a kind of statesman-like approach to different problems with each side gaining and losing at the same time. He saw himself as the leader of the Whig party, which had won the election; the one element that he had not factored into his presentation was that the man who had won the presidential election was Zachary Taylor, not Clay, who had been his opponent for the nomination. Old Zack may have been one of the few men in the South with more than 100 slaves working a large plantation in Mississippi, but he had spent a major part of his life as a soldier, seeing combat in the War of 1812 and in the various military skirmishes with the Indians. As such, he had risen to the rank of brigadier general and had led one successful campaign after another against the Mexicans in the recently-ended war. A good military man knows one basic principle. When an order is given, it is expected to be followed. When he was told to release most of the Army regulars under his command to his superior, General Scott, he complied — much as he might have disagreed. General Taylor took the view that his victory in the election made him titular head of the Whig Party as well as president of the United States.

As president, he controlled the appointments to all the major political offices which gave him enormous power. Clay had used the presidential power of Taylor to have one of his sons appointed to head up the legation to Portugal. But, and this was a big but, he had not consulted with Taylor prior to releasing his plan to the Senate. Perhaps Clay was naive enough to take seriously one of the pledges that Taylor had made during the presidential campaign: that he would not exercise his power of veto to forestall congressional legislation. More than likely, however, he probably considered Taylor to be an intellectual lightweight who would rubber-stamp any legislation coming out of Congress. That expectation was erroneous and would have been fatal had not the General conveniently died from an overdose of iced water coupled with raw fruits during one of Washington's proverbial summer heat waves. His death in 1850 opened the door for his replacement, Vice President Millard Fillmore, a staunch ally of Clay, to become president, which resolved that problem. Before the death of Taylor, however, the subject of Clay's resolutions was debated in the Senate. A few days after he proposed them, Clay took to the floor of the Senate to defend his eight propositions, speaking for two days and almost five hours. Clay's fundamental problem was to convince the Southerners, in both the Whig and the Democratic parties, that the propositions he had outlined were not inimical to the fortunes of the South. His first premise, which was totally specious, was that his proposals would once and for all eliminate the Wilmot Proviso, which had consistently passed the House and which called for the elimination of slavery in all the new territories. He then contradicted himself by stating that the New Mexico territory was totally unsuitable for agriculture, since it was largely desert. Since all the other territories which had yet to be settled were north of the line drawn by the Missouri Compromise, in effect he was saying to the South, that slavery had gone as far as it could go with the admission of Texas. As an appeasement to the South he attacked the decision of the Supreme Court in the case of *Prigg vs. Pennsylvania* which ruled that states did not have to aid in the hunting or recapture of slaves, greatly weakening the Fugitive Slave Law of 1793. Complicating the situation even further was the announcement by President Taylor that he had received the constitution for the state of California and forwarded it to the Senate for approval. Almost at the same time, Senator Henry Foote of Mississippi had questioned Clay as to whether his proposals were an omnibus bill or were to be considered one by one. Clay's response was that each of them should stand on its own feet. One by one, amendments were offered to the proposed legislation, which only served to further confuse the situation. It was then that Senator Foote called for a conference of 13 members of the Senate, one half Democrat and one half Whig, with Clay acting as the chairman. As a result, Clay's proposals were bundled into one package and would be treated as an omnibus bill.

Clay, after balking at the idea of lumping together all his proposals, changed his mind once he felt that the tide was turning in that direction; he assumed that the bill now would be able to pass the Senate without any problem. There was only one sticking point in the final legislation that would be offered to the Senate. The Committee of 13 had rejected the concept of popular sovereignty in determining whether a state would be free or slave. Stephen Douglas, the senator from Illinois, and a leader among the liberal Democrats, had attempted to restore this provision with no success. Clay now asked Douglas to reintroduce a motion which would strike out the prohibition against popular sovereignty in determining whether a state would be free or slave. Instead, Douglas chose to have Moses Norris, a senator from New Hampshire, introduce the legislation. Clay believed that without eliminating that amendment the omnibus bill could not pass. A number of reasons have been offered as to why the Senate now decided to strike out that part of the final bill: the failure of the Nashville conference of Southern diehards to come to terms on the concept of secession; the support of President Fillmore for its elimination; and the fact that the New Mexico legislature had already voted to ban slavery. (The ban was subject to a possible veto by the governor, which was unlikely since Fillmore would appoint him, or to disallowance by Congress.) Probably the major factor was the fatigue of the members of the Senate who had been wrestling with the legislation for more than six months.

Sensing that the last of the problems had been resolved, Clay made one final speech defending the omnibus bill and attacking those who threatened disunion. It was the last effort of an old, sick man to attack the concept that the states had an inherent right to secede from the Union. It was to be his last hurrah in which he excoriated those who spoke of secession as being nothing less than traitors to their country. It was a sincere and emotional call to the members of the Senate to remember that they were Americans first, and Kentuckians or South Carolinians second. The speech appeared to work, and the assumption by the opponents of the measure that it would readily pass seemed to be a foregone conclusion. And then the impossible happened. An amendment on deciding the final boundary line between Texas and New Mexico was offered by Senator James Bradbury of Maine, who suggested a joint commission made up of representatives from Texas and the United States. To that was appended a modification by Senator William Dawson of Georgia that New Mexico would not have jurisdiction east of the Rio Grande until the commission had decided. It was then that Senator James Pearce of Maryland threw a monkey wrench into the negotiations by challenging the senator from Georgia and moving that his amendment should be struck out. Clay begged the senator from Maryland to withdraw his motion but to no avail. His motion was carried by a vote of 33 to 22. The South, sensing blood, then introduced an amendment by Senator David Yulee of Florida to strike out everything related to Texas, and that passed by one vote, 29 to 28. Once Texas was eliminated, the opposition closed in, and a similar motion to drop California as well was introduced by Missouri Senator David Atchison; and, that passed as well, by a vote of 34 to 25. The omnibus bill was dead and the Abolitionists and the Southern fire eaters jumped for joy. Clay was thunderstruck. Nine months of labor had suddenly gone down the drain. The tangled web of alliances that he had put together between Northerners and Southerners, between Whigs and Democrats, had come apart, and there was no chance to put Humpty Dumpty together again. Clay left Washington in despair. Fortunately all was not lost. Stephen Douglas, who was chairman of the committee on territories in the Senate, never had believed that the omnibus bill would pass. Instead, in seven days he wrote five separate bills for each part of Clay's compromise, which he submitted for approval. One by one, all of the measures that had been incorporated in the one bill were passed separately. Douglas and Pearce fashioned a bill addressing the boundary of Texas which gave the state 33,333 square miles more than the omnibus had allowed and left New Mexico with all of its territory. For its sacrifice, Texas would receive $10 million in place of the $3.25 million under the omnibus bill. Four days later, California was admitted to the Union. The Fugitive Slave Law was enacted by a voice vote in the Senate; it required citizens to assist in returning runaway slaves regardless of a state's law. The District's slave trade bill was enacted a month later; it permitted slavery in the capital, but banned slave trading. While Douglas would give all the credit to Clay for the passage of the legislation, and well he should receive the plaudits from the point of view of steering legislation through a divided Senate, the kudos belong to Douglas. The facts support that premise. Only 16 senators voted for all the bills proposed by Douglas. The majority for each piece of legislation brought different supporters from different constituencies to reach a final accord. What it highlighted was the difference between conception, which was all Clay's, and execution, which belonged to Douglas. The Compromise of 1850 averted secession and war, and given the caliber of politicians at that time, the South might have been successful.

This was the first time since 1832, when South Carolina had threatened to secede over the issue of the "Abominable Tariff," that the concept of secession as a remedy for the South's ills had been raised. While all the slave states did not send representatives to the Nashville Conference and no consensus was reached by those in attendance, the fact that it did occur was reason enough for Clay to make his emotional appeal. As a slaveholder, Clay was well aware of the major problem that had led some members of the Southern establishment to discuss the possibility of secession. An economy based on slave labor had certain drawbacks. Foremost among them was the cost of feeding, housing and clothing an ever increasing slave population while at the same time the amount of land under cultivation did not increase. The Southern establishment had yet to fashion a rational answer for this conundrum. While only 15 percent of the Southern population owned slaves, this 15 percent accounted for more than 80 percent of the cotton produced and exported. Among that 15 percent, the largest plantations with the greatest number of slaves accounted for the bulk of that 80 percent. As was the case with the white population, the number of females equaled the number of males and the women were continually being impregnated by the males, either white or Negro, further increasing the Negro population. In 1850, cotton still was profitable enough to support this ever growing and aging slave population, so the concept of secession was placed on the back burner. But if the fire in their bellies had yet to emerge, the rage still remained.

While slavery was both an asset and liability to the Southern economy, a far more serious problem was the homogeneity of the population. Except for western Virginia and St. Louis, which attracted large numbers of German immigrants both before and after the 1848 revolutions that swept Western Europe, the Southern states did not benefit from the waves of immigrants pouring into America. While the population of the newly created Northwestern states grew at an extraordinary pace thanks to the influx of immigrants, growth in the Southern states was predicated on intermarriage between cousins, almost entirely of English, Scots or Scots–Irish descent. The census figures tell the story. In Wisconsin in 1840, there were 31,000 residents. Ten years later the figure had multiplied ten-fold to 305,000; by 1860, it had more than doubled to 776,000. The population figures for Minnesota were even more startling. In 1850 there were 6,000 inhabitants. Ten years later there were 172,000. Michigan, one of the early states, by 1860 had a population of 749,000; Illinois in that same year could boast of 1,712,000. The only state in the South that could match such numbers was Virginia, and it only exceeded a million in population because of its 500,000 Negroes. While these statistics confirm where the new immigrants were settling, they don't explain why the South was absorbing so few of them. Slavery, kinsmen, climatic conditions, large open expanses of land and the absence of large cities which could absorb people with specific trades already have been noted. Far more important in the decision-making of the emigrants was the industrialization that was taking place in the North and Midwest as opposed to the commodity agriculture of the South. In no way is the foregoing meant to imply that the Industrial Revolution skipped the Southern states. The construction of railroads was almost as much a priority in the Southern states as it was in those of the North and Midwest. The mining of coal took place not only in western Virginia but in Tennessee and Kentucky as well. Iron ore deposits were uncovered in Alabama. The longest rail line in the nation was constructed to link the Southern states with those in the North. Other factors, however, impeded the industrialization of the South. Of great importance was the attitude and financial condition of the Southern establishment. Geared to one-crop commodities, such as cotton and tobacco, the Southern states were at the mercy of market conditions in Britain and Europe. As a result most of them were heavily in debt to their British and continental factors. There always was a shortage of liquid capital, the necessary ingredient for industrial expansion. In addition, no effort was made to attract the engineers and craftsmen required to develop an industrial economy. While all the foregoing did impede the development of a mixed economy in the Southern states, the fundamental hindrance was the attitude of the Southern establishment. The elite took pride in the Southern way of life. Unlike the hustle and bustle common to the large cities in the North, with their foreign-born populations, the South was a relatively homogenous Anglo-Saxon rural society. On the large plantations sat huge mansions where friends and visitors were entertained for a week or more at a time, enjoying fox hunting and horse racing, with a bevy of Negro slaves to cater to their own needs and those of their guests. They, their wives and their children were outfitted with the latest fashions from London or Paris. It was a fairy tale world sustained by the cultivation of cotton, tobacco, rice and indigo and by a slave population. The only indigenous culture of the region would emerge later from its slave population. The strict enforcement of the Fugitive Slave Act was the only sop that the North could offer the South in the Compromise of 1850. While on the surface it appeared to have saved the Union, or at least the implied threat engendered by the conclave of Southern states meeting in Nashville, in reality it was only a temporary expedient. Far more important for the moment was the presidential election of 1852 and the question of which party would control the future destiny of the country.

When the Democratic Party held its convention in Baltimore there were five leading candidates for the presidency, all but one from the Northern wing of the party. These included Lewis Cass from Michigan, who had been defeated by General Taylor; James Buchanan, a leading politician from the large state of Pennsylvania; William Marcy from New York, who had been Secretary of War under Polk and three times governor of New York; William Butler from Kentucky, Cass's vice presidential candidate in 1848; and the new kid on the block, Stephen Douglas from Illinois, the youngest member of the Senate, and the man who had broken down Clay's omnibus bill into its separate elements and pushed its passage through the Senate. He was being backed by a new group calling itself Young America, but as far as the major politicians were concerned, he was not a serious choice. The man that most of the professional politicos were focused on, once again, was Levi Woodbury of Connecticut — a Yankee whom the South trusted and believed supported their point of view. To their dismay he upped and died before the convention. That left the battlefield to Cass, Butler, Marcy, Buchanan and Douglas, and with the two-thirds rule in place for nomination, none of the five were able to assemble the necessary votes. For three days prior to the actual voting, the wrangling between the politicians went on with neither side willing to give in to the others and settle on a candidate. As the balloting began it was obvious that none of the candidates would be able to attain the 197 votes necessary to have a two-thirds majority. All kinds of deals were offered by the contending candidates with none of them ready to concede. Meanwhile, Edmund Burke had appointed himself Franklin Pierce's campaign manager although his name had never been brought to the floor, and he had never been considered as a compromise candidate. Burke set to work, first in New England, prior to the convention, and then at the convention to tout Franklin Pierce as the presidential candidate who could unite the party. Edmund Burke had been a Congressman, the head of the U.S. Patent Office, and co-editor of a Washington newspaper. What Burke brought to his new role as a campaign manager was a deep understanding of how politics worked in Washington. To him, every delegate at the convention had one thought in mind, patronage — the awarding of political jobs within a new administration. Federal patronage was the mother's milk of national politics in this new, growing republic. It was the seat and source of all political power. Burke, a very astute politician, waited patiently as one ballot after another indicated that none of the candidates were prepared to drop out of the running. When the 48th ballot was taken, with nothing still resolved, he made his move. Burke, as a Washington insider, knew who was up for sale and what it would cost. On the 49th ballot, James C. Dobbin, the senator from North Carolina, made an impassioned speech for the nomination of Franklin Pierce and cast all the state's votes for his candidacy. This sudden move out of left field, worked. The delegates were tired, the impasse between the candidates showed no sign of being broken, and one state after another followed the lead of Dobbin. When the chair announced the results, there were 282 for Pierce, two votes each for Cass and Douglas, and one for Butler. To appease Buchanan, who all along had assumed that the nomination belonged to him, his political ally William R. King of Alabama was chosen for vice president.

Who then was Franklin Pierce, who emerged as the savior of the Democrat-ic Party? Not even mentioned as a dark horse for the nomination, he suddenly was unanimously elected the Democratic presidential candidate, following his nomination by one senator from the relatively small state of North Carolina. On the surface this drama has all the earmarks of a Hollywood movie script. Yet, while long removed from the limelight, Pierce wasn't exactly an unknown fac-tor. He was born into a political family. His father had been a general during the Revolutionary War, and while not a major figure in terms of overall American history during that period, he was well known within the state of New Hamp-shire and had been elected and served two terms as its governor. Franklin had attended college and become a lawyer. Through the influence of his father he had been elected to the state legislature. Through his family connections he became Speaker of the House, and in 1837 he was sent to the Senate. As an intellectual he was no great shakes, but he was sociable. His appearance lent him an air of respectability and confidence, and he seemed destined for some major role in the Democratic Party even if he represented a relatively small state. Unfortunately, as was the case with his father, he was an alcoholic, and his physical and mental deterioration caused by his excessive drinking forced him to resign from the Sen-ate. To all appearances his political career seemed to be over. He joined a tem-perance movement for a while; practiced law and seemed destined for political obscurity. Even his military performance during the Mexican war was disastrous. Enlisting as a Private when the hostilities broke out, through political connec-tions he suddenly became a Colonel. When President Polk, fearful of the fact that all the credit for the military successes in the campaign was being accorded to Whig generals, raised several Democrats to the rank of brigadier general, Pierce was one of them. But bad luck pursued him. He was thrown from his horse and suffered injuries in his pelvic region and his leg; when ordered by General Scott to retire to the rear, Pierce remonstrated with his commander-in-chief, harbor-ing the hope that he could achieve military fame by leading his 2,500 men into Mexico City. It was not to be. Poor Pierce, when he attempted to lead his men on the last thrust of the military campaign, he fainted from the pain in his injured leg, and this time he was ordered to the rear and sent home. With one failure com-ing on the heels of another, it appeared that Pierce's political career had come to an end. All this abruptly changed when the Democratic nominee for governor of New Hampshire came out against the recently passed Fugitive Slave Act; over-night, Pierce was back in the thick of politics, working to defeat this candidate's nomination, which sat well with the Southern wing of the party. There was even noise bruited around of his being nominated for the vice presidency, which he declined in no uncertain terms. But when his friend and political mentor, Ed-mund Burke, queried him as to whether he would accept the nomination for the presidency, he gave his accord provided that he would not have to campaign for the position. This was the man the Democrats had chosen to be their standard bearer. An ex-alcoholic who had joined the temperance movement and then slid off the wagon; insecure while at the same time egotistical, a contradiction which was to make a wreck of his tenure in office; a loyal party man; neither introspective nor intellectual — one could almost describe him as a party hack that had lucked into the nomination. Nevertheless, the choice of Pierce was not without reason. The Democrats were anything but unified; there was the Southern wing, many of whom were still angry over the admission of California as a free state in the Compromise of 1850. In the minds of these Southerners, the line between a slave and a free state had been established with the Missouri Compromise, and since almost all of California was below 36°30' latitude, it should have been designated automatically as a slave state. Also disturbing was that the legislation had been pushed through the Senate by a Northern Democrat, Stephen Douglas of Illinois. Finally, the split in New York State during the last election still upset the Southern establishment: Van Buren, considered to be a loyal Democrat, had abandoned the party which had elevated him to the presidency and ran for office on the Free Soil Party line. This had cost the Democrats the election by dividing the Democratic vote in New York. Worst of all was the belief that only a Northerner could head the ticket if the Democrats were to win the presidency. Of the five candidates who sought the nomination and the sixth who won it, all were Northerners. It was the South's sense of isolation, of no longer being a party to the nominating process, which would eventually lead to secession.

If the Democrats were disunited, the Whigs were in greater disarray. The Whigs never had been a political party. They were a loose amalgamation of anti-Jackson Democrats; the remnants of those who still believed that there had been a Federalist party; the old Southern establishment, which did not cotton up to Jackson's democracy, and Westerners like Clay, who believed that the federal government had an important role to play in the development of the nation. Some of them were for a national bank that would stabilize the currency; others were for cheap money and unlimited credit. They had taken the presidency in only two elections by nominating a war hero as their candidate. Now there were new elements that had crawled under their blanket. There were those violently opposed to the expansion of slavery, along with some of an even more radical persuasion, who wished to abolish slavery altogether. In lieu of five candidates, there were only two serious contenders for the nomination; General Winfield Scott, who believed he had been robbed of the last nomination when the party selected General Zachary Taylor; and of course, the sitting President Millard Fillmore. Daniel Webster, once again, had thrown his hat into the ring, but the old man was dying and soon would join the other two great senators of the nineteenth century, Calhoun and Clay, to the grave. Since nomination for the candidacy in the Whig party involved only a simple majority of the delegates, it was assumed that one of the two would get the nomination. The problem was that the votes for the two candidates were evenly divided. And, with Webster still hoping for the nomination and refusing to release his 32 delegates, the party had yet to select a candidate after 46 consecutive ballots. Finally accepting the fact that he had no chance for the nomination, Webster released his delegates under the assumption that they would cast their votes for Fillmore. Instead, to his dismay, his adherents split their votes and Scott emerged as the victor. The Whigs wanted a man on a horse. As a portent of what was to come, the early congressional elections indicated a sweep for the Democrats, with nine states going for the Democrats and only Vermont for the Whigs. When the electoral vote was counted, it was worse than any Whig could have imagined. Pierce received 254 electoral votes to Scott's 42, with the latter only carrying the states of Massachusetts, Vermont, Kentucky and Tennessee. The Whigs, which had been more of an opposition than a political party, now seemed doomed to disappear from the political scene.

The return of the Democrats to power in Washington had one important meaning — thousands of jobs to be distributed to the politically loyal as a result of capturing the White House. The dispensers of all of these positions, except for the major ones controlled by the President, would be the members of the Cabinet, and the choice of the Cabinet would reflect the personal views of Pierce concerning how his administration planned to govern. Two things were mandatory in the selection of a Cabinet, geography and political views. Another factor that had to be considered was the political rivalries of Democrats within the individual states. This was particularly true in New York where the animosities between the supporters of Van Buren, and his defection to the Free Soil party in 1848, and those who remained loyal to the party never had healed. Thus Pierce's choice of Marcy as Secretary of State, even though he was a Hunkerer, aroused opposition within that element of the party because he wished to make peace with the Barnburners. Marcy, who had been governor of New York five times, had sat on the State's Supreme Court, and also had been Secretary of War under Polk during the Mexican War, came to his new job without any experience in foreign affairs. Despite this apparent weakness, he soon mastered his job and was considered to be close to the President. The job of attorney general was given to Caleb Cushing of Massachusetts. A former Whig, he had become an ardent disciple of states' rights, was violently opposed to the Free Soil elements of the Democratic Party in Massachusetts and was the only member of the Cabinet to have experience in foreign affairs, having served as US Minister to China. He too was close to Pierce. The third member of the inner circle in the Cabinet was Jefferson Davis. A graduate of West Point, seriously wounded in the Mexican War, he had met Pierce when the latter came to the Senate. A pronounced advocate for states' rights and slavery, who had voted against the Compromise of 1850, and a devout believer that the aim of the North was to expunge slavery, he was very close to Pierce, both in terms of politics and also on a social level, which included their two wives. For the postmaster general, where there were thousands of positions to be doled out, Pierce selected James Campbell, the only Catholic in the Cabinet, who had been backed by James Buchanan. For Secretary of the Treasury, he chose James Guthrie from Kentucky, a Southern Border State, but unlike the other Cabinet members, he was a very successful business man, with interests in railroads, real estate and banking. Under his leadership, the Treasury Department finally became an efficient tool of the government as he eliminated waste and did not curry favor with the private banking interests. For Secretary of the Navy, Pierce repaid his debt to Senator James C. Dobbin of North Carolina, whose change of vote had started the stampede towards Pierce's nomination. Finally, for Secretary of the Interior, to placate the Cass faction, he chose Robert McClelland, who had voted for the Wilmot Proviso, later changed his mind, but did vote for the Compromise of 1850.

The US of the 1850s had little in common with the nation's previous profile. At the turn of the nineteenth century there were approximately 1,000 cotton textile wage earners. Sixty years later, at the outbreak of the War Between the States, there were 122,000, almost all of them women and children. The mining industry was no different. In 1800 there were 10,000 employed compared to 176,000 in 1860. This growth in non-agricultural labor was confined largely to the Northeast, the Mid-Atlantic and the Northwestern states. Every industry above the Mason–Dixon Line was growing by leaps and bounds. The fishing industry, which formerly employed 5,000, now had a workforce of 31,000. All of the cities in the North were expanding at an incredible rate to keep pace with the flood of immigrants. As a result, the construction industry, which wasn't reported as being part of the labor force until 1840, employed 620,000 people by the time the war broke out, or more than the entire non-agricultural wage force 20 years earlier, if domestics weren't counted. By the outbreak of the hostilities, there were 43,000 iron and steel workers engaged in producing raw materials to expand the railroads that traversed the country, including the South. The railroads, prior to the outbreak of hostilities, employed 80,000 workers. America's ocean-going fleet, almost all of it in the Northeast with the exception of New Orleans, now employed 145,000 men. Only in the area of domestic labor, where the South enjoyed the advantage of a huge female slave population, did it remain on a par with the North. Even in the area of education, which had grown along with the expanding population, of the 115,000 who listed teaching as their profession, a far larger majority were in the North than in the South. As far as trade was concerned, which employed more people than any other industry, both wholesale and retail, once again the North with its far larger population dominated this category. The nation's financial market was concentrated in New York City with the New York Stock and Exchange floating securities for the individual states and for the nascent corporations that the burgeoning railroad industry had set in motion. The major newspaper, periodical and book publishing industries all were located in the Northeast, again with New York City playing the dominant role. America's great novelists, poets and essayists were all Northerners.

It is within this framework that the great domestic crisis of the Pierce administration was played out. Stephen Douglas, the senator from Illinois, was a young man in a hurry. Short in stature, only five feet four inches tall, he made up for his height with a huge head topped by a large mass of hair, which sat upon a squat body. A great believer in national expansion and popular sovereignty, he was elected to Congress in 1842 and became one of the youngest senators in 1846, at the age of 36. Before he had completed his first term in the Senate, he was an active candidate for the presidency in 1852, the year Pierce was nominated and elected as the compromise candidate. Just a first-term member of the Senate, he was awarded the all-important chairmanship of the Senate committee on territories, which enabled him to devise the strategy for the Senate's acceptance of the Compromise of 1850. One thing was obvious about the "Little Giant," the name ascribed to him by the press, from the very beginning of his political career he had his sights set on the presidency. Every step he took during his political career reflected that goal. A transplant from the Northeast, he immediately attached himself to the fortunes of the party in power in Illinois, the Democrats. As the political divisions within the country intensified, Douglas was well aware that in order to be nominated for the highest office he stood no chance without the support of the Southern delegates. His only pro-slavery credential was that his wife owned slaves which came with her dowry. When his father-in-law, a wealthy North Carolinian planter offered him the opportunity to operate a successful plantation he owned in Mississippi, Douglas turned it down. Politics was his lifeblood and the presidency was his target. The presidential bug is lethal. It delivers a poison which blinds even the most rational of human beings to abnegate their most profound beliefs in order to catch the magic ring. Stephen Douglas had ingested a huge quantity of that toxin, and if the times had been ordinary, he probably would have attained the presidency. But times were not normal. The country was growing and expanding at a prodigious rate, and those who had been in power could sense that it was slipping through their fingers. At least that was the feeling among the Southerners.

The problem was the Nebraska territory which had been divided into two states, Kansas and Nebraska. Congress had made the decision to move the Indian tribes located there either north to the Dakotas or southwest to the Oklahoma territory, both of which had been set aside for them as permanent places of abode. When it came to the Native Americans not only was the memory of the white establishment short but it kept changing to fit the circumstances. Nor was there a dearth of rationalizations for this new attitude. First, if Congress was to pass legislation authorizing the construction of a trans-continental railroad, it would have to pass through these territories, thereby disturbing Indian settlements. Second, those settlers moving westward to California had been harassed by the Indians. Most important of all was that this was fertile land best left to the exploitation by white American settlers. The sticking point to the settlement of these new territories as far as the South was concerned was the Missouri Compromise of 1820, which had restricted slavery to all lands below 36°30' latitude, which ended at the northern border of Missouri. Given the Southern predicament of a growing slave population, this legislation was the only impediment that stood in the way of the slave trade expanding to the new territories that would eventually become states. Herein lay a marvelous opportunity for Douglas to become a champion of Southern rights without destroying his personal integrity. If the Missouri Compromise was repealed, while at the same time insisting on the sovereignty of the people in determining whether a state should be free or slave, Douglas could have his cake and eat it as well. The South no longer would be restrained from growing by an artificial line drawn in the sand, while at the same time the wishes of the people who populated the new territories would be paramount. It was the majority of the residents of the new state that would decide on the final disposition of whether free or slave. The first obstacle to be removed if his plan was to succeed was the Missouri Compromise; after much haggling and debate, that was accomplished. What happened next was something he had never anticipated. Senator Atchison of Missouri, a vigorous proponent of slavery, saw in the new legislation an immediate opportunity. By moving quickly, he attempted to establish the foundation for the admission of Kansas as a slave state. Since Missouri bordered Kansas, he would move settlers from Missouri into the new territory with their slaves and establish as quickly as possible a temporary legislature for the territory, along with a judicial system, and pronounce a pro-slavery position for the state's future. While the pro-slavery settlers were establishing their own government in Leavenworth, the Free Soil settlers were establishing theirs in Lawrence, Kansas, aided by funds and propaganda from the Emigrant Aid Society, an organization formed in Massachusetts. This was not an Abolitionist organization since its constitution called for no Negroes in the new territory, whether slave or free.

With two competing legislatures, each of which declared itself to be the legitimate representative of the people of Kansas, the stage was set for conflict as well as corruption on the part of officials sent from Washington to adjudicate the competing claims. While Congress had set aside a certain portion of the lands to be settled by half-breeds (those who were half Indian and half white), the speculators only were interested in enriching themselves. The first governor that Pierce appointed to act as chief executive of the territory was Andrew Reeder, a Pennsylvanian who was pro-slavery in his political views. Reeder, after finally reaching the territory, discovered that in fact the Missouri-sponsored Southern legislature was a sham. When voting was to take place, thousands would come up from Missouri, cast their ballots and then return to their homes. Every time he tried to veto a piece of legislation passed by the pro-slavery legislature, his veto would be overridden. Reeder, after insuring the legitimacy of his own land speculations in the divided territory, returned to Washington and was replaced as governor by Wilson Shannon from Cincinnati, another pro-slavery appointee. The problem actually lay with Franklin Pierce. Having accidentally stumbled into the presidency as a compromise candidate backed by the South, not only was he indebted to them for his present position but since he had a hankering for a second term, it would be in his self interest to support the minority govern-ment in the south of Kansas. The concept of Kansas being able to support a slave-based economy was absurd. The climatic conditions were such that none of the commodities that dominated the economy of the South were practicable in this region. Even in Missouri, the cut-off line for the admission of a slave state, most of the Negroes were employed in the southern tier of the state. A perfect example of this futility was that at the height of the controversy, fewer than 200 Negroes had been brought into the state by those Southerners who had established a fraudulent legislature and wished to be recognized as the official government of the state. Stephen Douglas, the great compromiser, stepped into the picture. His solution was two-pronged. First, recognize the Lecompton Constitution (named for a town between Lawrence and Topeka), which was written by the pro-slavery legislature and ratified in late 1857 after voters were given a choice only between limited or unlimited slavery — with free-state advocates refusing to vote. Second, following a census of all the inhabitants of the state, a decision would be made as to whether the state should be admitted as free or slave. After some amendments by Alexander Stephens of Georgia, the bill passed the Senate, but in the House, where a combination of Free Soil members, Republicans and Know-Nothings had taken over during the mid-term elections, the bill was killed. John Geary, the last of the governors appointed by Pierce, did try to bring some order out of the chaos of two competing legislatures. He was offered bribes by the Free Soil party if he would support their position in Washington, one tempt-ing him with the governorship, the other with a senatorial appointment, both of which he turned down. The disposition of the future of Kansas would be left to the next administration.

In 1854, in Michigan and a few other Northwestern states, a new political party was about to be born. The evolution of the Republican Party was an entire-ly new phenomenon in American politics. Its origins were not in the Northeast or the Southwest but in the Northwest, which had previously been the home of the Democratic Party. It was a party that recognized that the fringe political parties — the Liberty Party, the Free Soil Party and the Know-Nothings — did not reflect the point of view of the people in the West. They were Eastern parties, representing the specific needs of the disenfranchised in the Eastern states. As for the Whigs, they would pander to any group that would vote them into office. Just like the Democrats, they were trying to straddle the fence between the views of their Southern and Northern constituencies. It was the issue of Kansas that galvanized these independent farmers and business men into the realization that they alone had no voice in the federal government. Like sheep, they had been voting the straight Democratic ticket under the illusion that the Democrats represented the average man as opposed to the Whigs who represented the money interests in the East. It was a *coup de foudre*, an instantaneous realization that the party of Jefferson and Jackson no longer was the old Democratic party of the individual but merely represented the interest of the slave owners. Furthermore, the Whigs were no better. The birth of the Republican Party was a phenomenon that could have taken place only in this country. When Lincoln had been invited to join, he turned his friend down. He had been a Whig all of his political life. His idol was Henry Clay. When he made his first run for the Senate in 1854, it was as a Whig. What convinced Lincoln and hundreds of thousands of others to leave the Whigs was the incredible showing of the Republicans in the presidential election of 1856. Carrying the new party's banner was a relatively unknown figure from California, John Fremont, who despite the fact that he was a Californian and had been instrumental in the founding of the state, ran behind the Democratic and Whig candidates in the vote count in California. What astounded most political pundits of 1856, if there were such animals, was the ability of this newly formed Republican party, not only to launch a presidential candidate in the 1856 election on a national level, but at the same time, to field candidates for governorships and for the House and the Senate. There were several factors that contributed to the sudden success of the newly formed Republican Party other than the bankruptcy of the Whigs as a political organization. There was a growing sense among Northern Democrats that they were being used by the Southern wing of the Democratic Party solely to advance the agenda of the South. This was particularly the view of those in the Northern industrial states. Equally important were the close economic ties between the Northwest and the Northeast as a result of the railroads and the enormously successful Erie Canal. Both groups of states came to realize that they shared a commonality of economic interests that transcended the West's past affiliation with the Democratic South. The basic sticking point that broke their loyalty to the Democrats was free soil. Now that the states west of the Mississippi were open to development, the issue of free versus slave states no longer could be resolved by past loyalty to the Democrats. This was a fundamental issue upon which there was no ground for compromise.

It is only with this background kept in mind that one can understand how the Republicans, literally overnight, could emerge as a major political party in the North and Northwest. Both the Whigs and the Democrats were victims of the new alliance. In the presidential election of 1856, Millard Fillmore, the Whig candidate, came in third in the popular vote with 870,000 as compared to Fremont's 1.3 million and Buchanan's 1.8 million. Even more devastating were the electoral results, where Buchanan captured 174 votes and Fremont garnered 114, while only Maryland supported Fillmore. One thing was clear. For Fremont to garner one-million-plus votes it had to come from disaffected Whigs such as Lincoln, along with former supporters of the Free Soil party, the Know-Nothing party, now renamed the American party, and disillusioned Northern Democrats fed up with the Southern dominance of their party. They were certainly not Abolitionists since their platform did not call for the repeal of the Fugitive Slave Act or the elimination of slavery within the District of Columbia. In addition, the Republicans had the support of the Temperance party, which viewed the Democratic base in the North as composed of drunken Irishmen and other day laborers who spent their life and savings on the consumption of alcohol. There also was a smattering of Abolitionists, who did not follow the example of William Lloyd Garrison, who remained aloof from the political scene. Finally, there were the free Northern Negroes, at least in those New England states where they had the right to vote. If the Republican Party in 1856 was an amalgam of various dissidents, the same could not be said of the Democratic Party. In theory the majority party in the nation, it had clobbered the Whigs in the 1852 presidential election, limiting the Whig electoral vote to just four states. Then two years later it had lost control of the House of Representatives by a wide margin and barely held a majority in the Senate. A year later, in state and local elections, it had recovered somewhat as a result of the temporary depression of 1854. But the results of the 1856 election demonstrated that the Democratic Party had lost a major part of its supporters in the North and the West. While its base was in the Southern slave states, without the support of Northern Democrats it could never have elected the president.

To the Southern establishment, the rise of the Republicans in local elections was an indication that time was not on its side. It had lost control of the House of Representatives and barely had a majority in the Senate. Once again, it would have to nominate a Northerner if it was to control the presidency. Among the three men vying for the presidential nomination in 1856 were President Pierce, Cass, Douglas, and Buchanan, the final choice, all of whom represented either the North or the West. Where then did the power of the Southern bloc lie? Part of it was tradition. It was the party of Jefferson, Madison, Monroe, and Jackson; all of these leaders were slaveholders who were dedicated to the concept of states' rights within the framework of the Constitution. When Jackson left the presidency in 1836, the US still was an agrarian society. Twenty years later, not only had the frontier disappeared from the eastern bank of the Mississippi River, but the western side had been settled with the admission of Iowa and Minnesota, not to mention Oregon and California. Kansas was ready to be admitted once the southern states recognized reality. When Jackson left office, he had inaugurated the first 12 miles of rail track to have been laid; two decades later there were thousands of miles of rail track linking the states. Samuel Morse had invented the telegraph which provided instant communication over hundreds of miles. Cyrus McCormick's reaper had revolutionized agriculture in the states north of the Ohio River. And the gas lamp had replaced candles. In the North, thanks to the railroad, what once had been towns had become small or large cities.

The massive waves of nineteenth century emigration to this country of Irish Catholics and those from Germany and central Europe had settled mainly in the North and Northwest. While the Southern states did receive a certain percentage of the new immigrants, the growth in population in the region was limited largely to internal growth. The result was a very stable establishment uncontaminated by new blood or new ideas, except in some of the Border States of Missouri, Tennessee, Kentucky and Maryland, which did receive an influx of immigrants but where slavery still remained an accepted institution. Except for Charleston, South Carolina and New Orleans, the South was a landlocked society where political power resided in the large landed establishments and the lawyers who represented them and their interests. If all the foregoing is factual, then what accounted for the continued support the Democratic Party received in the North and the Midwest? There were two basic reasons for the success of the Democrats in these regions. First, the collapse of the Federalists, following the defeat of John Adams in his quest for a second term, left but one political party in this country, the Democrats. His son, John Quincy Adams ran for the presidency as a Democrat. In other words, it was by default that only one political party existed. It was only with the advent of Jackson and his policies that the Whig party emerged as a competitor to the Democrats. Second, it was only in the late 1820s and early 1830s that the North began to develop industries whose aims and goals differed from those of a largely agrarian society. With the advent of first the canals and then the railroads, an economic alliance between the Midwest and the Northeast ensued. Prior to that, the Midwestern states were basically rural, and as such, adherents of the Jeffersonian philosophy of the independent yeoman. With the advent of the Whigs, however, the Democrats faced competition not only in the Southern states but among those in the Northeast as well, where the commercial interests were centered, who sought the return of the national bank. Moreover, the key swing state had become New York because of its large and growing population and its substantial number of electoral votes. Clay had been defeated by Polk only as a result of the Free Soil party's strong showing in New York, which enabled the Democrat to carry the state. This simple fact of arithmetic did not go unnoticed among the Southern, Democratic establishment. If the Democratic

Party was to hold onto the White House, it needed a Northern candidate who would pander to the basic views of the slave states. The one subject that united the Northern, Southern and Western Democrats was the political spoils that accrued to the winning party in the presidential elections.

Demographics and the changing pattern of the Northern economies were working against the party of Jefferson. Start with changing population trends. Using South Carolina as an example; in 1830, the population of the state was 581,000, including 258,000 whites and 323,000 Negroes. But if each slave was counted as representing three fifths of a white resident, then the representation of South Carolina in the House of Representatives would be based on a total population of 452,000. Now compare that with the state of Maine where there were 399,000 residents, all white. Twenty years later, however, the population of Maine had grown to the point where there were now 583,000 whites as compared to South Carolina's combined population of slaves and whites of 669,000. But when you break it down into races, there were 275,000 whites and 394,000 Negroes. When you apply the three-fifths rule for congressional representation, there are now 510,000 who can be counted as residents of the state, or fewer than those of Maine. This comparison illustrates the different patterns of growth in population between the North and the South. In the North, the population was increasing because of an influx of immigrants; in the South, population growth was almost totally dependent upon the fertility of the slaves. Furthermore, the growth of railroads was playing an important role in the distribution and movement of people. In Illinois, in 1830, the most western of the states admitted to the Union at the time, the total population was 157,000, with 155,000 white and 2,000 Negro. Twenty years later, the white population was 846,000 and the Negro population only 5,000. Compare that with Georgia. In 1830, the white population of that state was 297,000 and the Negro was 220,000; using the three fifths rule, population adjusted for the congressional representation was 429,000. Twenty years later, the white population had increased to 592,000 and the Negro to 355,000. But when you factor in the three-fifths rule, the state is only represented by a population of 805,000. In each instance, the South was on a downward slide in terms of proportional representation within the House of Representatives.

The same pattern of population growth holds true throughout the Southern slave states with the exception of Texas, only admitted to the Union in 1850. Without the support of the Democrats in the North, the South would become a minority party, and as a result, lose all the important committee chairmanships in the House and the Senate. Whether the Southern establishment was cognizant of these demographic changes and how they would affect its power base is certainly probable. All the new political parties coming upon the scene were emanating from the North, albeit there was a Southern branch of the Know-Nothing party. The South remained the stronghold of the slave-owning Democrats and the fading slave-owning Whig party. The former already was leaning towards secession while the latter was not prepared to leave the Union. The election of 1856 would be nothing more than a temporary holding pattern. The power base of the South was already eroding with the results of the off-year congressional elections of 1854. With the presidential election of 1856, and the incredible political strength shown by the new political party, the Republicans, the Southern Democrats were losing their hold on the Northern branch.

James Buchanan, the thirteenth man elected to the presidency, was a self made man who had built up a personal fortune of more than $300,000. Originally a Federalist, when that party vanished, by default he became a Democrat, the only party still in existence. Elected first as a Congressman and then a senator, he had served as Secretary of State in the Polk administration, unsuccessfully opposing the President on the dividing line for the Oregon territory. Buchanan had also been against engaging in the Mexican War; and then, after the success of the campaign, believed that the US should incorporate all of Mexico within the Union. He had unsuccessfully run for the Democratic nomination in 1848 and 1852 and succeeded in 1856, when it became apparent that the party was unhappy with Pierce running for a second term and not yet ready to accept Stephen Douglas, the other viable candidate. Buchanan seemed to be an ideal choice for the Southern wing of the party. He had been Minister to England, during the fracas over the question of Kansas and therefore had avoided the debate over whether the state should be admitted as free or slave state. He was important because it was assumed that he would bring to the Democratic electoral column the votes of Pennsylvania, the second largest Northern state, and because he always had been pro-Southern in his views on slavery. While the question of Kansas had yet to be resolved when he assumed office, the overnight success of the newly formed Republican party at the polls, with its basic theme that Kansas should be admitted only as a free state, would dominate the presidency of Buchanan.

Just prior to Buchanan's inaugural address, given on March 4, 1857, the Supreme Court was poised to rule on a case that might have a bearing on the issue of slavery in the free states. The case involved a 62-year-old slave, Dred Scott, whose owners had moved along with Scott to a free state and stayed there for several years before returning to Missouri. Since he had lived in a free state for that period of time, Scott claimed that he no longer was a slave. A lower court upheld his petition but when the case was remanded to the Supreme Court of Missouri, it was overruled. Scott's lawyers appealed the verdict to the US Supreme Court. Roger B. Taney, the Chief Justice, was from Maryland and the other members of the court were divided — four Southerners and four from the Northern states. In fact, two of the four members from the Northern states tended to be pro-slavery. Shortly after Buchanan was elected, he wrote to Justice John Cantron, inquiring whether a decision would be handed down before inauguration day; further,

Buchanan convinced a Northern justice to join the Southern majority. With advance knowledge of the court's predisposition, Buchanan proposed in his inaugural address that whatever the court's decision, he and his administration would abide by it, and he asked the public to do so as well.

Two days after the inauguration, the decision of the Supreme Court was announced, with only two Northern justices dissenting. The first question addressed by the court was whether Dred Scott could be considered a citizen. The court ruled that no Negro, whether free or slave, could be considered a citizen and therefore could not bring suit. In writing the majority decision, Taney, who had freed his own slaves, stated: "Negroes had always been considered unfit to associate with the white race ... and so far inferior, that they had no rights which the white man was bound to respect." However, Taney and the majority did not stop with Scott's petition for freedom. Instead, they used his petition to make far-reaching decisions on the question of slavery itself. Invoking the due process clause in the Constitution, which concerns the protection of property, the court ruled that it applied within territories as well as states, and asserted that neither the federal government nor a territorial legislature had the right to bar slavery from any territory. To add fuel to the flames, the court went on to declare that the Missouri Compromise had been unconstitutional from the beginning. The decision on the territories, while it seemed to advance the cause of slavery by allowing it in any territory, in reality was a toothless tiger since it did not prevent a territory from prohibiting slavery within its borders once it became a state. Nor had the decision called for positive federal protection of slavery within the territories. But Taney and the majority on the court seem to have forgotten something. By classifying the Negro as property, they were challenging the Constitution which, when tabulating the number of citizens in each state, had allowed the Southern states to count their Negro males over 21 as three fifths of a white man. The legal implications went beyond that potential threat to Southern political interests. Could a US Supreme Court ruling on a case overturn what was part of the Constitution, or did it require an amendment to that document, as the Constitution stated? Except for the Abolitionists, the public ignored the plight of the Negro, and nobody paid much attention to this ruling.

Meanwhile all of Buchanan's efforts to turn a sow's ear into a silk purse collapsed under the weight of political and economic reality. Even with forging names to increase the rolls of those who supported the Lecompton Constitution, the votes weren't there either in Kansas or in Congress. In the spring elections of 1858, the Republicans captured such Democratic strongholds as Toledo, Cincinnati, Chicago and St. Louis. It was in desperation that Buchanan finally decided to accept a compromise to avoid losing face. A new bill was offered in the House, after obtaining an agreement from the administration and the Senate. Kansas should hold a referendum on its land grant. If the people voted to accept the four million acres provided in the Senate bill, plus five percent of the proceeds from two million acres to be sold in July, the state would be immediately admitted under the Lecompton Constitution. If they rejected this offer, they could not apply for statehood until the population had increased significantly. The final bill offered by an anti-Lecompton Democrat, William English, was passed in the House by a vote of 112 to 103 and in the Senate by 31 to 22. While Kansas Governor Robert Walker endorsed the bill and attempted to get Senator Douglas to back the legislation, Douglas, who had opposed the President in his efforts to get the Lecompton Constitution passed, would not alter his fundamental belief in the sovereignty of the people. He told them he could not support a bill based on unfair conditions and which offered only an indirect choice to the voters. In effect, the bill was nothing more than an attempt to buy off the heavily indebted settlers with promises of land and money. Three months later, in August 1858, the people of Kansas rejected the land grant and with it the Lecompton Constitution by 11,812 to 1,926. The issue of slavery was dead as far as Kansas was concerned, but more importantly, it announced to the Southern establishment that the extension of slavery in the new territories was a dead issue.

Likewise, much as the nascent Republican Party liked to assume that their electoral victories in the 1858 congressional elections could be traced to the debate over the future of Kansas, the real issue was the financial panic of 1857. Unlike the panics of 1819 and 1837, it differed not only by the number of people affected, since the population especially in the cities had expanded enormously, but in the amount of money and credit involved. As the US continued to grow in terms of population and wealth, any sharp decline in the economy would affect more people than previous ones. In theory, the panic was launched by the failure of the New York City branch of the Ohio Life Insurance & Trust Co., which despite its name, did not deal in insurance. Rather, the New York branch, which was capitalized at $2 million, was considered to be a conservative lending operation investing largely in railroads and other securities. When it unexpectedly declared bankruptcy, owing between five and seven million dollars as a result of non-payment of loans, it would bring down its headquarters in Cincinnati and set in motion a financial crisis that started in the New York banking system and gradually swept across the country, resulting in bank and railroad failures, along with the bankruptcies of 5,000 businesses both large and small. Foundries, textile mills and mines either would close or cut down on production, in either case producing massive unemployment. The big cities were the hardest hit, in particular New York, where it was estimated that between 30,000 and 100,000 people had been thrown out of work. There was a run on the 60 banks located in New York City as people rushed in to convert paper money into gold and silver. For a while the banks held firm, making payment in specie to all their depositors, but then one bank gave way and a chain reaction was set off affecting the other New York banks, which had repercussions throughout America. The credit system in the country was close to collapse, and in its wake not only were some wealthy men suddenly pauperized, but tens of thousands of people were literally without any means of staying alive other then charities. Meanwhile one farm after another in the Midwest found its mortgage foreclosed and all of the farmers' labors washed down the drain.

There were a host of reasons offered at the time and later on by historians for the collapse of the nation's credit system and foremost among them was the degree of wild speculation on land and securities and the speculation of individuals within corporations that dominated the American economy. However, there were global reasons as well: the end of the Crimean War, which had reduced the American export of wheat now that Russian wheat was available; the excessive investment in small railroad lines which never could prove to be profitable; and the reduction of British investment in this country as funds were diverted to pay for the cost of the Crimean War. All of these were valid reasons for placing a strain on the American economy, which created the Depression of 1857–58, but they didn't touch on the fundamental cause for the crunch on national credit — an overly optimistic view of the future. The Gold Rush began in 1848; by 1850 the US Treasury, for the first time in the nation's history, had a surplus of $50 million in gold. These funds were deposited in state banks throughout the country but especially in New York, the financial capital of the nation. Now able to draw upon this hard currency, the number of loans being extended by the banks increased. The slight recession of 1854 should have been a warning sign that the banks were overextending themselves, but when that downturn proved to be only a ripple on the waters, the banks no longer felt any restraints and assumed that the economy was on the right course. As a result, all too many Americans had become obsessed with the idea of instant wealth. A large dose of this rosy future for the fortunate few was to be found in speculation on farm land and on real estate in the newly created cities which had once been frontier towns. Another huge chunk of disposable income was invested in that greatest of panaceas, the railroads, which not only were uniting the country in terms of travel, but were expediting the transportation of wheat, corn and cotton from the hinterlands to the nation's cities, and from there to overseas destinations. Jefferson's yeoman farmer, cultivating his crops to take care of his own needs and that of his extended family, now was thinking like a capitalist — exporting excess crops for consumption elsewhere. While at an earlier period of American history only the Southern states had been subjected to the rise and fall of commodity prices, now the West was as well. The American economy was growing to the extent where it was now part of the European economy. As such, it was subject to the ups and downs of the economies of Great Britain and those countries on the continent. The Northern and Western U.S. economies had outgrown their period of isolation. From a society of self-sufficiency had emerged capitalism. The success of capitalism was contingent upon continued growth. Furthermore, growth involved risk. In the midst of this economic euphoria, the element of risk was dismissed. American business and especially agriculture were determined to board the gravy train before it pulled out of the station. Unfortunately, too many people boarded the train, and the irrevocable laws of supply and demand kicked in, bringing the train to a screeching halt.

The man responsible for this transformation of the American West from self-sufficiency to that of nascent capitalism was Cyrus McCormick. McCormick was to wheat and corn what Eli Whitney had been to cotton. His invention of the reaper provided the flat plains of the West with the tool for mass production. In the same way the railroad replaced the horse, the reaper replaced manual labor using the scythe. But McCormick was more than an inventor of machinery. He was the progenitor of advertising and promotion of big-ticket items — he developed the installment plan. After demonstrating the reaper to a large group of farmers, he explained that its cost was no different than the mortgage on their land. Even though his patent had expired, his Chicago factory was selling 4,000 reapers every year.

The key element in the expansion of the US during this period was credit. It provided for the expansion of the railway and telegraph lines; it was the engine for land speculation. Therein lay the weakness of the credit system in this country. If the credit system was used for speculative investments in land or real estate and the property could not then be sold, and if the bank foreclosed on the borrowers, the bank had used up some of its financial reserves and was left with unsold land still waiting to be purchased. If a bank extended credit to build a rail line or to purchase stock in a rail line, and the rail line either wasn't completed or wasn't profitable when completed, once again the bank's reserves were being depleted. On the other hand, the bank could not make a profit unless it lent out its reserves. But paper money was worthless unless it was backed by gold and silver, the only hard currencies acceptable to investors; and there was no standard regulation requiring banks to hold a specific percentage of hard currency to back the emission of paper currency.

There were 1,500 banks in America when the Panic of 1858 engulfed the nation. There were state banks, chartered by states, and private banks. What was missing, except in rare instances, was a regulatory agency that would oversee the loans issued by the banks in relation to the hard currency backing the loans. New York was the financial center of the nation, and as such it set the scale for the interest rates paid on deposits and the interest rates charged on loans. A good percentage of the country's banks kept a portion of their deposits with New York banks, either because of the interest paid on their deposits or because it was assumed that they were the most fiscally conservative. Thus, when the New York banks, one by one, closed their doors and refused to redeem any deposits, the entire banking system of the country was affected. First hit were the New England banks, but the panic soon spread to the West and the South as one bank after another closed its door to depositors. At the same time, the New York banks raised interest rates on any loans, thereby further contracting the money supply. Unlike the panic of 1837 which produced a depression that lasted for seven years, this one lasted barely a year and a half. There was a sound reason for its brief impact. Gold from California continued to flow into the Treasury. The damage done to individuals was not forgotten. The success of the Republicans in the elections of 1858 was breaking the hold the Democrats held on the working class in the large cities. Even in those days, the woes precipitated by a sharp decline in the economy and the resultant unemployment paid off at the ballot box.

As the economy began to recover, and with the fate of Kansas finally decided, the one dark cloud on the horizon was the coming election of 1860 and the possibility that the Republicans might win the presidency. To say that Buchanan had recovered from his stinging defeat over the results of the Kansas referendum would be to imply that he was a giant of man, far above the fray, rather than a petty politician who had been treated to a severe drubbing by a Congress that was ostensibly controlled by his own party. The person he had singled out for his wrath was Stephen Douglas, who had been instrumental in his being nominated by releasing his delegates at the Democratic convention of 1856. To Buchanan, Douglas represented everything that Buchanan himself lacked. Douglas was a brilliant speaker, who when he took the floor, the galleries would be crowded with an audience eagerly awaiting his words of wisdom; in contrast, when Buchanan held the floor, when he was a senator, few bothered to listen and the galleries were empty. Douglas was married to a beautiful woman whose salon rivaled that of the President's, where his niece had to perform the social functions since he had never married. But worst of all, in the President's mind, Douglas had led the opposition to the adoption of the Lecompton Constitution, thereby making a fool of him and his presidency and the laughing stock of Washington society. Nor did Buchanan hold a grudge lightly. During the 1858 campaign for Douglas's Senate seat, he not only removed from office all of the political appointees whom he granted to Douglas in Illinois, but set up a rival candidate on the Democratic line who would drain away enough Democratic votes to give Lincoln the popular majority in the election. But Buchanan's terrible, swift sword of justice would wait to be unsheathed during the nominating process for the Democratic candidacy in 1860.

Much ado was made throughout the twentieth century about the famous Lincoln–Douglas debates for the Senate seat in Illinois in 1858, and in particular Lincoln's often quoted statement: "A house divided against itself cannot stand. I believe this government cannot endure permanently half slave and half free. I do not expect the Union to be dissolved — I do not expect the house to fall — but I do expect it will cease to be divided. It will become one thing or the other. Either the opponents of slavery will arrest the further spread of it, and place it where the public mind shall rest in the belief that it is in the course of ultimate extinction, or its advocates will push it forward till it shall become alike lawful in all the states, old as well as new, North as well as South." It was Lincoln's most telling argument in his debate with Senator Douglas. While his language and metaphor were brilliant and later would be interpreted as a devastating attack on the institution of slavery, that was not his purpose. Lincoln was not speaking for posterity but to the voters in Illinois, and his words were designed to destroy Douglas's ability to represent the interests of the farmers of Illinois. To appease the Southerners, necessary to receive the Democratic nomination, he supported the revocation of the Missouri Compromise which had prevented slavery from being admitted into any territory above 36°30' latitude. Both Douglas and Lincoln were aware that climatic conditions above that parallel were inimical to the expansion of slavery from an economic point of view. The rejection of the Lecompton Constitution by an overwhelming majority of the voters in Kansas proved his point. On the other hand, the Supreme Court decision in the Dred Scott case, which altered the Negro's status to that of a piece of property, would have allowed slave holders to bring their slaves into any territory.

Douglas's answer, which has come to be known as the Freeport Doctrine, since it was delivered in a debate with Lincoln at Freeport, Illinois, was that the Supreme Court ruling on Dred Scott did not impose on the territories the laws they wrote with regard to the Constitution. Thus, if a territorial government did not provide for the enforcement of slavery, no slaveholder would dare bring his slaves into that territory. Therefore, a territorial government could exclude slavery without violating the Dred Scott decision. Douglas was attempting to walk an imaginary chalk line. Once a territory was admitted to the Union as a state, the Dred Scott decision on slavery would become the law of the state.

Nor was this the first time that Douglas had proposed that argument. On the other hand, by illustrating the weakness of the Supreme Court decision when it came to protecting slave property, it only served to further alienate him from any strong Southern support. The dilemma for Lincoln, on the other hand, was how to temper his personal belief that slavery, by itself, was immoral, with the attitude of the citizens he was addressing; while they might condemn slavery in the Southern states, they were terrified at the thought of all those Negroes, once liberated, moving north and challenging them as potential cheap labor. For Lincoln, slavery was to be contained within the slave states, and as a result, it would gradually wither away. When or how long its demise would take he did not bother to say. In reality, the Lincoln–Douglas debates proved nothing more than that both men were politicians pandering to the public for their votes. Lincoln, in order to get votes from central and southern Illinois, had to back off from his House Divided speech. Whereas in Chicago, he had promoted the concept that all men are created equal. In central Illinois, Whig territory, he announced that he was "not now or ever had been, in favor of bringing about in any way the social and political equality of the white and black races. I am not now nor ever have been in favor of making voters or jurors of Negroes, nor of qualifying them to hold office, nor to intermarry with white people; and I will say in addition to this, that there is a physical difference between the white and black races which I believe will forever forbid the two races from living together on terms of social and political equality. And inasmuch as they cannot so live, while they do remain together there must remain the position of superior and inferior and I as much as any other man am in favor of having the superior position assigned to the white race. I do not perceive that because the white man is to have the superior position that the Negro should be denied everything. I do not understand that, because if I do not want a Negro woman for a slave, that I must necessarily want her for a wife. My understanding is that I can just let her alone." In fact on many occasions Lincoln would contend that the Negro was not his equal when it came to intelligence. Throughout his campaign for the Senate seat held by Douglas, other than the debates, Lincoln was at pain to explain his attitude towards Negroes. It was a touchy subject, and like any politician — and above all, Lincoln was a master politician, even before he arrived at the White House — he had to be circumspect in order to avoid alienating potential voters.

In Massachusetts, where the soul and spirit of true Abolitionism was born, nurtured and propagated, the attitude of the state's residents towards the Irish immigrants differed very little from Lincoln's attitude towards slavery. Social prejudice was not limited to the Negro race but was extended to the influx of Germans and Irish who had arrived in the country during the 1840s and the early 1850s. The Declaration of Independence might state that all men were created equal, and for certain, the Founding Fathers did not include Negroes in that category, but as America was to evolve, and one ethnic group after another emigrated to this country from Europe, the original Anglo-Saxon majority did not cotton up to the presence of Catholics and Jews. Today, the US takes great pride in being the only melting pot in the world, but in the middle of the nineteenth century, this was far from the case. Religion was not the sole factor in excluding people; ethnicity and customs also played a role.

What was most remarkable about the Lincoln–Douglas debates was not the content of the speeches delivered by the two candidates for the Senate, which focused on the issue of slavery expanding into the new territories, but their failure to address the real problem — the distinct possibility that the issue of slavery in the territories might lead to the end of the Union. While it is true that their arguments were directed solely to the electorate of the state of Illinois, which would decide which candidate should represent the state as their senator, they were not discussing the issue of slavery for the state of Illinois but for the territories that had yet to be settled and finally admitted to the Union. The paranoia that had gripped the Southern states over the issue of slavery in the territories was nothing more than a red herring. Nor was the Southern establishment really concerned about the Abolitionist tracts sent through the mail. What disturbed the South was the growing sense of political isolation. Each state carved out of the newly settled territories brought with it two senators whose views would have nothing in common with the economic interests of the Southern states. Douglas certainly was aware of their attitude, as was Lincoln to a lesser degree. As a political party, the Whigs were on their way out. The presidential election of 1856 announced their demise. It had been the alliance with the Southern Whigs that had enabled the Southern states to control the Senate.

It was not the threat to the institution of slavery that eventually led the seven states of the Deep South to secede, the reason propagated by their politicians and subscribed to by most historians. As previously noted, slavery had been written into the Constitution and could only be banned if three fourths of the states voted for an amendment, an impossibility in 1861 with 12 slave states certain to vote against it. The real reason was political and in turn economic. The presidential election of 1856, when the only state to cast its electoral votes for the Whigs was Maryland, made it crystal clear that the Whigs were no longer a viable political party, and in the North had been replaced by the Republicans and their fringe party allies. Faced with this prospect and not yet willing to abandon the Union, Jefferson Davis, soon to be elected as President of the Confederacy and at that time a senator from Mississippi, took the floor and made the most absurd proposal imaginable. What Davis offered as a solution was that each new state admitted to the Union should have one senator who represented the interests of the North and one who represented the interests of the South, in order for the current balance in the Senate to be maintained. The South had made its position clear. Either they maintained their strength in the Senate or they would leave the Union. For the first time, a Southern politician had laid his cards on the table faces up and spoken the truth. It was not the issue of slavery that threatened the dissolution of the Union but control of the Senate. Foremost in his mind and among other major producers of cotton was the tariff. With the Republicans in control of the presidency and both Houses of Congress, in order to protect their industries they would impose exorbitant tariffs. In retaliation, Britain would raise the duties on cotton imports, cutting into the cotton producers' profitability. In 1832, the passage of the Abominable tariffs had led South Carolina to take the initial steps to secede.

CHAPTER 13. THE INEVITABLE DEMISE OF ONE NATION

While both Lincoln and Douglas were ardent believers in the Union — and as proof, once the war broke out Douglas immediately offered his full cooperation to Lincoln and accepted the role of rallying the Northern and Border Democrats to support the Union cause — yet neither candidate would allude to the topic of secession albeit both were well aware that this threat loomed over the nation. It was as though the thought of such an event occurring was too horrendous to imagine or face. Yet, in all his debates with Lincoln, except for implying that Lincoln was a Black Republican, an Abolitionist, a lover of Negroes, Douglas never touched on what was moving the Southern establishment in the direction of secession. It was as though the subject of the tariff was too contentious for open debate

As for Lincoln, in his now famous "A House Divided Cannot Stand" speech, by even the most generous interpretation, he certainly sent a signal to the South that slavery had to be uprooted throughout the country. Since slavery only existed in the Southern states, this only could be taken as a threat to their institution. Lincoln would spend the rest of the campaign in an effort to disclaim that statement by reiterating he was not referring to the South, but to the territories, but since slavery only existed in the Southern states the damage had been done. Why Lincoln would go out of his way to pacify the South when he was running for the Senate in Illinois where slavery was non-existent brings up the question of Lincoln's motive. In 1858 both men were actively running for the presidency. To understand why to equate Lincoln with Douglas as presidential candidates in 1860 it is necessary to go back to 1854 and even earlier to follow the careers of these two men. The one trait common to both Lincoln and Douglas was that the two of them were political animals. A political animal is a man or a woman whose fundamental ambition in life is to use the political process in order to gain power, and once having attained that power, use it to impose, as much as possible, his or her point of view upon society as a whole. Whether his or her point of view has a moral base to it is immaterial. The important thing is to have one's hand on the lever of power. Moreover, the closer the individual comes to reaching that goal, the greater the necessity to concentrate on the means in order to attain the end. The action taken by Douglas, as Chairman of the Senate Committee on Territories, in pushing through the adoption of the Nebraska Act, which in turn led to the abrogation of the Missouri Compromise that had limited slavery to 36°30' latitude, was a prime example of his efforts to appease the South. As the senator from Illinois, Douglas was more than aware that the climatic conditions in Kansas were such as to prohibit the mass production of cotton or tobacco, the profitable commodities of the South. Given that fact, there was no possibility of any mass Southern migration to the new territory even with the lifting of the Missouri Compromise, which he hoped would pacify the South without alienating the North. Likewise, when Lincoln informed Judge David Davis, his campaign manager in the 1860 campaign for the Republican nomination for the presidency, not to commit him to any deals in order for him to receive the nomination, Lincoln was well aware that without satisfying the demands of the Republican leaders in the individual states, whose support he would need in order to attain the nomination, that Davis would disregard his instructions and commit Lincoln despite his protestations, to commitments which he would have to honor. Lincoln was no more naive about politics than Douglas. In attempting to assess Lincoln and Douglas, outside of their political ambitions, there were certain similarities and certain differences. While both of them practiced law, neither one of them was very learned on the subject, their legal educations having been deficient. As a result, both gravitated to state politics early on in their careers. Both had moved to Illinois seeking their fortune. Lincoln arrived by way of Kentucky and Indiana; Douglas from Vermont and upstate New York. Lincoln arrived totally without means; Douglas, although poor when he arrived, could call upon his family to send him money. Both considered themselves to be westerners, and as such, until late in life were indifferent in their dress. Lincoln was physically healthy but suffered from deep depressions. Douglas, although stocky in build, was continually sick throughout his career, often being obliged to be absent for three months in order to recuperate. Both men married women from slave-owning families. The major differences between the two men were equally stark, in addition to Lincoln being unusually tall and Douglas rather short. Douglas had married the daughter of a wealthy planter from North Carolina who had given the married couple as a dowry a huge plantation in Mississippi with 100 slaves, and while he rejected the idea of personally operating this generous grant, he did draw an income of 20 percent of the profits from the sales of cotton, corn and some sugar cane. Lincoln enjoyed nothing of the sort. Douglas had been educated and exposed to Latin and Greek; Lincoln was self educated. Douglas was a high liver and a major speculator in lands, garnering huge profits from his acquisitions. If Lincoln did dabble in speculation, it was on a small scale. Douglas was a heavy drinker; Lincoln abstemious. Lincoln had been a volunteer in the Army during the Black Hawk War and had been elected Captain of his company. Although he and his company never saw active duty, he had a military record. Douglas had never served or volunteered.

Douglas rose rapidly in the political ranks of the Democratic party, and despite his young age, had his sights set on the Senate before he had even reached the minimum age of 30, a requisite in order to sit in that body. Lincoln after three terms in the state legislature was elected to Congress for one term on the basis of an agreement with his friend Edward D. Baker and John Hardin. Since there was only one safe seat for a Whig in Illinois, the decision was made that each of them would have a turn at being a Congressman. Lincoln's turn came third, after those of Baker and Hardin, and it was only with difficulty that he convinced the other two to honor the agreement. As was the case with the other previous holders of the one Whig seat from Illinois, Lincoln got bitten by the bug of being part of the national government, from which all decisions affecting the nation were decided and from which all appointive offices in the individual states flowed. As a good Whig, he opposed the Mexican War, lobbied for internal improvements and when his term was over campaigned extensively for the Whig candidate for president, Zachary Taylor, in the hope of getting a political payoff. For his efforts, Lincoln expected to be appointed to the post of Land Office Commissioner, which provided an excellent salary and would obviate the necessity of traveling continually to maintain a law practice. Instead he was offered the governorship of the Oregon territory which his wife vetoed.

For Lincoln, it was back to his law practice with his partner William Herndon. He had a family to support and that meant being on the road most of the year. In a sense, his travels from one district to another, while difficult and arduous, would pay off one day in the future. At the same time, Douglas was serving three terms in Congress before being elected senator. Lincoln's idol was Henry Clay, one of the founders of the Whig party, the great senator from Kentucky, who had been instrumental in establishing the Missouri Compromise and the Compromise of 1830 with Calhoun, which introduced a gradual reduction in the tariffs and which put an end to South Carolina's threat of secession. Clay had also been the author of the Compromise of 1850 and when it failed to pass as one measure, as previously noted, it was Douglas who picked up the ball and had the Compromise passed by one bill at a time. Douglas's idol was Andrew Jackson, and he supported his policies with the same fervor he had given to picking up the pieces of Clay's 1850 Compromise and ramming it through Congress. Lincoln in his speeches often made his point through the use of humor and parables. Douglas, on the other hand, could hold the Senate spellbound by the intensity of his arguments and by the timber of his voice. When the debates and the campaign were over, and Lincoln had lost in the legislature even while winning the popular vote, Lincoln's first step was to inform Lyman Trumbull, ostensibly a Democrat, but who differed with Douglas on the Nebraska Act, that he would not challenge him for his Senate seat in 1860. Instead, Lincoln was determined to run for the Republican nomination for president in 1860. Given his political credentials, a one-term congressman from Illinois, who had been defeated twice in a run for the Senate, it would appear to be the height of chutzpa for a relative unknown to be contemplating such a leap in political fortunes, and to expect this nascent political party to take his candidacy seriously. Ordinarily, it was assumed that a candidate for the office of the presidency, in either the Democrat or Whig parties, would not be treated seriously as a potential candidate if he did not bring to the table in his background either one or more examples of having served as a governor, a senator, the Speaker of the House or at least a Cabinet member. The trump card that Lincoln's supporters brought to the Republican convention was the history of his debates with Douglas, the leading senator in that chamber, the expected nominee for the Democrats and the man Lincoln had defeated in the popular vote.

The coverage of the Lincoln–Douglas debates was not limited to the newspapers in that state. So great was the reputation of Douglas and so crucial the direction the country would take with regard to the free territories, that the debates were carried in newspapers throughout the country. And since Douglas had agreed to seven debates, the coverage was that more widespread. Lincoln had the taste of blood in his mouth. He had met the grandest poobah in the nation on a one-to-one basis, and not only had he more than held his own, he had beaten him in the popular vote. Despite Lincoln's amazing triumph on the stump, he still remained largely a local hero. What he needed for a successful run for the Republican nomination was to gain national publicity; the door to that was unexpectedly opened by an invitation to address the Republicans in New York City, the home state of the Republican front runner, former Governor William Seward and now one of its two senators. New York was the largest state in the Union, and naturally, had the largest number of electoral votes. In the 1856 presidential campaign, the relatively unknown presidential candidate, James Fremont, had captured them. New York also was a place where political animosities ran high, whether the candidate was a Democrat or a Republican. While Seward appeared to have the Republican nomination sewed up, at least as far as New York's favorite son was concerned, he still had his enemies; among the most influential were William Cullen Bryant, the editor of the *Evening Post*, and Horace Greeley, editor of the *Tribune*. Both men were working with James Briggs, the eastern campaign manager for Salomon Chase, the fiery abolitionist from Ohio, who would be that state's favorite son. Their goal was simple: to stop Seward from gaining the Republican nomination on an early vote. Seward had a big lead. He not only was strong in New York but had a large following in New England, including the important state of Massachusetts, as well as the northwestern states of Michigan, Minnesota and Wisconsin. By inviting Lincoln, the more than likely favorite son for the state of Illinois, to address the Young Men's Republican Union, Seward's foes hoped that Lincoln might serve as a chink in the seemingly impregnable armor of Seward. Originally scheduled for Henry Ward Beecher's church in Brooklyn, the event was moved to the Cooper Institute in Manhattan where it could acquire far more publicity. This was the break Lincoln needed. For the first time he would be personally exposed to the Republican establishment in the key state of New York. Trying to make the most of this unexpected invitation, Lincoln journeyed first to Philadelphia in the hope of meeting with Simon Cameron, Pennsylvania's favorite son, but he failed to make a connection. Lincoln's speech in New York City advanced his moderate attitude towards slavery. He went so far as to condemn John Brown's raid on Harper's Ferry in his effort to create an insurrection by the slaves in Virginia.

Having portrayed himself as a moderate Republican who had no intention of disturbing slavery where it already existed, Lincoln moved on to New England, ostensibly to visit his son, Robert, a student at Exeter, New Hampshire, but stopping along the way in Connecticut and Rhode Island. These three states were not aligned with the candidacy of William Seward. Given the favorable reception Lincoln had received in New York and the contacts he had made in Connecticut and Rhode Island, he no longer perceived himself as a dark horse but as a moderate second choice to Seward. Nor was he alone in sensing his importance to the Republican Party. One of Senator Simon Cameron's aides had inquired what Lincoln's attitude would be towards a Cameron–Lincoln ticket. Lincoln, ever the deft politician, didn't commit himself further than to say that if the Republican convention so wished it, he would be available. Four states seemed to hold the key to a Republican victory in 1860: Pennsylvania, Illinois, Indiana and New Jersey. If they had gone Republican in 1856, Fremont would have been elected president without a single vote from the South. The Electoral College was the key to Republican strategy. By 1860, given the enormous growth in the population of the North and the West, the electoral votes from the Southern states no longer were required to be elected. Next to New York, Pennsylvania had the largest number of electoral votes required for victory. It also was the major industrial state in the Union; thus, the overriding issue as far as its voters were concerned was the tariff. Only a high tariff could keep out British imports. As a disciple of Henry Clay, Lincoln had campaigned vigorously for protective tariffs for industry. He may have been a resident of Indiana for 14 years, but his best hope for winning that state was the basic antagonism between Indiana's Democratic senator, Jesse Bright, and Stephen Douglas. New Jersey was not quite as pivotal as the other three since Minnesota now had been added to the Union in 1858, and Oregon in 1859, and it was assumed that both of these states would wind up in the Republican column. While Lincoln took an active interest in gaining the presidential nomination of the Republican party, once he had garnered the Illinois party's support as its favorite son, the lining up of delegates from other states was left entirely in the hands of Norman Judd, the head of the Republicans in that state, and David Davis, his friend for years and a Justice on the Eighth Judicial circuit. There was no doubt in terms of experience and position that Seward was the leading candidate for the party. With the backing of Thurlow Weed and Tammany Hall, and taking into consideration New York's 35 electoral votes, he should have been the natural leader of this young party. Despite his seeming impregnability, the Republican Party was not a monolith, which is why Lincoln was invited to speak at Cooper Institute. What stood in Seward's way were the candidacies of other favorite sons. There was Chase in Ohio, Cameron in Pennsylvania, Edward Bates in Missouri and Caleb Smith in Indiana. Each of them carried a certain amount of negative baggage. Chase was even more radical than Seward in his opposition to slavery; Bates had backed Millard Fillmore and the Know-Nothing party in 1856, which made his candidacy inimical to the foreign born, especially the Germans; Cameron had a seedy reputation for his financial dealings, and Smith aroused no enthusiasm among the delegates. But the most important work was in the hands of Judge Davis and Norman Judd. They promised Cameron, in the important state of Pennsylvania, a Cabinet post and did the same for Caleb Smith in Indiana. On the first ballot, Seward backed by New England and the upper Midwestern states of Wisconsin, Michigan and Minnesota as well as New York, had a commanding lead over Lincoln with 173 1/2 votes to Lincoln's 102, with 233 votes needed to obtain a majority of the 465 delegates. On the second ballot Seward's lead had increased to 184 1/2 but Lincoln with the addition of Pennsylvania and Indiana now stood at 181. At this moment in time there was little doubt who would be the final candidate. The impetus was all on the side of Lincoln, and on the third ballot Lincoln's bandwagon carried the day when it was announced that Lincoln now had 354 of the 465, or more than 100 more votes than necessary for the nomination. New York then made his nomination unanimous, and the news went over the wire service, reaching Lincoln patiently waiting in Springfield. The one-term Congressman, the relative unknown, had been selected to carry the Republican banner in the forthcoming election.

James Buchanan was a man of so many contradictions that it is impossible to understand what he had in mind when as titular head of the Democrats he selected Charleston, South Carolina as the site for the Democratic convention. A staunch believer in the Union, which he would support even before hostilities began, he had chosen the one city in the South whose citizens openly declared their intention to secede if a Republican was elected president. While his intent was to prevent Douglas from obtaining the nomination, he ignored the more than likely possibility that it would divide the Democrats into Northern and Southern wings and insure the election of a Republican. Douglas understood that his motive was to prevent him from getting the nomination, and when the party split over the platform, he offered to withdraw in favor of Alexander Stephens, a moderate southerner. His backers concerned with their reelection knew it would ensure the election of Lincoln, and therefore their defeat. Buchanan never gave any thought to that possibility because he assumed he understood the mind of the South. To him there was no rationale for the Southern states to secede. Even Jefferson Davis had openly stated that climatic conditions obviated the expansion of slavery into the northern territories. Kansas, however, was not what the southerners had in mind. Their interest was California, and if the Democratic platform did not support slavery in the territories or states, they were prepared to secede. What Buchanan never grasped was that the firebrands in the states of the Deep South wanted to secede and were looking for an excuse to remove their states from the Union. To them cotton was King, and Britain's, France's and New England's mills were dependent upon them for the magic fiber. Once free from the Union, the issue of tariffs would become a moot point. The Northern banks were not about to drop them as customers since they made money from the loans they extended. Moreover, British banks could replace them if necessary. The morality of slavery no longer would be an issue since slavery was taken for granted. When the Northern delegates rejected the plank in the platform that called for slavery in all the states or territories, with or without majority approval, the delegates from the states in the Deep South left the hall and decided to set up their own convention. But not all of the delegates from these states left. A minority from the seceding states still remained, along with all the delegates from Virginia, North Carolina, Tennessee and Kentucky.

Caleb Cushing, a loyal Buchanan man who had been named chairman of the convention and who would later support the Union, initiated two rulings that ensured the success of the departing delegates. First, he ruled that those delegates from the departing states who had remained in the hall could not vote on the presidential nomination because they did not constitute a majority for those states. Next, given the departure of the delegates, he decided that instead of a two-thirds rule for nominating a president a five-sixths majority now would be required. Since the delegates from four Southern states were still in the hall, it was impossible for Douglas to win the nomination. Therefore, the decision was made to adjourn and a new convention was called to convene in Baltimore. The departing delegates would hold a separate convention in Richmond, Virginia.

Those in the North who continued to believe that the states of the Deep South were not intent on leaving the Union for the aforementioned economic reasons, soon came to understand their rationale, once the November election results were counted. Despite the fact that Lincoln won a majority in the Electoral College, in the congressional elections, the Democratic Party would have had a majority in both the House and the Senate if the South had remained in the Union. Since the election results were known November 6, and South Carolina did not secede until December 6, South Carolina and the other states that followed its example were obviously well aware that the new Republican administration would be hamstrung about passing any legislation that would be inimical to the basic interests of the South, including enacting high tariff legislation, which was part and parcel of the Republican platform and which the South vehemently opposed. Nor did the election portend that the Republicans would be able to find party regulars in the South upon whom to bestow the role of Postmasters and thereby flood the South with Abolitionist literature. In other words, the decision to secede had nothing to do with the election. No matter what the election results, the states of the Deep South had decided that their future lay in their independence. And, no matter the Dred Scott decision, which determined that the Negro was property and as such could be transported anywhere, and that previous state laws banning slavery were unconstitutional. It was the Constitution that stated that the decisions of the US Supreme Court superseded state laws when they conflicted with the laws of the Constitution. Equally ironic, the court's decision violated the same Constitution that allowed the slave states to classify their Negroes as three fifths of a white citizen. In the heated atmosphere that marked the election of 1860, the states of the Deep South had no interest in the law of the land. Their bags already were packed, and it was only a question of when they were going to leave the Union.

Following the decision by the radical Southerners to vacate the convention hall in Charleston and hold their own convention in Richmond, they proceeded to nominate John Breckinridge of Kentucky, Buchanan's vice president, as their standard bearer. Breckinridge was an odd choice for the radical firebrands. He had not supported Buchanan on the Lecompton Constitution; he had endorsed Douglas in an 1858 letter, and when nominated, he denied that a Lincoln victory justified the doctrine of secession. Even more peculiar was the decision by the old-line Whigs to form a third party. Led by John Crittenden of Kentucky, along with John Bell of Tennessee, Edward Everett and Amos Lawrence of Massachusetts and John Rives of Virginia, they held a convention in Baltimore and nominated Bell for the presidency and Everett for the vice presidency. Calling the new party, the Constitutional Union, their platform was reduced to the platitude of calling for sectional peace. To Buchanan, the emergence of a third party seemed to be a perfect addition to his long-range plan which would throw the results of the election into the House of Representatives. The result of this new party was that it now pitted three parties against the Republicans. The Northern Democrats led by Douglas; the Border States who would support the Whig candidate, John Bell; and the Deep South with Breckinridge heading the ticket. Buchanan, more determined than ever to destroy Douglas, not only announced his support of Breckinridge for the presidency but enlisted the support of former President Pierce of New Hampshire and defeated presidential candidate Lewis Cass of Michigan. Furthermore, to prove that the Democratic Party in the North was behind Buchanan's candidate, he enlisted the support of eight Democratic senators and four fifths of the Democratic representatives in the House. Buchanan was on a suicide mission, and he was using all the power and prestige of the administration to lead the party over the cliff.

The early congressional results from Maine seemed to presage a major Republican victory in the North. It was at this moment that Jefferson Davis, of all people, the future president of the Confederacy, once again would step forth as the great compromiser. What Davis suggested to Bell, Douglas and Breckinridge was that all three candidates should resign in favor of Horatio Seymour of New York and actively campaign for his election to the presidency. Both Bell and Breckinridge agreed but Douglas refused, contending that a watered down candidate only would ensure the election of Lincoln. What never was addressed in the proposal of Davis was the platform that the new candidate would support in relation to slavery in the territories. What Davis failed to comprehend was that the forthcoming presidential election would be decided by the electoral vote in the Northern and Western states; even if the South joined with the Border States, without making a serious dent in the Northern and Western electoral vote, the election would go to Lincoln. Horatio Seymour, as a compromise candidate, now supported by the South, would stand no chance. Douglas was the only man capable of rallying these voters to the Democratic column. As the election date drew closer, the major financial interests in the North began to panic. The large Southern planters were indebted to the Northern banks and the large textile mills for upwards of $200 million. If the South should secede upon the election of Lincoln, what would happen to the monies owed them? Given the Northern interests' power in terms of financing the Democratic Party, they attempted to cobble together the electoral delegates from the three parties competing against Lincoln to consolidate their votes for one candidate in a desperate effort to stop Lincoln and throw the election into the House of Representatives. It proved to be a vain effort on their part. The Republican tide was too strong to be stopped. Meanwhile Douglas, whether consciously or unconsciously, realizing that Lincoln would be elected, made a last ditch effort to prevent the Southerners in the Deep South and the Border States from seceding from the Union in the event of Lincoln being elected. Traveling with his second wife and his secretary, he attracted reasonably large audiences since he was well known and admired in the South. His message was clear. The mere election of a Republican president did not of itself call for secession. The Union was the strength of this nation, and to dissolve it would constitute a repudiation of everything the Founding Fathers had created. He referred to Andrew Jackson, the patron saint of the Democratic Party, reminding his audiences that when South Carolina had attempted nullification in 1832, Jackson had succeeded in keeping the state in the Union. All of Douglas' speeches were to no avail. The establishments in the deep Southern states had made the decision that the future of the South lay in secession. While Douglas toured the country speaking throughout New England, the Mid-Atlantic and the Western and Border States as well as the Deep South, Lincoln remained silent. When the Homestead Act, a basic plank of the Republican Party, passed Congress, Buchanan vetoed it. Once again he had cut the rug from under the Democratic Party in its efforts to gain votes in the West. On November 6, the nation went to the polls. The results came in as expected. Lincoln won a majority of the electoral votes, with a total of 180. Breckinridge, the candidate of the South, was second with 72; John Bell of the Constitutional Union party was third with 39 votes, capturing the ballots of the Border States; Douglas was a distant fourth, winning only Missouri and a few electoral votes from New Jersey under the fusion ticket. However, in terms of the popular vote, Lincoln garnered only 40 percent. His total was 1,865,908, compared to that of Douglas at 1,380,202, Breckinridge at 848,019 and Bell at 590,901.

The internecine warfare between the two elements of the Democratic Party had resulted in the loss of California and Oregon, normally Democratic states. In New York, the last minute effort by the financial community to create a fusion ticket between the backers of Buchanan and Douglas was too late. While Douglas amassed 46 percent of the vote in that state, it was not enough. In Pennsylvania, Buchanan had used all the power of his administration to inflict a major defeat on Douglas. On the other hand, while Breckinridge carried 11 of the 13 slave states, he won a majority in only seven of them. The combined vote of Douglas and Bell in that region far exceeded that of Breckinridge. He received only 570,000 votes while the combined ballots of Douglas and Bell in the slave states was 705,000. Even in those states that were the first to secede, the combined vote of Bell and Douglas was 48 percent, with the exception of South Carolina where the population didn't have the ballot, the electors being appointed by the legislature. Finally, as previously noted, the Republicans failed to capture a majority in either the Senate or the House. Lincoln and the Republicans might have won the presidency, but without control of either the House or the Senate, it would be difficult to legislate against Southern interests. Add to this that the Supreme Court still would be dominated by the Southerners, and any legislation coming under its review would be subject to critical scrutiny. Lincoln's metaphor that a house divided could not stand had come to fruition, not over any particular policy that his administration would attempt to enact but because the establishments in the states of the Deep South had decided to cut the umbilical cord that bound them to the Union.

While the threat of secession if Lincoln was elected had long been enunciated by the states of the Deep South, it wasn't until six weeks after the election that South Carolina formally removed itself from the Union by an act of its legislature. It would not be until January 1861 that the other states would follow, with Texas being the last one before Fort Sumter was attacked to approve secession in February. In between the election and Lincoln's inaugural, the only major stance by President Buchanan in the light of this impending disaster was his last State of the Union message to both houses of Congress, and in effect to the nation. Buchanan was the last man in this country who might have brought the two sides together. He was a Unionist who was pro Southern. He had labored personally to destroy the unity of the Democrats in order to have his vengeance on Douglas. Nor did he comprehend the rationale for secession which lay behind all the flamboyant rhetoric of the seceding states. Finally, being obtuse, he counseled restraint on his Southern friends by advising them to wait until Lincoln had done something that would warrant their leaving the Union. The overt cause for the war, which no one wanted or expected, was the attack on Fort Sumter, a federal fort situated on a piece of rock in Charleston harbor. But the taking of this fort, which did not surrender until April 14, was only a symbol of the birth of the Confederacy, which had been in existence for several months. The question, still unresolved when the fort capitulated, was whether or not the seven states that comprised the new government had the right to secede under the Constitution. The major fallacy used by the Unionists against the right of any state to secede was that the Constitution had been ratified by the American people and not by the states. But, for the Constitution to have been ratified by the electorate would have required a referendum. The facts belie that assertion. Had the proponents of the Constitution called for a referendum by the voting electorate of the 12 states that originally ratified the document, it never would have been approved. Americans in 1787 were oriented towards their individual states, not towards a national government. On the other hand, the position taken by the seven states of the Deep South was just as specious. Once the legislatures of these states had ratified the Constitution, there was no clause in that document that allowed for secession. There was nothing unconstitutional in the election of Lincoln. He had won the necessary majority of the electoral votes.

The event leading up to the surrender of Fort Sumter, not only includes the final days of the Buchanan administration but the early weeks of the Lincoln administration when the fate of the fort was anyone's guess. If the war that followed hadn't been so tragic, that piece of history would have made a wonderful farce.

Neither the leadership of the Confederacy nor the Lincoln administration sought war until the symbol of Fort Sumter took on such monumental proportions that there was no alternative. The fort was federal property, but so too were the Custom House and the Post Office, which already had been appropriated by the state of South Carolina with no notice taken by either the Buchanan or the Lincoln administrations. Moreover, once the other six states joined South Carolina, all the federal property within their states, including federal fortifications, now were claimed to be the property of the Confederate government. Fort Sumter and Fort Pickens, off the west coast of Florida, were the only federal properties still in the possession of the federal government. No effort had been made by President Buchanan to protest these seizures. Suppose President-elect Lincoln had abandoned Fort Sumter — which was the opinion voiced by his entire Cabinet, with the exception of Montgomery Blair, who threatened to resign unless the fort was defended — and Lincoln was faced with the fact that a new nation existed side by side with the old Union: would he have had the rationale to launch a preemptive war? At that moment in time, the Confederacy consisted solely of the seven states of the Deep South with its capital in Montgomery, Alabama. There was no possible way of attacking them by land without the approval of those states that bordered those of the Confederacy. Furthermore, an act of war only could be approved by Congress, and while there was no longer a Democratic majority in either the House or Senate, following the organization of the new nation and the resignations of its delegates from Congress, it is highly doubtful that a vote could have been passed since it might have induced the Border States to join the Confederacy.

Given these circumstances, what could the Lincoln administration have done, and what contingency plans had been formulated? The terrible answer is nothing. To blockade the Southern ports would be an act of war requiring a two-thirds approval of Congress, and worse yet, might bring all the Border States plus North Carolina into the Confederacy. If, on the other hand, the remaining states in the Union reluctantly accepted the act of secession, then the seceding states, in all likelihood, would have gained recognition by their major European customers, Great Britain and France, and would have become a viable nation. In other words, Fort Sumter was the last and only opportunity Lincoln had to initiate a legitimate war since it was the last piece of contested property still held by the Union. At that time, he was naïve enough to believe that the Border States, especially Virginia, never would abandon the Union that their former sons had given so much of their lives to create. The Lincoln administration was between a rock and a hard place. If it did nothing, the secession of the seven Southern states would succeed. If it precipitated a conflict, it might lose all the Border States to the Confederacy and find itself to be a country without a national capital. It was a venture fraught with risk. All six slave states had large Negro populations — Virginia, 549,000,

Tennessee, 283,000, Kentucky, 236,000, Maryland, 171,000, Missouri, 119,000, Arkansas, 111,000 and North Carolina, 362,000. All of these states had a vested interest in perpetuating slavery. But the Lincoln administration had no alternative. It assumed that given the advantages that the North had in terms of manpower and wealth, the conflict would be short. Of more immediate concern was Fort Sumter, which the government of South Carolina demanded should be evacuated since it lay within the boundaries of its territory. In reality there were a number of forts within Charleston harbor. In addition to Sumter, there were Fort Moultrie, Castle Pinckney and Fort Johnson. The latter had been abandoned; Castle Pinckney was guarded by one sergeant; Fort Moultrie, where the troops were stationed, not only was understaffed but was situated among a group of summer cottages, and was so run down that the sand had piled up against it sides, making it almost impossible to aim at a target. Finally, there was Sumter, which was not yet a viable fortress and was being renovated by the federal government. It was a touch of irony: a fort still under construction would become the *cause célèbre* for the War Between the States. If ever there was a sense of black humor exposing the stupidity of the human race, this had to be the apex of asininity. The completion of the fortifications was being paid for by the federal government but the fulfillment of the contract to complete the fort was assigned to the state of South Carolina. To put the subject matter in the simplest terms, at any moment in time the governor of South Carolina could have stopped all work on the fort, and it would have been useless. This was a federal fort paid for by federal dollars, and even though South Carolina had seceded from the Union and demanded surrender of the fort, the workforce completing its fortifications were dispatched every day to fulfill the contract that had been signed by the federal government. Placed in perspective, with the possibility of a potential war looming, it was in the interest of the state of South Carolina to have the federal government pay for its renovations. The War Department, having allocated the funds for Sumter's renovations, insisted that the work be completed. As far as Governor Francis W. Pickens of South Carolina was concerned, once having initiated the project it was up to the government to fulfill its obligation.

Weeks before December 24, when the South Carolina legislature officially seceded from the government of the US and declared itself to be a separate nation, it sent commissioners to Washington to deal with President Buchanan over the status of the forts in the Charleston harbor. Their goal was to have the President surrender the forts in Charleston harbor, which they considered to be a threat to their state. Buchanan informed them that he had no authority to turn over the forts to South Carolina and that his oath of office precluded him from taking any such action; that the matter at hand would have to be taken up by Congress. The delegates from South Carolina then stated that they would take no action against the forts provided that there would be no change in the current disposition of US forces within the forts and that no attempt would be made to reinforce them.

Following the meeting with the delegates from South Carolina, in early December Secretary of War John B. Floyd sent a special emissary, Don Carlos Buell, to visit with US Army Major Robert Anderson in command of Fort Moultrie with oral instructions. Whether Buell accurately interpreted the oral instructions given him by the Secretary of War or not, he left the distinct impression with Anderson that if attacked he was to defend himself, and if he believed that an attack was imminent, he had the option of choosing whichever fort would best serve his means. What Buell had either stated or implied was that it was up to Anderson's discretion as to which fort — Moultrie or Sumter — would best serve his defense. To Anderson, the choice was obvious. At Moultrie, with his undermanned garrison located on a sand bar, he had no chance of defending himself, whereas at Sumter, built on a rock in the harbor, where the guns could point in all directions, his force would be relatively secure. Thus, in the middle of the night, despite the Southern patrol boats cruising in the waters of the harbor, he skillfully and luckily managed to transfer the entire garrison at Moultrie over to the almost completed Sumter. When Governor Pickens of South Carolina and his delegates learned what had occurred, they believed that Buchanan had gone back on his word and purposely deceived him.

The man sent to confront the President was Senator Jefferson Davis, of Mississippi, who related that Major Anderson not only had disobeyed the President but in leaving Fort Moultrie had spiked the guns and burned the gun emplacements and destroyed the flag pole. The President, having no knowledge of what had taken place, was visibly upset. South Carolina, Davis continued, would obviously seize Fort Moultrie and Castle Pinckney and only the word from Buchanan ordering Anderson to restore the status quo would prevent South Carolina from attacking Sumter and seizing the other forts. Buchanan informed the senator that he would take no action until he had conferred with his Cabinet. But the Cabinet had changed. His good friend Howell Cobb of Georgia had resigned; his attorney general also had resigned and had been replaced by Edward M. Stanton, an Ohio lawyer.

During all this time, Lieutenant General Winfield Scott, the commander of the US Army, had remained relatively silent. Although born in Virginia, he was an out-and-out Unionist and had been the Whig candidate for the presidency in 1852. Laughed at and mocked with the sobriquet of "Old Fuss and Feathers," he may have made a lousy politician but he was the best general this country had ever produced and had risen in the ranks by means of merit rather than political favoritism. He had performed brilliantly along the Canadian border during the War of 1812, and it was he who had led the armed forces that brought the Mexican War to a successful conclusion. Despite his social affectations he was the only man in the country with a clear vision of what had to be done militarily. He had warned Buchanan early on, that the US forts were undermanned and prone to easy capture if the South decided to secede. The problem, of course, was that Congress saw no need to spend any more funds on an Army of now 16,000 men and officers, whose main role was to protect settlers and voyagers in the Indian country. Instead of increasing appropriations for the military, Congress was cutting back on them. Now the six-foot five-inch general, so obese that he had to be lifted onto his horse, wrote to Buchanan on two separate occasions that it was necessary to reinforce Sumter not only with food and munitions but with armed personnel as well. He was prepared to send reinforcements from New York to supplement the forces already stationed at Fort Sumter. But first Buchanan had to deal with the plaints of senator Davis and the commissioners from the nation-state of South Carolina, which the United States had yet to recognize.

There were a number of factors that finally forced Buchanan to change his position with the Carolina delegates. First was the discovery of the letter of instructions that Buell had deposited in the war office box, confirming the actions taken by Major Anderson; second was the realization that South Carolina had been part of the Union when Buchanan had supposedly agreed to respect the status quo in the Charleston harbor and now it was no longer a part of the United States; third was the total arrogance of the representatives from South Carolina who appeared to be charging him with dishonorable conduct; finally was the language of his Attorney General, Edward Stanton, who went so far as to charge him with being a worse traitor than Benedict Arnold. The decision was made. Buchanan no longer would deal with the commissioners from South Carolina, and Fort Sumter would be held. With John Floyd having resigned his post as Secretary of War, owing to his being implicated in a scandal, and with a Northerner as his replacement, the attitude of the Buchanan administration towards appeasing the South, now that it had seceded from the Union, took a 180 degree turn. The administration had finally decided to reinforce Major Anderson at Fort Sumter with men and supplies. The warship Brooklyn was then outfitted with all the necessities, and 200 armed men from Fort Monroe were piped aboard with supplies for 90 days. And then, just as this wooden steamship was about to depart, the President put a hold on it for three days. Why? Although, personally, he no longer would treat with the commissioners, perhaps they might have something to say to him indirectly. Throughout his four years in office, Buchanan had leaned over backward to curry favor with the Southern establishment, and all his efforts had proved to be in vain. Because of his close relationships, he also knew their mentality. To Governor Pickens and the hot-headed Carolinians, a relief ship with men and supplies meant that the US government intended to hold onto the fort. Buchanan did not want to bear the onus of having precipitated a war.

So the three days passed, and when he heard nothing from the commissioners, the Brooklyn was scheduled to depart when General Scott stepped into the picture. Since the ship was departing from Hampton Roads, Virginia, word certainly would be passed to the authorities in Charleston that a relief ship was on its way. Perhaps it would be better to send a merchant ship from New York, whose ordinary run was from New York to New Orleans. The government would charter the boat, and this time 200 soldiers from Governor's Island would be sent as reinforcements. The idea that this could be kept a secret was as preposterous as the withdrawing of the warship Brooklyn. As if to compound this change of orders, a message now was received by the War Department from Major Anderson, reporting that at this time he required no reinforcements. What was a serious matter had degenerated into a charade. The left hand and the right hand were not communicating. To complete this farce, every day workmen from Charleston were being ferried out to the fort to complete its fortifications. The rationale of Governor Pickens was that South Carolina was saving money by having the federal government pay for the labor and material. At the same time, he continued to demand that the fort either be evacuated or surrender since it represented a threat to South Carolina's existence as an independent nation. The Buchanan administration, on the other hand, insisted that the fort was federal property, having been erected and paid for by the citizens of the United States, and therefore outside the jurisdiction of the state. Moreover, the United States had not recognized the independence of South Carolina, and there had been no exchange of ministers, as there were with other countries. While the ambivalent attitude of Buchanan is explicable, given the debt he felt he owed the South, that of Scott remains a mystery. Why would he dispatch the Star of the West, a merchant ship designed to carry only freight and passengers between New York and New Orleans, in place of an armed warship capable of defending itself? Why issue the orders to slip surreptitiously into the Charleston harbor in the middle of the night, deposit the supplies and military contingents, and then slip out of sight as though it had never been on a mission? If the Buchanan administration, representing the federal authority, continued to take the stand that Fort Sumter was federal property and at the same time refused to recognize the independence of South Carolina, why this subterfuge? Finally, why did Major Anderson send the telegram stating that he did not need reinforcements when, during the bombardment of Fort Sumter several months later, he would complain that he did not have sufficient personnel to man all of his guns?

The farce had only begun. New players would be added to the plot in order to keep the audience laughing. If its denouement hadn't been so tragic, people would have left the theater wondering how the author could have come up with such black humor. Once Major Anderson's telegram had been routed to General Scott with the information that he required no reinforcements, Scott ordered the warship Brooklyn to intercept the Star of the West and turn it back from its mission. Behind all of these orders and counter-orders was the hope that some miracle would intercede that would prevent the other states in the Deep South from seceding and establishing a Southern confederacy. The warship Brooklyn did not arrive in time to intercept the Star of the West. The merchant ship gingerly made its way into the harbor, following its instructions, and prior to reaching its destination, Fort Sumter, was discovered by the Carolinians who now occupied Fort Moultrie and opened fire on the ship. Immediately, upon hearing the shelling, which first fell far from its mark, Major Anderson and his officers and men rushed to their stations to man their guns. The rockets sent up by the Carolinian gunners highlighted the ship, and the Captain immediately raised the American flag. A shot from the enemy crossed the bow of the ship as a warning shot. If the ship advanced any further, it would come under direct fire from Fort Moultrie. Before proceeding any further up the harbor, the Captain of the Star of the West waited for the return fire from the far larger guns on Fort Sumter to clear his path. The cannons on the fort were loaded, the lanyards were ready to be pulled, and in a minute, the far superior fire from the fort's guns would have destroyed whatever artillery was on the opposite shore. The men and officers were literally begging Major Anderson to give the order, and yet he refused. The reason, he later stated, was that he did not wish to feel responsible for starting a war between the US and South Carolina. In his defense, it must be noted, that he had no idea that a relief ship was on its way. His last message to the War Department had been that he had no need for supplies or reinforcements. On the other hand, he was an officer of the US Army and in command of the fort. If the Captain of the ship, upon hearing no response from the fort's guns, had not made a quick 180 degree turn, and steered the ship out of Fort Moultrie's range of fire, Anderson would have been personally responsible for whatever lives were lost since the ship had shown its colors. No matter how many excuses Major Anderson might have offered for his failure to give the order to fire the fort's guns, the fact was that as an officer he had pledged his life to defend his country and its flag. This brave soldier, who had more than proved his heroism during the Mexican War, had lost his nerve. Worse yet, he had lost face among his officers and men. The next morning, whether it was whiskey courage or an attempt to recoup his reputation, he dispatched a letter to Governor Pickens advising him that if he personally had given the order to fire on the ship of the United States, then from now on Fort Sumter would fire on any ship attempting to enter the harbor. Those were fighting words — or were they? The Governor's answer was "no," he had not personally given the order; he was probably asleep in bed. But he had ordered the men stationed at Fort Moultrie to fire on any ship attempting to reinforce Fort Sumter. The Governor's reply was even more adamant. He called for the immediate surrender of Fort Sumter. He was carried away by his own rhetoric and that of the other firebrands in his state.

The total white population of South Carolina was 291,000, divided into half men and half women. In addition, there were 412,000 slaves. While bluster might go a long way among the citizenry of the state, the reality was different. Militarily, all it possessed was an untrained militia with an astonishingly brassy attitude. His own military advisor had tried to explain the reality of the situation to him; if that didn't make an impression upon the Governor's inflated ego, a letter of warning soon arrived from Jefferson Davis. The message urged him to hold his fire until the other states of the Deep South had joined the secessionist movement; until a government had been established; and until a military plan had been organized. Cautioned by these facts, the Governor tried a new ploy. He sent two of the leading citizens of the state to negotiate with Major Anderson the possible surrender of the fort. Major Anderson replied that he could do nothing without orders from Washington and that he would send a man there, and if the Governor so desired, he could send a representative along with the US officer. Meanwhile, the women and children living in the fort were evacuated and sent to their families. Governor Pickens, realizing he had committed an egregious error in acting so precipitously, since South Carolina still was the only state to have seceded, resumed supplying the fort with fresh food and water. At the same time, the Governor continued to surround the fort with new gun emplacements. As for the trip to Washington, it accomplished nothing. Buchanan refused to meet with the Governor's representative, and Secretary of War Joseph Holt told him that Fort Sumter was not up for sale, which completely confused the representative. He had been sent to Washington to discuss the time and terms for the fort's surrender, and the President refused to meet with him, and Holt had treated him as a commercial man haggling over the price of an article that was not up for sale. While this farce continued to play out, one by one the legislatures in the states of the Deep South were meeting and declaring for secession. By the month of February, when Texas voted to join the Confederacy, the seven renegade states had met, created a Constitution, elected a president and a Cabinet and decided on Montgomery, Alabama as its capital.

Meanwhile, President Lincoln sat silently in Springfield, Illinois, making the final decisions on his Cabinet and other important political appointments, but making no statement with regards to the fate of Fort Sumter. In private correspondence, however, he wrote in confidence that the position of the federal government should be to hold onto the fort, and if it was lost, retake it. Neither Buchanan nor Lincoln was ready to come to grips with the existence of a purported new nation that was threatening the very concept of the United States of America. As one state after another left the Union, the federal properties — which included forts and arms depots, Post Offices and Custom Houses — were being confiscated by the new government and made part of the treasury of the Confederacy. The only properties left were Fort Pickens on the Florida coastline and Fort Sumter. Union forces were ultimately able to seize the former; the demise of the latter brought on the war. It is important to bear in mind that in 1860, except for a few major cities, the majority of the population in this country still was rural. The federal government, unlike today, was an abstraction. Residents paid no taxes to the federal government; they paid them to the state in which they resided. The only laws that affected them directly were state laws. Judicial disputes were decided within the states, with only a rare few reaching the Supreme Court. While the wealthy few attended one of the rare private academies or had tutors, whatever education existed for residents was on a local level. Whatever debates took place in the halls of Congress, they had very little to do with the personal lives of the average citizen. Elections served as a break from the daily monotony of their lives. They offered entertainment in the form of speeches and free refreshments, especially liquor; games were played, and an opportunity was provided to meet old acquaintances and acquire new ones, and for boys to meet girls and vice versa. (Sunday church services did create a weekly occasion to socialize, but not everyone attended them. One of the reasons for the success of the religious revival meetings was that they brought people together.)

Viewed from this context, it was perfectly normal and natural for people to rally around the flag of their state. Patrick Henry may have aroused the delegates to the first Continental Congress in 1774 by declaiming that he was not a Virginian but an American, but when it came to adopting the American Constitution for the state of Virginia, he led the opposition to its ratification. In Texas, Sam Houston, who had fought so long and well for the independence of his state and then its admission to the Union, was bitterly opposed to Texas joining the Confederacy and tried to fight it, but in the final analysis he, too, capitulated. Northerners like President Buchanan, who still believed that some kind of compromise could be arranged, gravely underestimated the problem. When John Crittenden of Kentucky offered his compromise, it was rejected not only by the federal government but by the Confederacy as well. Once the Confederacy had been established, two unanswered questions loomed in the background. How would incoming President Lincoln and his administration react to the actual establishment of a new nation on the country's borders; and how would the other Western states that had yet to join the Confederacy react in the event that hostilities broke out? As previously noted, a land invasion was impossible since the states that had seceded were shielded from direct attack by the Border States and North Carolina.

General Winfield Scott had offered the only logical solution to this problem: a naval blockade of the Western ports and the collection of custom duties out at sea. While this action would certainly constitute an act of war upon the Confederacy and might bring some of the Border States to join the rogue nation, from a logical point of view it offered the best solution. As a matter of fact, the North did impose such a blockade on the Western ports once warfare on land had commenced, and it would be extremely effective in cutting off the South from needed revenues. The Northern shipyards certainly were capable of building the fleet of ships needed to form a tight ring around the few Western ports. If the conflict had been contained to the seven seceding states, then land warfare was out of the question. But Winfield Scott was an old man, and although he was in command of the Army, he was not the commander-in-chief of the armed forces. That role had been reserved for the president. If the overwhelming majority of the officers and men in the Confederate Army were certain that they could whip the hated Yankees, the same ardor and confidence existed in the Northern Army, as well.

When Jefferson Davis was inaugurated president on February 9, he proclaimed the Confederacy to be an independent nation no longer attached to the United States. Lincoln in his inaugural address, delivered on March 4, replied that the Confederacy was sheer nonsense; that the states that claimed to have seceded from the Union were still a part of it, despite all of their declamations, and would be treated as errant brothers who had somehow strayed from the true faith. Whether the speech was sincere or not, it certainly could be treated as a slap in the face to the pretensions of the Confederacy. Yet there was nothing in Lincoln's speech that was threatening. He delivered no "either–or" to the seceded states; nor did he establish a timetable for their return to the Union. His administration merely refused to recognize them as a political entity despite the fact that the seven states had established a Constitution; had appointed a president and a Cabinet analogous to that of the United States; had its own judicial and postal system; its own Army and its own flag. It had even gone so far as to write in its Constitution a law forbidding the further importation of slaves. As already noted, the excess of slaves was the bane of the economy of the Western slave states. Since the act of Secession wouldn't resolve the problem of an ever-increasing birth rate among the Negroes and of the lands devoted to the cultivation of cotton becoming less productive every year, how would secession ameliorate these fundamental problems? Several hypotheses have been offered: one emotional; the other somewhat rational. There is no doubt that a state of paranoia among many members of the Western establishment had been building up during the last decade fueled by frustration over the turn of events. They felt they had been duped into accepting the Compromise of 1850 since in the final analysis all they had received for their concessions was a supposed tougher stance on the Fugitive Slave Act, which had no relevance for the states of the Deep South; the same could be said for the repeal of the Missouri Compromise. On the rational side was a belief that because cotton from their states was the mainstay of the British textile industry, any blockade imposed by the North would be challenged by the British, allowing the new government to continue to export its major cash product, cotton. As for a land invasion, that action was impossible without the improbable collaboration of neighboring Western slave states.

Despite the letter Lincoln had sent to a friend detailing his position on what action his administration would take now that he was in office, and the responsibility for war or peace rested with him, he began to have his doubts. As already noted, with the exception of Montgomery Blair, the other members of his Cabinet were opposed to initiating hostilities. Prior to the surrender of Fort Sumter, another farce was played out, this time by Lincoln. The old cast of characters, with the exception of Major Anderson, had been removed from the scene. Governor Pickens had been stripped of his authority over the fate of the fort, which now had been placed in the hands of the new government in Montgomery. President Davis, after dispatching an Army engineer to make recommendations about the gun emplacements that the Governor had overseen, now dispatched General P.T. Beauregard, a native of Louisiana, a former captain in the American Army who had served in the Mexican War, to assume command. Beauregard brought the sophistication of New Orleans to the elite among Charleston and soon had them eating out of his hands and ready to follow all of his instructions. A war hero, and a professional soldier, he soon rearranged the gun emplacements so that the fort was entirely ringed by the artillery he set in place. Meanwhile, back in Washington, the debate within the Lincoln Cabinet continued over the question of whether to hold or surrender the fort. Inside the fort, however, now that Beauregard had taken command, Major Anderson discovered that the supplies of food from the Charleston markets had been cut off once again. Whereas a month before he had notified Washington that he needed neither reinforcements nor new supplies, it now dawned upon him that faced with a professional Army officer, his position had changed not only for the worse but would soon border on the desperate. Back in Montgomery, Jefferson Davis also was very concerned about the final disposition of Fort Sumter. He, like Lincoln, was faced with making hard choices. He was well aware that if he seized Fort Sumter by force, this act would more than likely precipitate a war with the North. He had no idea of how many of the Border slave states would join the Confederacy in the event of a conflict. It was one thing for emissaries from the other slave states to announce their solidarity with the Confederacy; it was quite another to be able to guarantee that the individual state legislatures would vote to join the Confederacy. On the other hand, if the new government did nothing and allowed the fort to stand, it would appear to the outside world that the new government, after all of its threats, was nothing more than a paper tiger. Not only would it lose face among the member states, but the possibility for recognition in Europe would be severely diminished. So he made the decision to send a delegation of three men to see if something could be worked out with the incoming Secretary of State,

William H. Seward, whom he knew from when they both served in the Senate; while they were on opposite ends of the spectrum when it came to slavery, there was still a certain degree of mutual respect among senators. Lincoln, on the other hand, was an unknown cipher, and besides, if you read the Northern newspapers, the consensus in many of them was that Seward was the Prime Minister and Lincoln, the titular head of the government.

In the light of what was considered to be reliable information, Davis then sent his representatives to negotiate with Seward over the surrender of Fort Sumter. Since the Lincoln administration did not recognize the Confederacy, negotiations would have to be carried out through a third party. Originally, Senator Robert Hunter of Virginia was appointed, but he found it awkward and the role was quickly assumed by Supreme Court Justice John Campbell. In the beginning of their conversations, Campbell was given to understand by Seward that Fort Sumter would be turned over to the Confederates, a message which he relayed onto the delegates sent by Davis. As the conversations proceeded and nothing happened, the word "certain" evolved into "almost certain" and finally into in "all likelihood." Robert Toombs, the Secretary of State for the Confederacy, rightly began to doubt the sincerity of Seward and believed that in fact, he was stringing them along. Finally, Seward announced to Campbell that in the event that the administration intended to re-supply Major Robert Anderson, Governor Pickens would be notified well in advance. The question that immediately comes to mind is: why would you notify the enemy what you were planning to do, thereby putting him on the alert? This sudden *volte-face* by Seward, after continually informing Judge Campbell that in all likelihood Fort Sumter would be evacuated, was the result of a conversation Lincoln had with Gustavus Fox. Fox, a graduate of Annapolis, who previously had served in the Navy for 15 years and then retired to become a successful textile manufacturer in Massachusetts, believed he could resolve the problem of Fort Sumter. He had been received by Lincoln by virtue of the fact that Fox and Montgomery Blair, the only member of his Cabinet who had offered to resign when the surrender of Fort Sumter was brought up at the first Cabinet meeting, were married to sisters. Fox, like his brother-in-law, was violently opposed to the surrender of the fort. He had a plan whereby the fort could be reinforced, thereby avoiding its surrender. It was Fox's contention that supplies could be sneaked into the fort, but in the event the plan went awry, he would back up the supply ship with a naval force. It was in light of this possibility that Lincoln decided to send Fox to Charleston to visit with Major Anderson. This meeting took place prior to Seward advising the Judge that in the event the fort was re-supplied, Governor Pickens would be notified. What remains incomprehensible is why Governor Pickens would allow Fox to meet with Major Anderson. Even more puzzling is why General Beauregard, ostensibly in command, would allow a former naval officer to visit the fort, assess its position in the harbor, and therefore become privy to the strength and weakness of Major Anderson's situation. Later on, the Governor would complain that Fox had violated his trust. The most important fact that Fox gleaned from his meeting with Anderson was that he barely had enough supplies in terms of food to hold out until April 15. Fox made this determination March 19. Something had to be done in a hurry or the fort would be forced to surrender or starve to death. In addition to the 80 officers and enlisted men still at the fort, there were 40 workmen whom Beauregard refused to have re-embarked to the mainland. As long as they were there, they were consuming Anderson's precious supply of dwindling food rations. Fox hurried back to Washington and met with Lincoln. If something was to be done to relieve the fort, they had less than a month's time. It was after the Cabinet meeting following Fox's return that the decision was made not only to reinforce Fort Sumter but also to reinforce Fort Pickens, located just outside of Pensacola, Florida. Seward informed Judge Campbell of Lincoln's decision. Since Lincoln had given his word that in the event of an expedition to reinforce the fort, he would notify Governor Pickens, Campbell was directed to pass along that information. If this sounds insane, it was part of a picture that had bordered on madness up until then.

The farce over negotiations had finally come to an end. Lincoln was putting the Confederacy on notice. Fort Sumter and Fort Pickens were federal property (the only federal forts that had yet to be seized by the Confederate states), and the government was prepared to defend them. If actual warfare was to break out, the onus would be on the Confederacy, not the Union. Fort Pickens presented no problem. There was a warship already in the area with troops aboard, and another warship was dispatched, so that within a short period of time the fort had been secured with 1,100 troops. Fort Sumter presented an entirely different and far more difficult situation. Fox would have to return to New York, charter a ship, fuel it up and have supplies and troops put on board. In addition he would have to send along two barges that would actually bring the necessary food to the garrison. He would have to station two warships just outside the harbor, ready to intervene in the event the vessel or the barges were fired upon. Anderson had warned Fox, when they met, that Fort Moultrie was directly across from the landing place and that the ships attempting to unload would be in a direct line of fire.

Fox was well aware of the potential for the destruction of the barges when they attempted to unload their cargoes, but he had convinced Lincoln that the time for inaction was over. General Beauregard and Jefferson Davis were of the same sentiment. On April 12, Beauregard wrote a rather formal note to Major Anderson calling for the surrender of the fort. It was delivered by Colonel James Chestnut and several Confederacy officers, in the best of military tradition. There was nothing contemptuous in the address to the Major. On the contrary, it was penned with dignity and magnanimity. What the note implied was that a brave officer was in an impossible situation. Therefore, he and his fellow officers and enlisted men should be accorded all the respect provided by rules of the game: to march out of the fort with their arms, to salute their flag before lowering it, and to be transported to any military base they desired. Major Anderson's answer was delivered in an equally formal way, in the negative. It was still a world of knights and paladins. Americans may have shucked all the European trappings of Kings and nobility, but in the military, honor among equals still had to be respected. The duel may have been outlawed, but a man still felt that his honor must be satisfied if the accused was considered to be his equal. American newspapers might have been notorious for their scurrilous depiction of individuals, but newspaper editors were not the equals of officers. All of this affected European gallantry would disappear under the gun smoke of four years of war.

On the way down to the boat that would take Colonel Chestnut back to the mainland, Anderson remarked casually that in a few days he would be forced to surrender, since they would be out of food. Colonel Chestnut abruptly stopped and asked Anderson to repeat his last remark. Anderson did and the Colonel then asked him if he would put it in writing. Anderson readily complied and his response was sent to Montgomery, where the final decision would be made. Davis was in favor of the proposed surrender but he wanted some amplification. Just how long would it be before he ran out of food and surrendered? They did not doubt Anderson's word in his reply to Colonel Chestnut, when he specified April 15, but warships had been sighted outside of the harbor, and it might be possible that during that interval of time he would be reinforced with food. Anderson was an equal, an officer in the American Army who played by the same rules as did Davis and Beauregard and other former members of the US Army. But the men in the ships outside the harbor were unknown. They might be officers, but they had not given their word. Ironically, the decision to attack the fort was not delivered by General Beauregard, but by Colonel Chestnut. Once again rowing out to the fort, he announced that without an immediate surrender, in one hour hostilities would commence.

The rest is well-known history. Outgunned and undermanned, Anderson and his men never had a chance. Beauregard was too good a general. The defenses of Fort Moultrie had been reinforced with huge bales of cotton so that the Union shells could not penetrate the fort. An iron-plated cannon, recently developed, had been sent over from England by a fellow South Carolinian, which could strike at the fort with impunity while Anderson's shells bounced off of its iron plate. As for Fox's relief fleet, everything that could have gone wrong did. The lead warship, with the largest and most powerful guns, instead of making the rendezvous with the other warships had gone directly to Fort Pickens to assist in reinforcing that facility. The barges that were supposed to transport the supplies to the fort never showed up. And the seas were so rough that all the military forces on board were seasick. But Fox was like a madman hell bent on a mission, no matter what reality dictated. He moved his ship over the sand bar and only stopped when he saw that the American flag was no longer flying over the fort.

Fort Sumter was not about to allow this farcical drama to be played out with such a conventional ending. In the midst of all the bombardment from both sides, one of the gunners on the lower level of the fort noticed a strange looking man through the embrasure. He was carrying an unsheathed sword with a white flag at its end and demanding entry since the shells were falling all around him. He identified himself as former Senator Louis Wigfall from Texas, now an aide to General Beauregard, and asked to be brought to Major Anderson. Upon being ushered into his presence Wigfall explained his position with respect to General Beauregard and detailed the hopelessness of Anderson's position and the futility of continuing to hold out. By now Anderson was more than well aware of the situation. Moreover, his instructions from the President had been not to hold out until the last man was dead. He lowered the American flag and raised his own white flag, signifying surrender. Captain Lee, who had accompanied Colonel Chestnut on the original visits, seeing the white flag, hurried out to the fort to determine what had taken place. When he learned that Wigfall had acted upon his own, he could not accept the surrender since it was not official. Wigfall actually was an aide to Beauregard, but he had not seen the General in days and therefore the surrender did not meet official military protocol. Anderson would have to haul down the white flag and raise the American flag, allowing hostilities to resume; but it was finally agreed that the terms on which Anderson had surrendered to Wigfall would be sent to Beauregard, and if he approved, the surrender would take effect. The white flag would still stay up until the General had approved the terms. With the General's approval, the following day, the American flag would be raised so that Anderson and his men could salute it before it was lowered again and the surrender became official. Despite all the shells lobbed on both sides, not one man had been killed until the hostilities were over, when an accidental explosion killed one victim and injured a few.

The Confederacy having taken the initiative, war now was on the horizon. Not because Lincoln or Davis wanted or willed it; nor even because of the actions of those firebrands, William Yancey and Robert Barnwell Rhett, who had preached secession; not even over the conflict over the extension of slavery into the new territories; and certainly not because of either slavery or the Dred Scott decision by the Supreme Court. All of these were merely symptoms of a great divide between the states of the North and those of the South. The divide was largely economic, which made it political. Was the war inevitable? Certainly Jefferson Davis hoped to avoid it. He was well aware of the difference in manpower and wealth between the North and the South, having served as Secretary of War.

As for Lincoln and his Cabinet, most were doves, with Montgomery Blair the only hawk. Lincoln himself, as he had written to a friend before taking office, believed that the stance of the federal government should be to hold onto the fort on principle. His approval of Fox's mission, as wild eyed as it was, certainly indicates his determination to hold onto Fort Sumter. On the other hand, Seward's negotiations with the Confederacy's appointed mediator had been carried out with Lincoln's approval, and had Fox not appeared, the surrender of the fort would have been negotiated peacefully. Could Lincoln have galvanized the Congress to declare war on the premise that the South had illegally dissolved the Union? If past history serves as an example, the answer is a likely "no." At that moment in time the secession of the seven states had no impact on the economies of the Northern or Western states. If Fox's ships had not appeared on the horizon, Colonel Chestnut never would have given the order to open fire, and Fort Sumter would have been abandoned under the terms offered to Major Anderson once he had run out of provisions. Both Lincoln and Davis had painted their respective governments into a corner by throwing down the gauntlet over a fort that had no strategic importance to either side. Lincoln and Jefferson Davis believed that the war would be of short duration. Even after Virginia, North Carolina, Tennessee and Arkansas had joined the Confederacy, Lincoln and most of the North and Midwest were convinced that given their superiority in manpower and sea power, the conflict would be brief. The South, on the other hand, was banking on recognition from Great Britain to compensate for its military weakness. That had been the game plan of the original seven states that had seceded from the Union. "Cotton is King" was their war cry, and the English mills would come to their rescue. This wishful thinking determined their decision to secede.

However, Virginia, North Carolina and Tennessee were slave states but had a mixed economy. What rationale did their citizens have to leave the Union and engage in a war to defend the economic interests of the Deep South? When the new Congress convened in March 1861 and its new members were sworn in, there was no indication that any of the elected Congressmen or senators from these states had any intention of resigning from their respective bodies of Congress. The issue of Fort Sumter was still up in the air. Except for Governor Claiborne Jackson of Missouri, who had attempted and been rebuffed in his effort to have his state align itself with the fortunes of the Confederacy, none of the other governors appear to have given this idea any consideration. While war was still possible, most people believed the situation could be resolved amicably.

RECOMMENDED READINGS

Larry H. Addington. *The Patterns of War since the 18th Century*, Bloomington, Indiana University Press, 1994

Tyler Anbinder. *Nativism and Slavery: The Northern Know Nothings and the Politics of the 1850's*, New York, Oxford University Press, 1992.

Fred Anderson. *Crucible of War: The Seven Years' War and the Fate of Empire in British North America, 1754-1766*, New York, A.A. Knopf, 2000.

John Ashworth. *Slavery, Capitalism, and Politics in the Antebellum Republic, Commerce and Compromise, 1820-1850*, New York, Cambridge University Press, 1995.

Victor Brooks and Hohwald, Robert. *How America Fought Its Wars, Military Strategy from the American Revolution to the Civil War*, Conshohocken, PA, Combined Publishing, 1999.

Richard L. Bushman. *From Puritan to Yankee, Character and the Social Order in Connecticut, 1690-1765*, Cambridge, Harvard University Press, 1967

Colin Gordon Calloway. *The Scratch of a Pen: 1763 and the Transformation of North America*, New York: Oxford University Press, 2006

Francis M. Carroll. *A Good and Wise Measure, The Search for the Canadian-American Boundary, 1783-1842*, Toronto: University of Toronto Press, 2001.

Sydney J Chapman. *History of the Trade between the United Kingdom and the United States with Special Reference to the Effects of Tariffs*, London, Routledge, 2005.

Ron Chernow. *Alexander Hamilton*, New York, Penguin, 2004.

Don Cook. *The Long Fuse, England and America, 1760-1785, a British perspective on the American Revolution*, New York, Atlantic Monthly Press, 1995.

Pamela C. Copeland and MacMaster, Richard K. *The Five George Masons, Patriots and Planters of Virginia and Maryland*, Charlottesville, University Press of Virginia, 1975.

Alan Dawley, *Class and Community, The Industrial Revolution in Lynn*, Cambridge, Mass., Harvard University Press, 2000.

David Detzer. *Allegiance: Fort Sumter, Charleston, and the Beginning of the Civil War*, New York, Harcourt, 2001.

Davis Rich Dewey, *Financial History of The United States*, New York, Longmans, Green and Co, 12 ed., 1934

Carville Earle. *The Evolution of a Tidewater Settlement System, All Hallow's Parish, Maryland, 1650-1783*, Chicago, University of Chicago, Dept. of Geography, 1975.

John S. D. Eisenhower. *So far from God: the U.S. war with Mexico, 1846-1848*, New York, Random House, 1989

John S. D. Eisenhower. *Agent of destiny: the life and times of General Winfield Scott*, New York, Free Press, 1997

Joseph J. Ellis. *American Creation: Triumphs and Tragedies at the Founding of the Republic*, New York, A.A. Knopf, 2007

Richard E. Ellis. *The Union at Risk, Jacksonian Democracy, States' Rights and the Nullification Crisis*, New York, Oxford University Press, 1987.

David Eltis et al., ed. *Slavery in the Development of the Americas*, Cambridge, UK, New York, Cambridge University Press, 2004.

Eric Foner. *Free Soil, Free Labor, Free Men, The Ideology of the Republican Party Before the Civil War*, New York, Oxford University Press, 1970.

Ronald P. Formisano. *For the People: American Populist Movements from the Revolution to the 1850s*, Chapel Hill, University of North Carolina Press, 2008.

William W. Freehling. *The Road to Disunion: Secessionists Triumphant, 1854-1861*, New York, Oxford University Press, 2007

Larry Gara. *The Presidency of Franklin Pierce*, Lawrence, Kan., University Press of Kansas, 1991.

Charles R. Geisst, *Wall Street, A History*, New York: Oxford University Press, 1997.

William E. Gienapp. *The Origins of the Republican Party, 1852-1856*, New York, Oxford University Press, 1988.

John Steele Gordon. *An Empire of Wealth: The Epic History of American Economic Power*, New York, HarperCollins, 2004.

James Grant. *John Adams, Party of One*, New York, Farrar, Straus and Giroux, 2005.

Allen C. Guelzo. *Lincoln and Douglas, The Debates that Defined America*, New York, Simon & Schuster, 2008.

Holman Hamilton. *Prologue to Conflict, The Crisis and Compromise of 1850*, New York, W.W. Norton, 1964.

Bray Hammond. *Banks and Politics in America from the Revolution to the Civil War, From the Revolution to the Civil War*, Princeton, Princeton University Press, 1957.

David Freeman Hawke, Honorable Treason, *The Declaration of Independence and the Men Who Signed It*, New York, Viking, 1976.

Michael F. Holt. *Political Parties and American Political Development, From the Age of Jackson to the Age of Lincoln*, Baton Rouge, Louisiana State University Press, 1992.

Michael Fitzgibbon Holt. *The Rise and Fall of the American Whig Party, Jacksonian Politics and the Onset of the Civil War*, New York, Oxford University Press, 1999

Daniel Walker Howe. *What Hath God Wrought, The Transformation of America, 1815-1848*, New York, Oxford University Press, 2007.

James L. Huston, *The Panic of 1857 and the Coming of the Civil War*, Baton Rouge, Louisiana State University Press, 1987.

James L. Huston, *Calculating the Value of the Union, Slavery, Property Rights, and the Economic Origins of the Civil War*, Chapel Hill, University of North Carolina Press, 2003.

James L. Huston. *Stephen A. Douglas and the Dilemmas of Democratic Equality*, Lanham, Md., Rowman & Littlefield Publishers, 2007

Nancy Isenberg. *Fallen Founder, The Life of Aaron Burr*, New York, Viking, 2007.

Merrill Jensen. *The Founding of a Nation, A History of the American Revolution, 1763-1776*, New York, Oxford University Press, 1968.

Howard Jones. *Crucible of Power, A History of American Foreign Relations to 1913*, Wilmington, Del., SR Books, 2002.

Mark A. Lause. *Young America: Land, Labor, and the Republican Community*, Urbana, University of Illinois Press, 2005.

David L. Lightner. *Slavery and the Commerce Power, How the Struggle Against the Interstate Slave Trade Led to the Civil War*, New Haven, Yale University Press, 2006

Leon F. Litwack. *North of Slavery, The Negro in the Free States*, Chicago, University of Chicago Press, 1965

Norbert Lyons. *The McCormick Reaper Legend, The True Story of a Great Invention*, New York, Exposition Press, 1955.

James Madison et. al. *Federalist Papers*, Harmondsworth, Penguin, 1987.

Jerry W. Markham. *A Financial History of the United States*, Armonk, N.Y., M.E. Sharpe, 2002.

Richard Middleton. *Pontiac's War, Its Causes, Course, and Consequences*, New York, Routledge, 2007.

Nathan Miller, *The Founding Finaglers*, New York, D. McKay Co., 1976.

Kenneth Morgan. *Slavery, Atlantic Trade and the British Economy, 1660-1800*,Cambridge, UK; New York, Cambridge University Press, 2000

Michael A. Morrison. *Slavery and the American West, The Eclipse of Manifest Destiny and the Coming of the Civil War*, Chapel Hill, University of North Carolina Press, 1999.

Jerome Mushkat. *Tammany, the Evolution of a Political Machine, 1789-1865*, Ithaca: Syracuse University Press, 1971

Allan Nevins. *Fremont, Pathmarker of the West*, Lincoln, University of Nebraska Press, 1992.

Lynn Hudson Parson. *John Quincy Adams*, Madison, Wis., Madison House, 1998.

Alvin Rabushka. *Taxation in Colonial America, 1607-1775*, Princeton: Princeton University Press, 2008.

Roger L. Ransom. *Conflict and Compromise, The Political Economy of slavery,*

Emancipation, and the American Civil War, New York, Cambridge University Press, 1989.

Robert V. Remini. *Andrew Jackson*, New York, Palgrave Macmillan, 2008.

Norman K. Risjord. *The Revolutionary Generation*, New York, Rowman & Littlefield, 2001

Michael P. Rogin, *Fathers and Children, Andrew Jackson and the Subjugation of the American Indian*, New York, Random House, 1975

David Lee Russell. *The American Revolution in the Southern Colonies*, Jefferson, N.C., McFarland & Co, 2000.

Carl Sandburg. *Abraham Lincoln, The Prairie Years*, Harcourt, Brace & Company, New York, 1954.

Robert Seager. *And Tyler Too, A Biography of John & Julia Gardiner Tyler*, New York, McGraw-Hill, 1963

Richard H. Sewell. *John P. Hale and the Politics of Abolition*, Cambridge, Mas., Harvard University Press, 1965.

Arthur Meier Schlesinger, *The Colonial Merchants and the American Revolution, 1763-1776*, New York, Atheneum, 1968.

Jean Edward Smith. *John Marshall, Definer of a Nation*, New York, Henry Holt & Company, 1998

Alan Taylor. *American Colonies, The Settling of North America*, New York, Viking, 2001

George Rogers Taylor. *The Transportation Revolution, 1815-1860*, New York, Rinehart, 1964

Richard H. Timberlake. *Monetary Policy in the United States, An Intellectual and Institutional History*, Chicago, University of Chicago Press, 1993

Robert W. Venables. *American Indian History, Five Centuries of Conflict & Coexistence*, Santa Fe, N.M., Clear Light Publishers, 2004.

Mark Voss-Hubbard. *Beyond Party, Cultures of Antipartisanship in Northern Politics Before the Civil War*, Baltimore, Johns Hopkins University Press, 2002.

Anthony C. Wallace, *Rockdale, The Growth of an American Village in the Early Industrial Revolution*, New York, Norton, 1980.

Eric H. Walther. *The Shattering of the Union, America in the 1850s*, Wilmington, Del., Scholarly Resources, 2004.

David Ward. *Cities and Immigrants, A Geography of Change in Nineteenth-Century America*, New York, Oxford University Press, 1971